Hertfordshire
COUNTY COUNCIL
Community Information

738
2
DRA

1 9 NOV 2002	- 8 AUG 2003	
17 Dec 2002	2 8 NOV 2003	
8 Jan	- 6 MAR 2004	
	- 8 JAN 2005	
1 4 MAR 2003	1 2 JAN 2005	
1 1 APR 2003	- 6 AUG 2006	
2 7 MAY 2003		

Please renew/return this item by the last date shown.

So that your telephone call is charged at local rate, please call the numbers as set out below:

	From Area codes 01923 or 020:	From the rest of Herts:
Renewals:	01923 471373	01438 737373
Enquiries:	01923 471333	01438 737333
Minicom:	01923 471599	01438 737599

L32   www.hertsdirect.org   HCM

CIRCULATING STOCK ROUTE   17

SPODE

TRANSFER PRINTED WARE

1784–1833

A new, enlarged and updated edition

SPODE

TRANSFER PRINTED WARE

1784–1833

A new, enlarged and updated edition

David Drakard and Paul Holdway

Antique Collectors' Club

©2002 David Drakard and Paul Holdway
World copyright reserved

ISBN 1 85149 394 8

British Library Cataloguing-in-Publication Data
A catalogue record for this book is available from the British Library

Printed and Published in England
by the Antique Collectors' Club Ltd., Woodbridge, Suffolk, IP12 4SD

*Frontispiece: **Garden Seat** in earthenware, 48cm. high. Peony (P808). The shape follows a Chinese original (see also page 308).*
*Title page: **John Bull giving Boney a Pull**. Mug printed with a typical Napoleonic cartoon (see also page 130).*

Publisher's Note: Readers are advised that a very small number of photographs used in this book lack definition and it has not been possible to obtain satisfactory replacements.

Antique Collectors' Club

THE ANTIQUE COLLECTORS' CLUB was formed in 1966 and quickly grew to a five figure membership spread throughout the world. It publishes the only independently run monthly antiques magazine, *Antique Collecting*, which caters for those collectors who are interested in widening their knowledge of antiques, both by greater awareness of quality and by discussion of the factors which influence the price that is likely to be asked. The Antique Collectors' Club pioneered the provision of information on prices for collectors and the magazine still leads in the provision of detailed articles on a variety of subjects.

It was in response to the enormous demand for information on 'what to pay' that the price guide series was introduced in 1968 with the first edition of *The Price Guide to Antique Furniture* (completely revised 1978 and 1989), a book which broke new ground by illustrating the more common types of antique furniture, the sort that collectors could buy in shops and at auctions rather than the rare museum pieces which had previously been used (and still to a large extent are used) to make up the limited amount of illustrations in books published by commercial publishers. Many other price guides have followed, all copiously illustrated, and greatly appreciated by collectors for the valuable information they contain, quite apart from prices. The Price Guide Series heralded the publication of many standard works of reference on art and antiques. *The Dictionary of British Art* (now in six volumes), *The Pictorial Dictionary of British 19th Century Furniture Design*, *Oak Furniture* and *Early English Clocks* were followed by many deeply researched reference works such as *The Directory of Gold and Silversmiths*, providing new information. Many of these books are now accepted as the standard work of reference on their subject.

The Antique Collectors' Club has widened its list to include books on gardens and architecture. All the Club's publications are available through bookshops world wide and a full catalogue of all these titles is available free of charge from the addresses below.

Club membership, open to all collectors, costs little. Members receive free of charge *Antique Collecting*, the Club's magazine (published ten times a year), which contains well-illustrated articles dealing with the practical aspects of collecting not normally dealt with by magazines. Prices, features of value, investment potential, fakes and forgeries are all given prominence in the magazine.

Among other facilities available to members are private buying and selling facilities and the opportunity to meet other collectors at their local antique collectors' club. There are over eighty in Britain and more than a dozen overseas. Members may also buy the Club's publications at special pre-publication prices.

As its motto implies, the Club is an organisation designed to help collectors get the most out of their hobby: it is informal and friendly and gives enormous enjoyment to all concerned.

For Collectors — By Collectors — About Collecting

ANTIQUE COLLECTORS' CLUB
Sandy Lane, Old Martlesham, Woodbridge, Suffolk IP12 4SD, UK
Tel: 01394 389950 Fax: 01394 389999
Email: sales@antique-acc.com
Website: www.antique-acc.com
or
Market Street Industrial Park, Wappingers' Falls, NY 12590, USA
Tel: 845 297 0003 Fax: 845 297 0068
Email: info@antiquecc.com
Website: www.antiquecc.com

To our wives
for putting up with us again

Contents

Authors' preface   8

Acknowledgements   9

Introduction   10

An outline of the history of printing at Spode Work, 1784–1833   13

Chapter 1   17
People and places 1733–1833

Chapter 2   31
Transfer printing processes

Chapter 3   43
Art forms and engraving techniques
   The copperplate makers

Chapter 4   60
Patterns and proofs, shapes and sizes

Chapter 5   73
On-glaze Bat printing
   Catalogue of Bat prints
   Shapes of wares decorated with Bat prints

Chapter 6   171
On-glaze Pluck and Dust printing
   Catalogue of Pluck and Dust prints
   Shapes of wares decorated with Pluck
   and Dust prints

Chapter 7   186
Underglaze printing
   Catalogue of underglaze blue prints
   Shapes of wares decorated with
   underglaze blue prints

Chapter 8   313
Marks and marking, dates and dating

Indexes   326
General
Named patterns and prints

Authors' preface

The subject of this second and enlarged edition of the history of Spode transfer printed ware again covers the period from 1784 to 1833 when control of the Works remained in the hands of the Spode family before passing to that of the Copelands. The pieces illustrated were all made by the Spodes, yet some of the patterns and shapes and all the methods of manufacture were those used throughout the Potteries and in many parts of the British Isles during that period. We are fortunate that much of the early history and products of the first two Spodes has been pieced together and a wide variety of printed wares made in those years can be illustrated together with a selection from the original copper plates which are still held at Spode Works. Today Bat printing and Pluck and Dust printing are no longer practised and the flat press underglaze printing illustrated in this book is giving way to a variety of printing methods using hand engraved copperplates or copper cylinders. The latter are designed to speed up the printing process without forfeiting the advantages of translucency of cobalt achieved by variations in depth of cut of properly hand engraved coppers that transfer without a loss to the crispness and quality found in the best original Spode. The present production of the Spode Company is once again marked with the name of Spode and we trust this history will throw further light on the many long-vanished manufactories of those times now known only by their surviving printed wares.

David Drakard
Paul Holdway

March, 2002

Acknowledgements

First we must acknowledge our debt to the Directors of Spode Ltd. and the Trustees of the Spode Museum Trust in allowing us to make use of and illustrate documents and items still held in the archives and museum as well as those Spode copperplates still remaining in Spode Works. We are particularly indebted to Harold Holdway lately a director of Royal Worcester-Spode Ltd., for the photographs of the factory and Spode wares and for information gained during his many years as art director of the Spode Company. We are similarly indebted to Peter F.C. Roden, a descendant of the Spode family, whose meticulous study of the life of Josiah Spode gives a better understanding of the early years at Spode Works. We must extend our thanks to the officers and members of the Spode Society, founded in 1986, and Pam Woolliscroft editor of the *Spode Recorder and Review* in which are published articles and illustrations of Spodes' and Copelands' wares, factory conditions and history up to the present day. We are grateful too for the help given to us by the Victoria and Albert Museum, the Potteries Museum and Art Gallery at Stoke-on-Trent, and to the Wedgwood Museum for use of their archives and to Dreweatt Neate for the supply of information and photographs of the rare Spode pieces appearing in their auction catalogues. Finally, but by no means least, are that body of collectors and friends who have been generous both with their knowledge and photographs of their pieces and to whom we are both greatly indebted. In this respect and before listing those deserving our gratitude, we must particularly thank Michael Attar for giving us free rein with his magnificent collection, illustrating many of his rare pieces.

Derek Andrews
Nick Berthoud
Winifred Bowden
Bill and Marguerite Coles
L.A. (Comp) Compton
Robert Copeland
Geraldine Drakard
Tony and Barbara Field
Geoffrey and Penny Fisk
John des Fontaines
Rodney and Eileen Hampson
Gordon Hewitt
Peter Higgins
Tim Holdaway

Margaret Ironside
Henry Irvine-Fortesque
Trevor Kentish
Pat Latham
Terry Lockett
Rustom and Rachel Patel
C.D. Pike
Martin and Rosalind Pulver
Alison Quinn
Stephen Robinson
Peter and Janis Rodwell
Allan Townsend
George Worlock
Colin Wyman

Josiah Spode, the second, 1755–1827, in a portrait by Michael Keeling painted in 1806.

Introduction

Portrait miniature of Josiah Spode, the first, 1733–1797.

It is astonishing that Josiah Spode, the first, 1733–1797, a man of the eighteenth century whose father died a pauper should rise to command the services of the portrait miniaturist who provided the illustration. In that century in the Potteries his success was only surpassed by Josiah Wedgwood but who can say that Spode's personal achievement was not greater than that of Wedgwood. Wedgwood was born into a long established family of master potters. Spode, in an age of influence, advanced unaided from obscure penury to proprietorship of a most extensive pottery and had said of him 'with his wealth increased his kindness', an epitaph of which any could be proud.

Joined with his father, we also portray Josiah Spode, the second, 1755–1827, shown in a portrait by Keeling painted in 1806. After nearly twenty years in London ever increasing the sale of Spode wares, the second Josiah on the death of his father, returned to Stoke to oversee the family manufactory. There he built upon his father's firm foundation of fine earthenwares and added with vigorous production and marketing, Spode porcelain, later universally known as fine bone china. It is obvious from the full length portrait of him, then aged fifty one, that he was a man of substance and purpose and a leading figure in the industry. Some three years earlier in 1803 he purchased a seventeen acre site in Penkhull, then still a separate village half a mile from Spode Works. Having demolished the previous building on the site, he erected in stone a splendid mansion with a domed roof known as 'The Mount'. By then this forcible man of purpose had rapidly eclipsed all rivals to become the premier manufacturer in the kingdom.

Thus in two generations the enduring reputation of Spode was built up to be carried on through the next hundred years by the Copeland family. In the last forty years great changes have taken place at Spode Works under new invigorated management which once again trades under the name of Spode.

The introduction to the first edition in 1983 opened with the words, 'In this book are listed, as far as the authors are able to ascertain, all Spode's plain printed decoration.' In this new and enlarged edition are listed many more patterns in each of the three categories of On-glaze Bat prints, On-glaze Pluck and Dust prints and Underglaze blue prints. Yet the authors can be no more certain that further examples will not be found and triumphantly appear published in the *Spode Society Review* or similar publications.

Purposely excluded from the first edition were those prints that were especially designed and used solely as a basis for hand-painted decoration. This has remained true except for the much extended range of Napoleonic Bat prints now numbering fifteen different designs being pattern numbers P380 to P394 inclusive. Of these, eleven appear as plain black Bat printed designs with an additional four printed in black and then over-painted in full colour and one design, P392, is known in plain black and over-coloured. The extreme rarity of these designs, with but a single copy known in some cases, has prompted us to include the over-painted designs so that the full range, as known at the present time, could be included.

Some difficulty occurs with the numbering of the illustrations in this book. Spode's Pattern Books, which are a record of painting and gilding, are numbered in series with plain numbers and do not include underglaze blue printed designs nor the separate designs of Bat printing and Pluck and Dust printing. To overcome the difficulty, we adopted a comprehensive three-figure system to cover all Spode's plain prints. These print references are prefixed with the letter P to avoid confusion with Spode's Pattern Book system of plain numbers. Where a print, particularly those in underglaze blue, is named this is included in the reference system. Minor variations and re-engravings of prints are listed as subdivisions of the main print number, as are the separate scenes from the underglaze blue multi-scene patterns. The P numbers system for differing prints remains unchanged in this edition and new prints have been allocated numbers not previously used.

The shapes illustrations, which immediately follow their respective prints catalogues, are designed to show a general and varied selection of all the major types of Spode print decorated ware and include examples of rarer shapes not previously included. The illustrations shown as examples of Spode shapes are prefixed with the letter S (for shapes) placed before the number of the illustration. A different selection of shapes is shown slightly more numerous in total than those previously used in our first edition. The shapes are again numbered consecutively commencing with S1 to S71 for Bat shapes in Chapter 5, proceeding with S72 to S80 for Pluck and Dust shapes in chapter 6. The shapes illustrations for underglaze blue are numbered S81 to S229, the largest section of shapes illustrations shown. To make clear which of these numbers are completely new illustrations not appearing in our first edition the bracketed word (New) has been added to the number shown below the actual illustration. Two examples of these can be seen below illustrations S20(New) and S97(New). Illustration numbers not marked as (New) will be found in our first edition but not necessarily with the same number used in this edition. This is particularly true of the illustrations of underglaze blue shapes which are all taken from fresh photography.

An outline of the history of printing at Spode Works 1784–1833

Before examining the lives of the Spode family, their Works and their workpeople in the following eight chapters, it seems sensible to set their lasting achievements with printed ceramics which once more now continues under the proud name of Spode.

1784	First underglaze blue printing, on earthenware. Dinner plate shape probably Early Indented. Prints in hard, dark, flat tones of blue from copperplates heavily line engraved copies of Chinese patterns. Occasional SPODE maker's marks type 1. There is no certain date that can be noted for Spode's commencement of On-glaze Bat printing since no marked pieces appear much before 1800. It would seem probable that this simple hand printing method was used by the partnership of Spode and Tomlinson or by the 1772 partnership of Mountford & Spode neither of which partnerships appeared to have marked their wares.
1789	French Revolution.
1790	Maker's mark becomes more regular in use with introduction of mark 2a.
1793–97	War with French Republic and with the Dutch.
Before 1796	First printed maker's mark on copperplate for pattern Rotunda P907.
1797	Death of Spode I. Spode II returns from London to take charge of Works. It would seem reasonable to suppose that this double event hastened the introduction of new dinner ware shapes, new tea ware shapes and of bone china all of which were in production by about 1800.
1798–1802	First War with Napoleon now first Consul of France.
1799–1800	Development and introduction of bone china with major tea ware pieces in Old Oval shape with Bute teacups and coffee cans. Introduction New Indented earthenware dinner plate and dish shape with re-engraving of underglaze blue patterns with improved technique to fit the new shape. The New Indented dinner plate is the first plate shape shown in the Pattern Books which do not show the Early Indented shape.
1800	Union of Great Britain and Ireland.
1800–1801	First underglaze blue printed patterns for bone china tewares.
1803	Introduction of Bat printing on bone china Pattern 473 with flower sprays in intense black and Pattern 500 with flower sprays in charcoal black and pattern 557 and 558 with landscapes in charcoal black and 523 in French brown.
1803–1815	Second war with Napoleon.
1804	First blue Bat printed pattern 613 with landscapes.
About 1805	New Oval shape for tea wares supersedes the Old Oval shape. The New Oval shape is that most commonly found with Bat printed decorations. Bute shape teacups, coffee cans and saucers continued in use with the new shape.
1806	Engraving technique for underglaze blue printing now fully developed. First underglaze blue printed service Greek P906 and first European Castle P711 introduced, thus heralding the change from Oriental art to European art on earthenware. Initiation of Pluck and Dust with an all-over design Bamboo P501 and the border designs Rose and Vine borders P521 and P522.
1807–08	Introduction of Bat printed Animal series P400.
1809	Double Indented earthenware dinner shape printed with multi-scene Caramanian service P905.
1810	First appearance of Bat printed fruits, P161–P196, printed in black, pattern 1513 and then in chocolate-brown, pattern 1516.

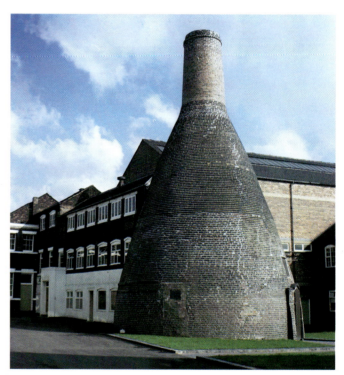

The final firing of a bottle oven at Spode Works commenced over forty years ago on 13th June 1960 in the No.2 china oven known as the Pump oven. The pair of photographs illustrating the event show the oven being filled with bungs of stacked saggars and being cleared after firing. The fires were kindled at 7am on Monday, and stoking by the fireman Jim Evans ceased at 12pm Wednesday 15th June. The oven was allowed to cool before being drawn on 20th June. The congested site can be seen during the last firing of no. 3 china oven with packing hogsheads still stacked about. After demolition of no. 3 oven, no. 2 oven was retained standing next to the company headquarters building until it collapsed in February 1972 leaving only the foundations which can just be seen in the final illustration of the Works to-day.

1811	Gold Bat printing with Fruit, Landscapes and Animals.
About 1812 or later	Although the first original prints, from which Spode's Indian Sporting P904 were copied, were issued in monthly parts by Edward Orme commenced on 4th January 1804, it would appear that Spode's most collected series was not first manufactured until some years later.
1812–13	New series of Contemporary Humanity P300, Bat prints introduced on pattern 1922.
1813	Spode produces Stone China in imitation of Chinese porcelain, together with orientally inspired underglaze blue printed patterns for its decoration. London shape teacup and saucer were first marketed. This shape was not much favoured for Bat printing and examples are rare. It is more easily found with underglaze blue decoration.
1815	Battle of Waterloo and end of Napoleonic Wars.
About 1815	Spode's underglaze blue printing reaches its pinnacle of excellence.
1816	Introduction of Italian pattern P710, Spode's famous underglaze print which is still in production. Special dated Wheal Sparnon mark used during this year only.
1818	Purple Bat printing introduced, followed by Rose colour in the following year.
1819	Peterloo Massacre and continued civil unrest.
From about 1820	Introduction over a number of years of new underglaze printing colours, of which green was the most popular, and new floral underglaze designs to meet changes of fashion.
1821	Felspar porcelain first produced with puce Bat printed makers' mark.
1822	New formulation of stone china marketed as Spode's New Stone. Blue-printed orientally inspired designs continue on New Stone body, with some floral designs added.
1822–23	Gadroon Edge tea and dinner ware introduced and becomes one of the most popular shapes for blue underglaze prints.
1825	The Great Money Panic, with between sixty and seventy banks stopping payment followed by distress and riots.
1827	Pembroke shape teawares first manufactured, with a revival of Bat printing as a decoration for tea and dessert wares. Death of Josiah Spode II.
1828–31	Four new multi-scene underglaze printed dinner ware patterns brought on to the market, Floral P901, British Flowers P902, Botanical P903 and Aesop's Fables P907.
1832	The Third Reform Bill finally becomes law.
1833	In March 1833 COPELAND AND GARRETT take over the Works and the firm ceases to trade as SPODE.

This outline history of the Spodes as manufacturers, although only covering their printed wares, gives some idea of their progress set against the adverse background for trade during the times in which they lived. It is not known how many were employed by Spode I when in partnership with Tomlinson or with Mountford nor later at the main Spode Works, but at the death of Spode II in 1827 it was over 700 which must be a vastly different number than were employed by his father. The Spodes were not the only family that prospered in the first Industrial Revolution despite a background of war, riots and unrest, yet it speaks well of the father and the son that their products continue to be as highly prized as they are today and that their Company, re-adopting the name of SPODE, should remain successful still.

Chapter 1

People and Places

The history of the Spode family as potters from the birth of Josiah Spode (the first) in 1733 to the final withdrawal of the family from the factory in 1833 covers exactly 100 years. It is now some 270 years since the birth of Josiah Spode I and 170 years since the change of ownership of the factory, yet the name lives on as strongly as ever and the present successors to the Spode and Copeland families once again mark their wares with the single name of Spode.

There is no doubt that at least a part of this lasting reputation rests upon the excellence of the printed wares produced by Spode, father and son, in the late eighteenth century and the first thirty years of the nineteenth century and are the subject of this book. However, before plunging headlong into the pleasures and technicalities of these printed wares, it would seem sensible to give a brief resumé of the manufacturers and the times in which they lived.

Much recent detailed research has been undertaken and published by a descendant of the Spode family, Peter F.C. Roden regarding the life of Josiah Spode I and to him we are indebted. It is our intention here not only to give a brief outline of the life of the first Josiah and his sons, as can be ascertained from documentary evidence, but also to place them within the potter's world of the eighteenth and nineteenth centuries.

Josiah Spode I was born in 1733, an only son but with three elder sisters, in the then tiny hamlet of Lane Delph, about a mile from the centre of Stoke and long since engulfed by the city of Stoke-on-Trent. He sprang from old Staffordshire stock, recorded close by at Biddulph as early as 1568 and where his father, another Josiah, was born in 1695.

In 1739, when Josiah was six, his father died a pauper. How Josiah was educated and how the family was supported is not known. However, his eldest sister, Anne, was then nineteen and his younger sisters aged fifteen and ten, all of working age, and this may supply the answer.

No record of the family has been found for a further ten years until, on 9th April 1749, Spode was fortunate to be hired by the leading Staffordshire potter of his day Thomas Whieldon. An entry in Whieldon's notebook reads:

1749 April 9th
Hired Siah Spode to give him from this time to
Martlemas next 2s. 3d. or 2s. 6d. if he deserves it.
2nd year   2s. 9d.
3rd year   3s. 3d.
Paid full earnest   1s. 0d.

Spode was then sixteen, long past the age when a pauper's son could be expected to start work, indeed past the usual age for apprenticeship. We can only speculate but the very hiring speaks of previous experience, if only of the

menial tasks reserved for children in the pot banks of the times. It was said that about 1740 the wages paid to lathe treaders, usually boys of seven years of age, was 4d. per week and, even in 1766, a good treader had only 6d. per week. In this print published in 1827, the lathe treader is a young woman.

Simeon Shaw, in his *History of the Staffordshire Potteries* published in 1829, tells us that in 1740 Thomas Whieldon, such a master of his trade that a class of lead-glazed earthenware is named after him, was potting in a manufactory which 'consisted of a small range of low buildings, all thatched'. His productions were knife hafts for the Sheffield cutlers, snuff boxes for Birmingham hardwaremen, toys and chimney-ornaments coloured and glazed black, red or white lead and coffee cups, tea wares and other useful wares both in white salt-glazed stoneware and lead glazed tortoiseshell ware.

Although it is true that Josiah Spode, having already reached the age of sixteen and receiving payment for his labour could not have been apprenticed to Whieldon, nevertheless in some respects he does appear to have been treated as an apprentice. In his book in 1829 Simeon Shaw wrote that 'of the four apprentices to Mr. Whieldon, three commenced business and were eminently successful, Mr. Josiah Spode (the first), Mr. Robert Garner, Mr. J. Barker – but Mr. William Greatbatch, a person of great ability, was ruined by a bad debt.' No better evidence could there be to the quality of schooling in manufacture and management received by these fortunate employees. It is interesting to note how close these gentlemen remained. Thomas Whieldon witnessed a later partnership agreement for Josiah Spode I. Garner and Barker were partners in business together, Spode's second son, Samuel, married Garner's daughter, Sarah. The last record by Whieldon that he had hired Josiah Spode was dated 25th February 1749 with his status and wages having risen to journeyman at 7s. 6d. per week. Some six months later at the age of twenty-one, he married Ellen Finlay at Stoke Church, a lady some eight years his senior. Mr. Spode signed the register, his bride made her mark. Following the usual practice of newlyweds, they set up home in a rented cottage hard by.

It is not certain when Spode left the employ of Whieldon, but 1754 appears the most likely year, nor can any certain record be found of his further employment before 1767. However, on 13th September 1758, the married couple had prospered sufficiently to buy a new house lately built and with some land. This remained in the Spode family until 1831 when the estate of Josiah Spode II was divided up, the building being described then as 'Dwelling house and shop situate on the North side thereof and fronting to Church Street in Stoke-on-Trent, now in the holding of Thomas Holdgate, Ironmonger.' No record reveals where Spode worked or how he and his wife improved their lot during this the first four years of their married life.

It was not until 27th October 1767 that Spode rented a pot works for a period of seven years from Lady Day next at a rent of £9.12s.6d per annum. This was not the large pot bank worked by William Banks and fronting the North side of Stoke's Church Street purchased by Josiah Spode in 1776 and becoming Spode Works. This Works was smaller with a frontage on the South side of Church Street partly opposite the East end of Banks' Works and running to the East of it. It was worked by the partnership of Spode & Tomlinson from 1767 to 1774 and by Spode himself to 25th March 1775. It became known later as the Bridge Bank Works. No marked pieces are known of wares made by this partnership and the only record of their production is an invoice dated 7th September 1771 from Spode and Tomlinson to Josiah and Thomas Wedgwood for a quantity of tableware in what would have been the up and coming creamware of the day. The plates and dishes are shown as having the well-known feather edge.

It is interesting to speculate just how much Wedgwood creamware was made by Spode and other manufacturers. Buying 'in the white' for decoration and resale was a well-established and continuing business in the Potteries.

It is at this point, with Spode established as the senior partner in a manufacturing business, it would be as well to review, however briefly, the state

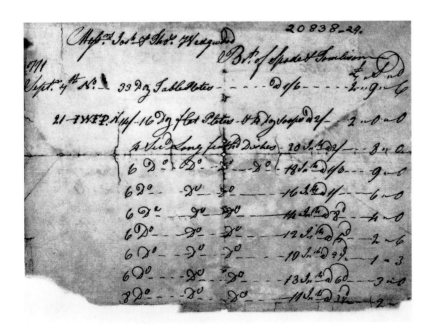

'Itinerant Dealers in
Staffordshire Ware'. Print
published in 1797.

of the pottery industry in Staffordshire. It was the beginning of the Industrial Revolution, which was to reshape the Potteries. The industry then still consisted of innumerable small undertakings, selling their wares through itinerant dealers who travelled the country with their merchandise carried on pack mules. This print, published in 1797, entitled 'Itinerant Dealers in Staffordshire Ware' depicts such a family some thirty years later.

In 1770 lead-glazed creamware had overtaken salt-glazed stoneware as the staple production for everyday table use. Some twenty-eight manufacturers of salt glaze stoneware entered into an agreement to avoid price cutting, an almost inevitable result of reduced demand. *(See page 21, opposite)*

This agreement reveals much of the methods of the trade and of the times. The inclusion of the wording 'Fifty pounds of good and lawful money of Great Britain' lead us to believe that payments by barter, exchange or token were still an everyday occurrence let alone the possibility of counterfeit or foreign coin. The pure impossibility of enforcing such an agreement is obvious. As can be seen, there were no less than six grades of plates. If you could not sell your wares as 'Best' at 2s.0d., no doubt you called them 'Best seconds' at 1s.9d. or, if this failed, 'Worser seconds' at 1s.6d. and so on down the scale. It is interesting to see the description of the lowest grade of plate 'none sold under 9d. and not to be pick'd, but took as they are put together'. Is not this still the method of many a market fruiterer? The fine peaches at the front must not be 'pick'd' but the bruised specimens at the back are to be accepted as they are 'put together' by the fruiterer.

This very multiplicity of grades of quality can cause doubt to the collector to this day. In the present keeping of one of the authors of this book is a Spode

We whose Hands are hereunto Subscribed do Bind Ourselves our Heirs, and Assigns in the sum of Fifty Pounds of good and lawful Money of great Britain not to sell or cause to be sold under the within specified Prices, as Witness our Hands,

This 4th Day of Feby. 1770.

John Platt, John Lowe, John Taylor, John Cobb, Robt. Bucknall, John Daniel, Thos. Daniel, Junr. Richd. Adams, Saml. Chatterley, Thos. Lowe, John Allen, Wm. Parrott, Jacob Warburton, Warburton and Stone, Jos. Smith, Joshua Heath, John Bourn, Jos. Stephens, Wm. Smith, Jos. Simpson, John Weatherby, J. & Rd. Mare, Nicholas Pool, John Yates, Chas. Hassells, Pr. Pro. of Ann Warburton, & Son, Thos. Warburton, Wm. Meir.

PRICES OF DISHES.

Best.		Seconds.	
	s. d.		s. d.
10 inches	3	10 inches	2
11 in.	4	11 in.	3
12 in.	6	12 in.	4
13 in.	8	13 in.	6
14 in.	10	14 in.	8
15 in.	1 0	15 in.	10
16 in.	1 4	16 in.	1 0
17 in.	1 6	17 in.	1 2
18 in.	1 9	18 in.	1 4
19 in.	2 0	19 in.	1 6
20 in.	2 6	20 in.	2 0
21 in.	3 0	21 in.	2 6

Worser Second Dishes half price of Best.

Prices of Nappeys and Baking Dishes.

7 inches	1 6	Seconds	1 0
8 in.	2 0	ditto	1 6
9 in.	2 6	ditto	2 0
10 in.	3 6	ditto	2 6
11 in.	4 6	d tto	3 6
12 in.	6 6	ditto	4 6

Tureens.

Best		Seconds
Large	3 6	2 6
Middle	2 9	2 0
Small	2 0	1 6

Best Stoolpans.		Seconds.
12 inch	1 4	1 0
11 in.	1 2	10
10 in.	11	9
9 in.	9	6
8 in.	7	4

Butter Tubs and Stands.

Large Best 9d. Seconds 6d.
Middle do. 7d. ditto 4d.
Small do. 5d. ditto 3d.

London Size Cups & Saucers, Best 1s. Seconds 9d.
Irish Size, Ditto and ditto ditto 1s. 2d. ditto 10d.

Sortable white ware, Best 1s. 6d. seconds 1s. 2d.
Covered ware ditto 2s. ditto 1s. 6.
Inlett Teapots ditto 2s. 6d. ditto 1s. 9.

Sortable Blue Flower'd, Best 1s. 10d. seconds 1s. 6d.

No Sortable under 8d. nor Cups and Saucers under 6d.

To allow no more than 5 per cent for Breakage, and 5 per cent for ready money.

To sell to the Manufacturers of Earthenware at the above Prices, and to allow no more than seven and a half per cent, beside Discount for Breakage and Prompt Payment.

Sauce Boats.

Best		Seconds
	s. d.	s. d.
Large	2 6	2 0
Mixt	2 0	1 9
Less	1 9	1 6
Less	1 6	1 3
Smallest	1 3	1 0

Twyflers.

Best	1 4
Seconds	1 0
Thirds	9
None less than	7
Best Plates	2 0
Best Seconds	1 9
Worser ditto	1 6
A degree worser	1 3
Ditto ditto	1 0

None Sold under 9d. and not to be Pick'd, but Took as they are put together.

Cups & Saucers Holland Size.

Mid. White best 10 seeds.	8
Small ditto ditto 9 ditto	7
Middle Blue do. 1 2 ditto	10
Small ditto do. 1 0 ditto	8
Three to Piece ware Best 1 4 seconds 1s.	
London Size Cups & Saucers	
Blue and White Best	1 4
Ditto Seconds	1 0
Holland Ware best	1 10
Ditto Ditto seconds	1 6
Covered Toys 6 seconds	4
Handled ditto 4 ditto	2½
Cups & Saucs. 3 ditto	2
Only twelve to doz.	

Policy of William Banks, Potter, Stoke-upon-Trent, 12 November 1763. Guildhall MS. 11936/150

204458	William Banks at Stoke in the County of Stafford Potter. On his buildings at Stoke aforesaid Viz!	
£1.5.0	On two Brick Hovels only not exceeding Thirty pounds on each	60
Xmas 1764	Two other small Brick Hovels only not exceeding fifteen Pounds on each	30
£1.8.0	Marle house only not Exceeding Five Pounds	5
	Barn only not Exceeding Fifteen Pounds	15
	Workhouse and Chamber only over to make dishes in not Exceeding	25
	On another Workhouse & Chamber only over not Exceeding Thirty pounds	30
	Cratemakers Shop only not Exceeding	15
	Plaining House only not Exceeding	20
	On one other Plaining House only not Exceeding	30
	Sagger house & Lath house only not Exceeding Thirty Pounds on each	60
	Long Lathouse only not Exceeding	40
	One Accounting house only not Exceeding	15
	Throwing house only not Exceeding	20
	Slip house only not Exceeding	30
	Slip Kiln only not Exceeding	10
	Slip Kiln only not Exceeding	15
	Slip house & Kiln only on the left not Exceeding	10
	Painting house only not Exceeding	10
	Smoak house only not Exceeding	10
	Large Smoak house only not Exceeding	30
	Smoak House only to make Plates in not Exceeding	20
		£500

P. Godfrey   J. Mason   J. Fisher

Mem^{dum} Endorsed to John Bourne of Newcastle under Line Cordwainer as Mortgagee. Ent^d 31 January 1764. J.W.

Sun Insurance policy dated 12th November 1763, taken out by William Banks some thirteen years before the premises was purchased by Spode I.

Agreement entered into by some twenty-eight manufacturers of salt glaze stoneware to avoid price cutting, an almost inevitable result of reduced demand.

earthenware vase-shaped coffee-pot, blue printed with Fruit and Flowers pattern P817. Spode earthenware coffee-pots are not easy to find; Fruit and Flowers pattern is not common. All is well until the hand touches the handle. The pot is unstable and rocks upon its base, which is not flat. Rejecting the first wild collector's hope that this pot was especially designed by Josiah Spode II no less, for use on antique gate-legged tables with uneven tops, sadly the conclusion must be reached, this is not a 'Best'. A 'Best second' perhaps, or a 'Worser second' or 'a degree worser', who can say? At least in the end it was 'pick'd' and perhaps owes its very existence now to the fault that must have relegated its first status to that of 'Worser Worser'.

Returning now to the affairs of Josiah Spode I, on 11th November 1772 a deed of co-partnership was duly signed for a period of seven years until 1779 between Thomas Mountford of Newcastle under Lyme in the County of Stafford, gentleman, and Josiah Spode of Stoke-on-Trent in the said county, potter. In this agreement Mountford, who is described as inexperienced in the trade of potter, was to provide £500 capital and in return he was to be instructed in 'the whole art and mystery of the aforesaid trade of potter as far as the knowledge of the said Josiah Spode extends'. The business was to be carried out at Shelton at a premises rented from Elizabeth Mountford, widow for a term of seven years. The partnership agreement included a restriction on both parties from trading or dealing separately in any trade or any of the wares or commodities in which the partnership had agreed to trade or deal. Two exceptions to this comprehensive restriction were Spode's partnership with Tomlinson until it ended on 11th November 1774 and the haberdashery business carried on by Josiah Spode's wife, Ellen.

Again the Wedgwood archives produced the only known invoice of Mountford & Spode to Josiah Wedgwood dated 23rd June 1774 for the very useful ware of two dozen chamber pots. At that time it would seem, no doubt, to Josiah Spode that a payment of 12s.6d. per week as 'an adequate compensation for his superior skill' plus a half share in the profits of the business was a very reasonable return from this second partnership which he had not had to finance.

Although Spode's agreement with Tomlinson terminated on 11th November 1774, his lease of the Bridge Bank Works extended to 25th March 1775 by which time his elder son, Josiah Spode II was almost twenty and within three months became a married man. His younger son Samuel was well over seventeen. It appears likely that they were employed with their father at Spode & Tomlinson or perhaps at Mountford & Spode.

On 29th February 1776 Josiah Spode I bought William Bank's old works from Jeremiah Smith who then owned it. Spode's partnership with Mountford had more than three years to run and there is no evidence to show how the Spode family overcame the restrictions placed upon the elder Spode by his partnership with Mountford. It would appear likely that the sons undertook the running of the pottery soon to become known as Spode Works. Situated on the North side of Stoke Church Street, the Works had been insured on 12th November 1763. From the policy, in the records of the Sun Insurance Company, now held in the City of London Guildhall Library, and reproduced here, it can be seen that William Banks ran a substantial business larger than, it would seem, both that of Spode & Tomlinson and Mountford & Spode.

Publish'd 25.ᵗ June 1777. **POT FAIR. CAMBRIDGE.**

A cartoon drawn by Henry Bunbury and dated 25th June 1777 is entitled POT FAIR,CAMBRIDGE. A portly don is about to be overturned by a pack of dogs chasing one of their number provocatively decorated by undergraduates all much to the detriment of the pottery, whether creamware or salt glaze.

There is nothing to suggest that Josiah Spode I did not meet his obligations to Thomas Mountford and, although owning the large pottery in the centre of Stoke, his conduct remained unchanged for the three years remaining of their agreement with neither partner making a complaint of conduct or duty. The most probable solution would appear to be that Josiah Spode II, perhaps with the assistance of his brother, took control of the new venture, a view possibly supported by the fact that it was he that paid off the mortgage on the property in the years to come.

On 9th July, 1775, at the age of twenty, Josiah Spode II was married to Elizabeth Barker who died of a fever in London some seven years later in 1782. At what age the younger Josiah left school and entered his father's business is not known, but it has been said that he had been employed in every branch of the manufactory and, at the time of his marriage, must have been well grounded in the trade of potter and thus be able to undertake the management of the manufactory his father purchased in the following year.

That the wedding pleased both fathers is clear. Elizabeth received a dowry of £500 and according to Simeon Shaw:

The parents judging this a proper opportunity to establish a regular London business, alike advantageous to themselves and the newly married pair, the younger Mr. Spode therefore commenced as a dealer in earthenware; and subsequently also of glass and porcelain; and the assiduity he manifested, to gratify the varying and wishes of purchasers in kinds, quality, and shapes of various articles; soon gained him extended connections, while the excellent Blue Printed pottery (recently introduced), supplied by the father, obtained such preference as to produce a considerable increase of business.

The move to London was not made immediately as might be supposed from Simeon Shaw's account. Their first son, William and their second son, Josiah III were both born in Stoke, in 1776 and in 1777. It was not until 1778 that Spode II became a freeman of the City of London, by then a simple matter to be bought from any City Livery Company, thus enabling him to enter the retail trade within the City. In 1778, no doubt with the help of his wife's dowry, he established himself in London at 29, Fore Street, Cripplegate, City, in quite a separate business from his father whose restrictive partnership in Stoke with Thomas Mountford still had a year to run. His business flourished; he twice moved in Fore Street to larger premises and finally, in 1796, he removed out of the City further west to the more fashionable area of Portugal Street, Lincoln's Inn. The premises in Portugal Street were nothing less than a converted Theatre (in fact the one in which Garrick had made his debut) with an attached house as living quarters in Lincoln's Inn itself. It should not be thought that the London business sold only the wares of the Spode factory. Particularly in the early days this would not be the case. From 1784 Spode's blue-printed pottery must have helped greatly with the sales of earthenware, but glass and porcelain must still have played their part. Indeed, first hand knowledge of demand would serve him well in future years.

Yet for all his involvement in the London business, Josiah Spode II remained a man of the Potteries. It was he who paid off the mortgage on the Stoke Works. It was he who joined with other potters to form Harrison Spode & Co., coal masters and miners at Fenton, and thus ensure cheap fuel for the Spode ovens. When Josiah Spode I, founder of this prosperity, died on 18th August 1797, to his elder son a return to Stoke would surely have been more a pleasure than a penance. His fortune was made in London; his heart remained in his place of birth. That his interest was centred in the Potteries can be judged from an entry in the *London Gazette* for 1798, the year following the death of his father. The entry confirms the commission of officers in the newly raised Staffordshire Pottery Volunteers, a body formed to defy the worst attentions of Napoleon. Of the nine officers named, all from the pottery industry, three held the senior rank of captain, of which Josiah Spode II was one.

Of Josiah Spode I it was said ' ...his loss was regretted, as a liberal master, a munificent benefactor and, above all, a truly honest man' — would that it could be said of us all! His obituary, published in *The Times* on 29th August 1797, duly noticed Mr. Spode's sons Josiah and Samuel. Of his widow and his daughters there is no mention — 'women's lib' and equal opportunities were yet to come!

The history of the Spode family has now taken us to the year 1797. Before particularising the continued expansion and development of the business, it

Spode's London warehouse in 1811, reproduced from a watercolour by George Shepherd. Built in 1714 as the Theatre Royal it was used as Thomas Turner of Caughley before being occupied by Josiah Spode II in 1796.

would be as well to remember the adverse circumstances for trade in which it was set. This was the period of war against the French and their allies; a war that was almost continuous from 1793 to 1815. In 1806, Napoleon in his Berlin Decrees, attempted to destroy our foreign trade and in all Europe only Russia remained open to our exports. Even victory brought no relief as it was followed by general distress and discontent with the Luddite and Spa Fields riots in 1816, the March of the Blanketeers and the Derby Insurrection in 1817, the Peterloo Massacre in 1819 and the Cato Street Conspiracy in 1820. Against this troubled background and stagnating trade, the leaders of the Industrial Revolution, by invention, application and determination, progressed and made their way. Amongst these was Josiah Spode II.

As can be guessed from his success, Josiah Spode II must have been a forceful and dominating man. He made early plans for his sons who, at a tender age, had lost their mother. William, the elder, was to enter and learn the merchant business and Josiah III was sent to Stoke to be educated and 'as soon as his youth permitted, initiated in the business of a Potter under his grandfather'.

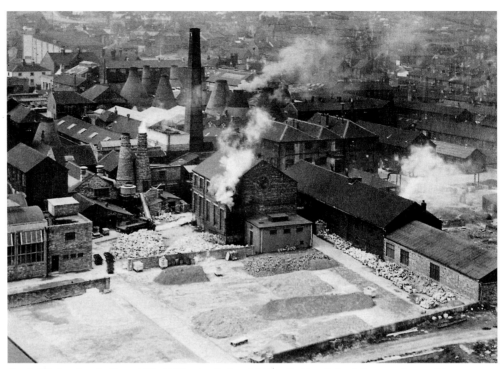

Spode Works after the Second World War in the late 1940s. Banks of clay left to weather and become more friable can be seen at the rear of the Works.

What a satisfactory arrangement this must have appeared to Josiah Spode II when, after the death of his father in 1797, he chose to leave London and return to Stoke.

William was now twenty-one and William Copeland, himself a native of Stoke and Spode's right-hand man in London, was thirty-two. They were left in charge of the London business. In 1805, Josiah II went one step further; he withdrew from London and made his son William and William Copeland partners trading as William Spode & Co. In 1811, William Spode retired and left London to live in Surrey and, somewhat later, changed his name to Hammersley the name of his maternal grandfather. Perhaps his life had been too well arranged by a dominating father. It would not be the first time, and will not be the last, that sons do not fit their father's cages.

From 1811, the year that the watercolour of the London warehouse was painted, Josiah Spode II again took up the partnership with William Copeland in London trading as Spode & Copeland. In 1824, William Copeland's son, William Taylor Copeland enlarged the London partnership which became Spode, Copeland & Son. William Taylor Copeland, the son, later became proprietor of both Spode Works and the London merchant business and a future Lord Mayor of London. Upon their shoulders rested much of the responsibility for marketing the new productions brought out by Spode II on his return to Stoke. They did not fail.

Turning back to 1797 after the death of Josiah Spode I, his son, Josiah Spode II then aged forty-two, returned to Stoke to take control of the manufactory in which previously he had more nearly been an absentee partner. He was to remain proprietor for thirty years. That he already knew the products and

Firing a bottle oven. Below, the fireman doing his job with those above wishing that he had not.

capacity of this, his family firm, is obvious. He also knew the London market for earthenware and for porcelain, two similar products which do not really compete. An introduction of porcelain would not endanger earthenware production. Spode porcelain would oust the wares of the existing manufacturers on the shelves of his London showrooms to his double benefit. To manufacture porcelain does not seem to be the decision of the long-established earthenware potter Josiah Spode I but rather that of a potter turned merchant turned manufacturer, Josiah Spode II. Be that as it may and some believe that Spode I initiated porcelain manufacture, about 1800, or a little before, the first Spode porcelain appeared using a formula containing bone ash. After a short experimental period, the fine body now known as 'Bone china' was produced and appeared as tea wares with the cups and cans of the new Bute shape with gilded band and line borders, the first being pattern 473 of about 1803. To decorate these wares the 'black printed' engraved copperplates were adapted at first with punched shading added to the 'black printed' technique of line engraving. Finally, to meet Copeland's death in 1826, the partnership reverted to the name of Spode and Copeland with Spode II and William Taylor Copeland as equal partners. These bald facts hide the true worth of William Copeland the father, and the demands of fashion. Copperplates, engraved entirely by punching, were printed in Spode's charcoal-grey rather than the intense black used in the past.

In the same year of 1803, a most unfortunate accident occurred to Josiah Spode III. When inspecting a recently installed steam-engine, driving throwers' wheels and turners' lathes, his hand was caught between the cogs, necessitating amputation; an early victim of industrialisation.

In 1806 the Works was visited by the Prince of Wales. Of this visit Simeon Shaw reports:

His Majesty George IV, while Prince of Wales, being on a journey of pleasure to Liverpool, in 1806, in company with his Royal Brother, the Duke of Clarence, visited the Marquis of Stafford at Trentham, on the way; where many of the Nobility joined the company. Having often intimated a wish to witness the manipulations and processes of Porcelain Manufacture, the opportunity was embraced, and their Royal Highnesses with the Nobility and suite visited the establishment at Stoke. Mr. Spode had so arranged, that all the persons employed, of both sexes, were in their best attire, to manifest their respectful and loyal attachment to the Heir Apparent, and the family on the throne; and as the Royal and Noble visitors passed thro' the different apartments, the appearance and demeanour of the working classes, drew forth repeated eulogiums. The large warehouse, (117 ft. long), was then visited where were arranged every variety of Pottery and Porcelain, in the most elegant and curious production, manufactured by Mr. S. whose loyalty and respect were so highly appreciated by the Royal visitor, that Mr. S. received the appointment of *'Potter to His Royal Highness the Prince of Wales'*.

In 1815, Josiah Spode III, then thirty-eight, was married and about this time retired from the business to take up farming. Perhaps this was another case of an over-dominant father. Yet even in those hard times Josiah Spode II expanded his business and produced 150 new decorative patterns each year, new shapes, new sizes and new bodies, stone china about 1813 and felspar

Spode Ware being sent for shipment on the maiden voyage of the RMS Queen Mary *in 1936 still packed in traditional hogsheads and packing cases with the Spode Ware protected by straw.*

porcelain in 1821. In 1820 his customers could choose from no less than nine sizes of chamber-pot, to fit all most comfortably, eight sizes of water ewer and handbowl and eleven sizes of Dutch jug. The list is endless; the customer is 'king'; the service absolute. Wedgwood, the leaders of the century before, were surpassed; thus did Josiah Spode II overcome all difficulties and progressed.

In July 1827 Josiah Spode II died, aged seventy-two. His obituaries speak highly of his abilities, his business acumen and his success, so richly deserved as we have seen. Perhaps it cannot be said of him, as it was of his father, that 'with his wealth, increased his kindness', yet his office staff and other dependants were remembered in his will, evidence of mutual respect between master and man.

During his last illness his son, Josiah Spode III returned to Spode Works and took charge continuing for two years as proprietor until his own untimely death, aged fifty-two, in October 1829. His heir, Josiah Spode IV was not yet six; late marriage and early death robbed the Spodes of a further generation of potters of renown.

For the next three and a half years the factory was the responsibility of the two trustees of the estate of Josiah Spode III, his brother-in-law Hugh Williamson and his uncle by marriage, Thomas Fenton. Neither of these two gentlemen, however worthy, were potters, and it has been said that the business 'languished' in their hands.

On 1st March 1833 the Spode family finally withdrew. William Taylor Copeland purchased the half-share of the London business and the manufactory complete. Thus ended the history of the Spodes as potters and that of William Taylor Copeland as potter began, first with Thomas Garrett as his partner and later with his sons.

The illustration here shows a Wedgwood creamware plate of about 1765 'black printed' by Sadler with exotic birds line engraved and coloured in black contrasted to a Spode bone china saucer bat printed with a stag, P408 of about 1807, stipple engraved and coloured with Spode's charcoal grey rather than black although this was occasionally used and named by Spode as 'intense black'. An enlargement of each reveals the change of engraving from Sadler's line engraving to Spode's softer stipple punching. The Sadler enlargement also reveals a fault in printing occasionally seen in Sadler's early prints. In the neck of the upright bird a section of the engraving has not been printed leaving a white space surrounding a double black dot. This is caused by minute specks of dirt on the engraved plate holding the glue bat away from the oil filled engraving on the copperplate and is a certain indication of printing using a sheet of solidified glue to transfer the design, engraved on the copperplate, to the surface of the ware to be decorated.

Chapter 2

Transfer printing processes

There seems little doubt that the first involuntary transfer of printing in England took place in late 1476 or early in 1477. William Caxton after learning the mystery of printing in Bruges, set up his press near Westminster Abbey in the autumn of 1476 when he first printed on vellum. Books, including *Canterbury Tales,* were printed from 1477. The very process of printing is the transfer of a liquid, nearly always ink, from a solid surface of the type or incised copperplate to a flexible surface of paper, cloth, rag or vellum which can be pressed upon it. Should the printed page be touched before the ink is dry, by careless handling or placing one upon another, a second involuntary transfer takes place be it only upon the thumb or hand or bench or upon the back of another sheet. Every printer knows it; every apprentice does it despite his master's best endeavours to eliminate the waste. Caxton must have suffered from it.

It was nearly 300 years before this simple fact was put to proper use. On 10th September 1751 John Brooks a Dubliner, who served an apprenticeship in Birmingham as an engraver, made the first of three unsuccessful petitions for a patent for transfer printing. Describing himself as John Brooks of Birmingham in the County of Warwick, engraver he claimed to have:

Found out a method of printing, impressing and reversing upon enamel and china from engraved, etched and mezzotinto plates and from cuttings on wood and metle, impressions of history, portraits, Landskips, Coats of Arms, Cyphers, Letters, Decorations, and Other Devices.

Brooks left Birmingham in 1753 to manage the Battersea Enamel Works in London and from there made two further applications in January 1754 and April 1755 both equally unsuccessful.

The second claimant for the invention of transfer printing was John Sadler, a printer of Liverpool, who on 2nd August 1756 swore an affidavit, as a preliminary to patent application, that, assisted by Guy Green and in the space of six hours, he had printed upwards of twelve hundred tiles of different patterns and that he had been upwards of seven years finding out the method. Although supported by Charles Poole, member of Parliament for Liverpool, in his intention to obtain a patent no such application appears to have been lodged. Thus despite four attempts at patents none was ever granted in the eighteenth century for transfer printing on ceramics however performed.

On 23rd September 1761, Josiah Wedgwood, the leading Staffordshire potter, reached an agreement with Sadler that the latter should print on Wedgwood's improved creamware known as Queensware. The prints on Sadler's tiles and Wedgwood's creamware were taken from line engraved copperplates and on-glaze transferred mostly in black although other colours were sometimes used.

The predominance of black prints in the eighteenth century accounted for the name of the process being termed 'Black Printed', rather than the nineteenth century name of 'Bat printing' which more accurately describes the transfer process. Black printing was said by Simeon Shaw in his *History of the Staffordshire Potteries* to have been undertaken by Josiah Spode I during his partnership with Tomlinson between 1767 and 1774. Regrettably Spode and Tomlinson did not mark their wares nor did the partnership of Mountford and Spode between 1772 and 1779. Black printing, in the meantime, had spread throughout the Potteries with numerous small undertakings decorating their pottery with a wide range of differing black prints. Very few of these pieces were marked, indeed, before 1800 marked pieces were the exception and only gradually did the practice of marking become the accepted policy of even the larger firms.

This on-glaze printing was rapidly followed by the development of underglaze blue printing used first at Worcester and at Thomas Turner's factory at Caughley in Shropshire, from whence it is said the process finally reached the Spode factory in 1784. On this event Simeon Shaw, writing in 1829, reported:

> About 1784, he (Josiah Spode I) introduced the manufacture of Blue Printed into Stoke; on the improved methods successfully adopted by Mr. Ralph Baddeley of Shelton. The patterns were — for Table Services what is now called Old Willow, with a border of a willow and a dagger; and for Tea Services the Broseley, from the Pattern used at Caughley. The engraver was named Lucas, and his first printer was named Richards, from Caughley. Specimens of this, shew the great strength of the engraving, and consequent deep blue of the ware. The first transferrer Mrs. Mary Broad, of Penkhull (recently buried at Stoke) informed us that she remembered the first dish printed in Blue, at Stoke, being long preserved as a specimen.

From the time that Spode's unmarked pieces can definitely be identified as manufactured by Spode, the two very different methods of printing, on-glaze Bat printing and underglaze Blue printing, had been joined by a third, a less used variation, known as Pluck and Dust printing.

On-glaze bat printing of the nineteenth century used the same printing technique as the 'black printed' of the century before. The difference in appearance stems not from the printing process but from the engraving technique and the necessity to meet the change of fashion brought about by the appearance of the softer look in engraved prints introduced by Francesco Bartolozzi with stipple punching replacing the use of line engraving.

There are several short eighteenth century descriptions of this method of transfer printing but regrettably none can be found in the Spode records. However, the *Official Descriptive and Illustrated Catalogue of the Great Exhibition of 1851* (three large volumes) includes a section written by Thomas Battam, art director at that time for William Taylor Copeland, successor to the Spodes. In this he states:

> The 'Bat printing' is done upon the glaze, and the engravings are for this style exceedingly fine, and no greater depth is required than for ordinary book engravings. The copper plate is first charged with linseed oil, and cleaned off by hand so that the engraved portions alone retains it. A preparation of glue being run upon flat dishes, about a quarter of an inch thick, is cut to the size required for the subject, and then

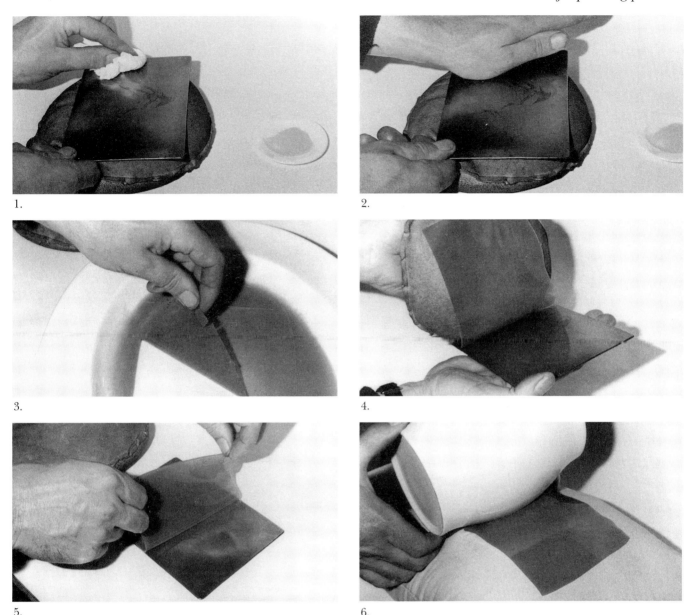

1.

2.

3.

4.

5.

6.

Bat Printing *The copperplate used in this series of illustrations is a Napoleonic print of 1803, P390, entitled* A STOPPAGE to a STRIDE over the GLOBE, *being one of the four Napoleonic coppers still held at the Works. As can be judged from Mr. Battam's description, the printing process is a simple hand craft with the printer undertaking all the steps of the process before the final firing of the transferred print.*
1. *First the copperplate is charged with a fine boiled linseed oil.*
2. *It is then cleaned off so that the oil is retained only in the engraving.*
3. *The transfer medium is formed by pouring onto flat dishes warm, liquid, gelatinous animal glue which on cooling becomes firm but flexible, resilient sheets of jelly of some elasticity and about 3mm thick. A section of this glue jelly, termed a bat, is cut to the size of the engraving.*
4. *Supported by a sawdust filled cushion, the bat is firmly pressed onto the charged copperplate.*
5. *The minute quantity of oil left in the engraving is picked up on the flat surface of the glue bat which is then carefully stripped from the copperplate and placed on the cushion, oily side uppermost.*
6. *The ware to be printed, in this case a jug, is rolled onto the bat with an even pressure to bring the oiled impression firmly in contact with the surface of the jug.*

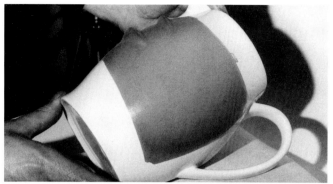

7.

8.

9.

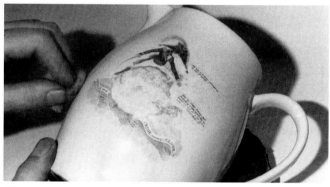

10.

11.

7. *The bat adheres to the surface of the jug and the transfer of the engraved design from the bat to the ware is completed.*

8. *The bat is then stripped away leaving the hardly visible oil on the glazed surface of the ware.*

9. *Colouring in the form of a very finely ground powder is dusted over the transferred oily impression.*

10. *The powder sticks to the oil but with careful cleaning can be removed from glazed surface leaving the transferred design now visible. The ware is then passed through the enamel kiln to fix the colour.*

11. *A print from the same copperplate can be seen transferred nearly 200 years ago to a Spode barrel shaped jug with the added decoration of a brick red band with black lines and the gilt name and date,* I. Topham 1804.

Printers' tools used for filling and cleaning off copper plates for underglaze printing. The circular backstone, upon which the colour is kept ready for use, is warmed on the corner of the stove to keep the colour workable. Colour is transferred to the heated copperplate by the spud, the smaller tool at the front of the backstone and then worked into the engraving by a wooden dabber shown behind. Surplus colour is removed from the engraved copperplate and returned to the backstone with the scraper, the larger instrument on the front of the backstone. On the left is the boss, a pad of flannel or cord, used to ensure that the unengraved portions of the copper are completely clean before printing. Compare this with the illustration of 1843 (page 36) which shows a knife rather than a scraper and a differently shaped dabber and boss.

pressed upon it, and being immediately removed, draws on its surface the oil with which the engraving was filled. The glue is then pressed upon the ware, with the oiled part next the glaze, and being again removed, the design remains, though being in pure oil, scarcely perceptible. Colour finely ground is then dusted upon it with cotton wool, and a sufficiency adhering to the oil leaves the impression perfect, and ready to be fired in the enamel kilns. (T.B.)

It is now 250 years since the first pieces of ceramic ware were decorated by this method of on-glaze printing and 150 years since Mr. Battam wrote this description yet we still do not know how thin sheets or bats of glue became the 'transfer' of a printing process or why the eighteenth century applications for patents were not granted. However, every step of the actual process is illustrated here demonstrated by Paul Holdway, the practical partner of this authorship, who first revived Bat printing after 100 years of forgotten slumber. He used Mr. Battam's description and many of the original copperplates still held at Spode Works as they have been for the last 200 years.

The second method of transfer printing greatly differs from that of Bat

The colour is being forced with the dabber into the engraved copperplate heated on the coal-fired stove. The thick iron-plate top of the stove is clearly shown in this 1920s photograph.

Bossing the copperplate after removal of surplus colour. Illustrated in the Penny Magazine *of May 1843 after a visit to the Works.*

printing It was used for transferring patterns on to the biscuit surface of the ware before the piece was glazed so that the print was protected by the subsequently applied glaze, a particular advantage for pieces subject to hard handling such as dinner plates. Although practised at Spode Works from about 1784, as reported by Simeon Shaw, the first description published in the Works is that of 1851 by Mr. Battam, who called the method 'press printing'. Today the process is known as flat-press printing and the term 'bisque' used in 1851 is now more usually called unglazed biscuit. Otherwise Mr. Battam's description is of the process fully developed by the beginning of the nineteenth century and still in use today although quicker modern presses and engraved rollers now print the transfers for today's productions. Mr. Battam's description reads as follows:

The engraving is executed upon copperplates, and for 'press' printing is cut very deep, to enable it to hold a sufficiency of colour to give a firm and full transfer on the ware. The printer's shop is furnished with a brisk stove, having an iron plate upon the top, immediately over the fire, for the convenience of warming the colour while being worked, also a roller, press and tubs. The printer has two female

Earthenware printing shop in the late 1920s. The method of printing and transferring is unchanged from Spode's times. The girl cutters stand dividing up the prints with their scissors just as shown in 1843. The women seated on the three-legged stools are transferring and rubbing down the prints.

assistants called 'transferrers' and also a girl called a 'cutter'. The copper plate is charged with colour, mixed with a thick boiled oil, by means of a knife and a 'dabber', while held on the hot stove, for the purpose of keeping the colour fluid; and the engraved portion being filled, the superfluous is scraped off the copper with the knife, which is further cleaned by being rubbed with a 'boss', made of leather. A thick firm oil is required to keep the different parts of the design from flowing into a mass, or becoming confused, while under the pressure of the rubber in the process of transferring. A sheet of paper, of the necessary size and of a peculiarly thin texture, called 'pottery tissue', after being saturated with a thin solution of soap and water, is placed upon the copper plate, and being put under the action of the press, the paper is carefully drawn off again (the engraving being placed upon the stove), bringing with it the colour by which the plate was charged, constituting the pattern. This impression is given to the 'cutter', who cuts away the superfluous paper about it; and if the pattern consists of a border and a centre, the border is separated from the centre as being more convenient to fit to the ware when divided. It is then laid by a transferrer upon the ware, and rubbed with a small piece of soaped flannel to fix it, and afterwards with a rubber formed of rolled flannel. This rubber is applied to the impression very forcibly, the friction causing

Earthenware printers in the 1930s engaged on teaware.

the colour to adhere firmly to the bisque surface, by which it is partially imbibed; it is then immersed in a tub of water, and the paper washed entirely away with a sponge; the colour, from its adhesion to the ware, and being mixed with oil, remains unaffected. It is now necessary, prior to 'glazing', to get rid of this oil, which is done by submitting the ware to heat in what are called 'hardening' kilns, sufficient to destroy it and leave the colour pure. This is a necessary process, as the glaze, being mixed with water, would be rejected by the print, while the oil remained in the colour.

As Mr. Battam's description and the illustrations show, the process of underglaze printing is that of an industrial team rather than the single person handcraft of Bat printing. The team of printer, cutter, transferrer and assistant divided the work yet each had their own particular skill. Of the four, the greater skill lay with the printer and the transferrer as would be supposed. Yet badly cut patterns with missing pieces and smudged impressions could mar the best of prints however well placed upon the ware. This early process of the Industrial Revolution was still far from the age of mere thoughtless repetition. Much skill and expertise were still required. The strength and tone of the colour were in the control of the printer. The true and proper fit of the pattern on the ware without wrinkles or tears, neither smudged nor smeared, tested the skill of the transferrer.

This method of transfer printing was used with prints of all sizes for

After printing, the copperplate is returned to the stove so that the heat will slightly soften the colour to release the printed transfer which can be carefully pulled away.

The method of laying a transfer has remained unchanged with the sticky coloured side of the transfer turned back over the hand, illustrated both in the 1843 print and this twentieth century photograph.

decoration of enormous dishes to tiny dolls' dinner plates and on earthenware, bone china and stoneware. The decoration by this method on Spode's eighteenth century wares was always in cobalt blue, the colour that could, at that time, withstand the high-temperature firing needed to develop the glaze. Towards the end of the Spode period other colours for underglaze printing were developed and introduced, of which green was the most popular, although it is blue that dominates.

Underglaze blue printing on dinnerware seems a logical progression from printing illustrated books. The transfer filled each 'page' with handsome patterns, flowers and scenes from far off places. In an age before easy travel, before photography, before universal literacy, a new world on your dinner table, produced at far less cost than anything yet made, could not fail to please. When it was the finest of its kind, as was Spode's underglaze blue ware, it not only pleased but its deserved reputation lives to this day.

The two, very different, main methods of printing in Spode Works before 1833 have now been described. The on-glaze Bat printing with its delicate, clean look blending so well with gilding on bone china and the bold underglaze blue printing, winning wide acclaim, both excelled within their limitations. The on-glaze Bat printing process could not produce all-over patterns or continuous borders. The underglaze process was at first confined to blue and only later were other colours added. No true red or orange colour was or is available that can withstand the high-temperature glost firing and so be used as underglaze.

A further illustration of 1843 again with the transferrer applying a printed border; her cutter stands behind. The two objects on the front of the bench are flannel rubbers with their ends bound to form handles.

Rubbing the transfer with a rubber to fix the colour firmly to the ware. A stiff brush dipped in soft soap rather than a flannel is used today. The final transferring process is to wash off the tissue in water leaving the print transferred to the ware ready for hardening on.

Printers' Square thought to have been built in the eighteenth century shown before demolition in 1922.

How then could these colours be offered on the cheaper printed wares when all-over patterns and borders were required? The solution was an on-glaze print neither as fine and delicate as Bat printing nor as bold and strong as underglaze. To place a print around a plate or cup a non-stretch transfer must be used. Glue bats distort and stretch when pulled around but tissue paper stays firm and thus neat joins can be made; tissue must therefore be used. The lightest prints that can be transferred by glue bats cannot be used with tissue paper and yet printing on the glaze does not require such a heavy print as underglaze. So a compromise was reached. A tissue paper transfer print was taken from the heated copperplate as in underglaze printing except that colour was not mixed with the oil. This allowed a finer print to be used than is possible with heavier oil and colour mixture necessary for underglaze. However, a little enamel colour was added to the oil so that the print was visible on the transfer paper, thus allowing the cutter to do her work and the transferrer to position the print correctly upon the ware. The tissue, after transfer to thoroughly clean glazed ware, was rubbed down with a flannel impregnated with soft soap to ensure close contact of the oil to the glaze. To allow easier removal of the tissue by reducing the viscosity of the oil, the ware was often warmed over the stove before the tissue was carefully plucked or pulled away leaving the sticky oil transferred to the glaze. Dusting the oil with finely ground enamel colour and cleaning off excess dust, exactly as the Bat printing process, was the last stage of this printing process to be followed by firing in the enamel kiln to remove all traces of the transfer oil and firmly fix the colours to the glaze.

This method was known as 'Pluck and Dust' or 'Pull and Dust' and was mostly used for iron-red and orange, a derivative of this colour although a wide range of other colours were used. However, 'The Red Shop' for Pluck and Dust printing established by the Spodes was discontinued in 1943 on health grounds. At its best the process produced a fine soft print but was more difficult to control than either Bat or underglaze printing and surviving Spode examples are of variable quality.

Both Bat printing and underglaze press printing were used to produce printed outline guides for the paintresses of enamelled ware. Bat printing was particularly used for badges, crests and coats of arms as a guide for repetitive enamelling. In this form the process lingered on into the 1870s. Colour dusting is gone forever, barred by the very proper health and safety laws. It is very interesting to note that one world-wide use remains for colour dusting on faint oil impressions. The world's police forces dust colour on the oily impressions of finger prints left on glossy surfaces, a transfer that many must have wished unmade.

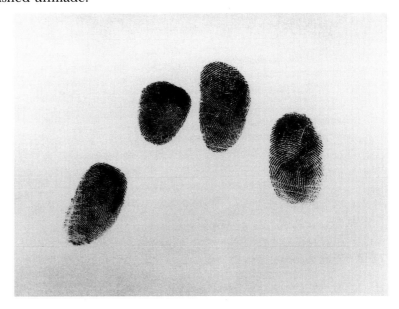

Chapter 3

Art forms and engraving techniques

It was no coincidence or chance that one of the possible 'Inventors' of transfer printing, John Brooks, was a copperplate engraver. It is obvious that without this craft transfer printing would not exist. However, the first step towards production of printed ware is to find a suitable design.

In the eighteenth and early nineteenth century, the time about which we write, this was of no difficulty. The present law of copyright did not exist. Any drawing, painting or paper print could be plagiarised and copied even line for line. One of Samuel Howitt's sporting prints had Howitt's name on the spaniel's collar. Spode's copy followed shape for shape except that only the collar plate is blank. Even then it was not quite so simple. Fitting flat designs to shaped pottery pieces calls for skilled adaptation of design, nevertheless nearly every print upon pottery or porcelain has an original in some other form.

Spode's designs themselves stem from two very different art traditions, that of the Orient, mainly Chinese, and that of post-Renaissance Europe, although Greek, P906 and Love Chase, P717 designs are based on ancient European art. The presentation of landscape views shows the most noticeable difference between the two main art forms. The perspective of a common vanishing point taught to and understood by the European mind is not used in the art of the Chinese. To western eyes their drawings of landscape views have a curious flat appearance. An island placed in a lake seems to hang in the sky or be a part of an unreal stylised design rather than the portrayal of a distant isle in a living landscape.

With the vast imports of blue painted Chinese porcelain in the eighteenth century, the Oriental art tradition, even if only partially understood, had in the western world become firmly established as an acceptable and, in many cases, a preferred decoration for dinner wares. It was to this ready-made market that the first Spode blue printed wares were addressed. These early printed wares followed Oriental designs and only later did European art reassert itself in printed wares to give the choice that had always been available in painted decoration.

The predominant colour for on-glaze printing in the eighteenth century was black as the term 'black printed' suggests. At Spode Works in the early years of the nineteenth century, to match the current fashion of the prints issued by London's print sellers, this was modified to the less startling charcoal grey obtained by mixing one part of dark yellow umber with one part of cobalt blue with three parts of flux. Black was still used at Spode on a decreasing number of prints and became known as intense black. For underglaze printing the main colour remained cobalt blue in a variety of shades although in both methods of printing other colours were sometimes used with slowly increasing frequency.

The charcoal grey used by Spode for the on-glaze printing had the same characteristics as the intense black favoured in the eighteenth century and still occasionally used. It was an opaque enamel colour. A very thin deposit soon built up to maximum intensity and further colour added did not change the tone. Cobalt blue, however, is a very different colour. It is translucent and allows the light colour of the body of the ware to show through so that varying the thickness of the deposit produces tints and shades of the same blue at a single print. Many readers may remember this phenomenon from their childhood days. The painted landscapes with green fields and yellow sun blazing from an intense blue sky. That awful struggle with the sky that never would become an even blue perhaps can still be well recalled.

On-glaze printing in black upon a white body is a simple adaptation of copperplate book engraving, a craft developed over many years before its advent into the potter's world. The difference in light and shade are controlled both by the weight of the line or dot and by their relative position to each other. A lighter shade can be produced by spacing more widely the same weight of engraving or by reducing the weight without altering the spacing. Skilled engravers use a combination of both techniques.

On the other hand, printing in cobalt blue belongs entirely to the ceramic field. The designers and engravers had no previous experience upon which to rely. As already seen, the Chinese blue painted ware, with which Spode set out to compete, was decorated with an even flat Oriental technique. This appearance was copied by Spode in the eighteenth century and the full potential of the translucent cobalt was not appreciated until the turn of the century. From about this time Spode's Chinese landscapes, although retaining the same Oriental style, benefited from improved techniques and showed differing tints and shades to enliven their appearance. These new techniques were used to great effect with the introduction of western perspective landscapes shortly to appear in underglaze blue printing.

Copperplates, before engraving work can commence, must have a perfectly flat, smooth and polished surface. First any bad flaws, pits or deep scratches must be removed. These marks are rubbed vigorously with a steel burnisher to round the edges and even out the indentation and then that section of the surface is levelled by 'knocking up'. To do this the exact position of the flaw or pit is found and marked on the reverse side using callipers. Then the copperplate is placed face down on a polished anvil and the copper is punched forward from the back with a hammer or hammer and punch so that the bottom of the flaw or pit is pushed up level with the face surface of the copperplate. In other words, the flaw or pit is transferred from the face of the copper to the back where it can do no harm.

The face of the copperplate is then brought back to perfection by 'planishing', that is rubbing backwards and forwards with a wet stone which removes the copper in a slurry. The stone must be kept very wet and passed evenly over the surface of the copper. Three grades of stone are employed with the delightful names of Middle Brook, Tam o' Shanter and Water of Ayr used in that order, with the last being the very finest. New copperplates are normally supplied ready faced by the coppersmiths but the engraver uses all three processes of burnishing, knocking up and planishing in his repair work to remove unwanted engraving or scars and cuts put in to existing plates by rough handling in the printing shop.

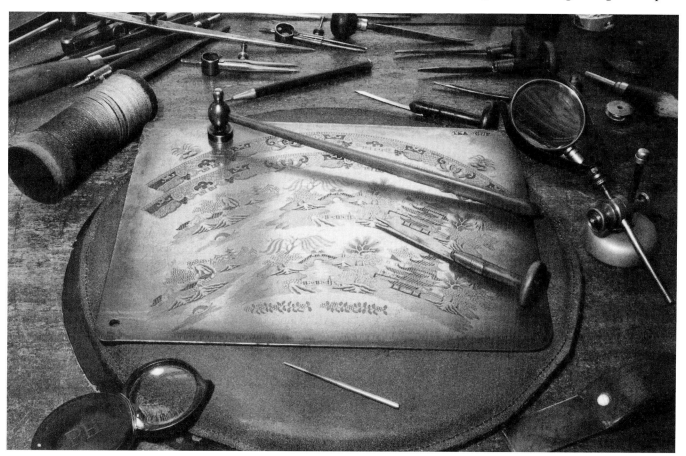

The engraver's tools. This small copperplate engraved with Broseley P614 is lying on the engraver's boss. This is a sand-filled leather pad onto which the copperplate is embedded and which forms a firm, even support for the copperplate when it is being worked. Lying on the copperplate is a graver or burin, with behind it a hammer used with a punch which itself is shown on the front of the boss. To the right of the boss is a scraper with behind it a magnifying glass on a stand. To the left of the boss a second, hand-held magnifying glass is the nearer object, with behind it an engraver's oil rubber. This is a roll of printer's flannel tied tightly and with the end trimmed flat. The flat end is rubbed on the engraver's sharpening oilstone to pick up oil and minute quantities of the abrasive stone. It is used first to remove any tarnish from the copperplate and further, during engraving, to dull any area of copper slightly so that a clearer inspection can be made of the engraving in progress.

The engraving on a copperplate for transfer printing must be designed to meet two basic needs. First, the engraving must accept the printing liquid quickly, easily and evenly. Second, the same liquid must be easily lifted out with a sharp clear print when the flexible transfer is pressed firmly on the copperplate. If these criteria are met, a good printed decoration can be produced quickly and with the minimum of wastage, both necessities for efficient swift production. The most successful forms of engraving that meet both needs are a 'V' cut line and, in the case of a dot, an inverted cone, again a 'V'. There is nothing in the shape to impede easy entry or removal of the printing liquid, and, by increasing the depth of the cut, additional colour can be held to give a darker shade of blue when printing with a cobalt mixture. This is also true, in some degree, of other colours. However, being more opaque than cobalt blue, they build up to full intensity more rapidly, thus shortening the range of shades available. This is particularly noticeable when comparing

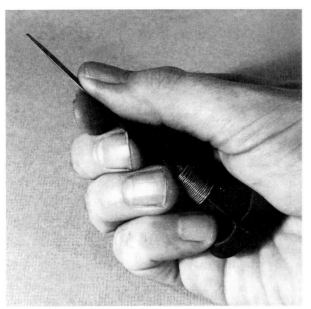

Holding the graver. The flat side of the graver is so shaped as to allow the tool to be held close to the copperplate.

Paul Holdway using the graver on a new modern size of copperplate for a larger plate for Waterloo P709.

underglaze blue with the later-developed underglaze green. The green, printed from the same copperplate, gives a flatter, less contrasting appearance than the blue, as can be seen when comparing prints of Aesop's Fables, P907, which were issued in both colours.

After approval of the initial design, the first step by an engraver, in the production of an all-over pattern for underglaze printing is to fit this design to the ware. To those not used to the difficulties of making a flat sheet of tissue paper cover a shaped article such as a jug or bowl, think back to the school-days atlas. There centuries of cartographers show their attempts to flatten the world's outer skin on to the flat printed page. How many of these atlas pages could be 'wall papered' back on to a globe without cuts or wrinkles? The transfer engraver has an advantage that the cartographer does not possess. The finished 'globe' is all his customer will see and the flat sheet 'map' is merely a step in the production. Its appearance may well be strange but of this no matter.

To find the outline shape of the transfer, an actual piece of ware to which the design is to be fitted is supplied to the engraver. The ware is rubbed over with a stick of fitting wax, a mixture of beeswax and tallow. Tissue paper is then smoothed on, sticking to the wax with the surplus paper carefully trimmed away during the fitting process. When the whole area that is to receive the pattern has been covered and all surplus paper removed, the shaped tissue is 'peeled up' carefully and re-laid on the flat surface of the copperplate. It often looks like a piece of the dressmaking patterns which tailors use in their endeavours to fit the human form. A line marked around the edges of the paper, known as the fit line, is then inscribed in to the copper with a sharp needle, or if a radius with dividers, thus permanently marking the outer shape of the engraving required.

The next step is to adapt the design to the outline shape, usually on a separate

Punching the background of the border for the modern plate of P709. As punching requires the use of both the engraver's hands it is not possible to use a hand-held magnifying glass. In this illustration the glass has been placed on a padded wooden block so that the engraver's view of the copper is suitably enlarged.

The completed copper is resting on Paul Holdway's bench. The first trial pull taken from it is shown on the left. The smaller antique plate of the same pattern on its right was made in the 1820s and was the model used for the modern enlargement.

drawing, marking in the main details. In the case of repeated border designs, only one complete section would be drawn in the size required with repeats being added later using prints from the first section. From this master drawing a tracing was taken on oiled tissue paper. In the eighteenth and early nineteenth century a sort of home-made carbon paper of tissue rubbed all over on one side with lampblack was made and placed, black side down, on the copperplate which had been sized with a mixture of turpentine and resin. The tracing was placed over the carbon and the design again traced through using a blunt needle or stylus leaving a black imprint on the copper. This was then permanently marked on the copper with a sharp needle or cut with the graver if it was to be a bold pattern. In the case of Bat printed designs, which are small, no 'fit' was usually needed and the engraver's work commenced with his tracing. With coppers intended to be produced using punched dots alone, the outline would be very lightly marked with a sharpened needle, so as to avoid over-facing the delicate design.

The engraver was then ready to begin 'getting in' on the copper, with the original design, his master copy and the marked copy before him. It is worth noting that all engravers' work is so detailed that it is usually undertaken with the aid of a magnifying glass. The hand tool used to make a 'V' cut line is termed a graver or burin. It is a slightly curved length of steel of diamond section fixed into a round wooden handle, which is flattened on one side. It is pushed along the surface of the copper, cutting and removing the metal to form a 'V' shaped groove in the copperplate. An engraver employs several sizes of graver and of different angular section in his work, but the force required to push the tool by hand through the copper limits the width of each cut. The same tool can be used with a picking or flicking action to produce a dot but for this indentation it is more usual to use a sharpened steel punch which is tapped with a hammer. Although the graver cuts and removes the metal from the

Spode copperplate to print decoration for 15.5cm plate GROOM LEADING OUT of Indian Sporting P904-16. The original Spode copper has been halved and reused on the reverse side. As was common for small items, it was originally a double copper for printing two of the same plate transfer at the same time. The dark patch on the left of the engraving are the dents of 'knocking up' put in when the copperplate was reversed and the original back was faced for new engraving. After printing, the cutter would first divide the double transfer into two sections each of a complete plate. Next, using the opening on the right in the border, the centre and the border would be separated and each in turn transferred to the plate as illustrated in Chapter 2.

copperplate, the punch does not. In the latter case the metal is forced up around the punched indentation into a raised rim called a burr. These burrs are cut away and removed using a sharpened steel scraper which will also remove any roughness on the edges of the graver cuts. Burrs can also be removed by planishing with stone and water. Thus the surface of the copper is made smooth, leaving only the cut grooves and punched indentations below the surface ready to accept the printing liquid.

However, it is very probable that much of the engraving will have to be re-entered with the graver or punch to clean out metal pushed back into the lines and indentations by the punch. In the case of coppers for blue ware, those portions of the engraving requiring a darker appearance will need to be cut more deeply by the graver or punch to allow them to hold more colour. Each time the graver or punch is used the scraper must follow until a perfect clean edge is left with each cut line or punched indentation. Engraving cut with a graver is called line engraving. In Spode's time, and continuing in Spode Works to this day, the punch used had a single point, which produced one dot at a time, as against a later development of multiple-pointed punches. Engraving with a hammer and punch is termed 'single punching' or just 'punching'. The very light, delicate punch work on bat coppers to be used with

A plate transferred from this or the twin engraving. The position of the join in the border depended entirely on the transferrer. On this plate it is at the bottom and neatly made. The centre and the border fit more tightly on the plate than on the copper where allowance has been made for the cutter's scissors.

charcoal grey impressions is termed 'stipple punching' or 'stipple engraving'.

In the preparation of a blue printing copper of fully developed technique, the engraver would first cut in the outline with the graver and then undertake the punched tones and removal of its burr. Punching is very close work and could only be undertaken in good daylight. On completion of punching, line shading follows using the graver and then re-entering the graver lines where extra strength is needed. Next, cross shades are added and finally 'cutting up' to produce shadows both using the graver. On reading this description and examining the illustrations on these pages the thought may well occur — what skilled, painstaking work this is. It is just that. A copper for a blue printed dinner plate with an all-over design such as Italian, P710 is about two months' work for an engraver. That for the largest dish would take perhaps six months. Transfers for a full dinner service could not be printed without the use of some fifty different coppers and a simple service used half this number. As can be seen, in terms of engravers' time, the introduction of just one new printed dinner service was a lengthy task.

In the forty-eight or forty-nine years in which Spode printed wares were produced, well over two hundred different designs of underglaze blue were produced and are listed in this book, not all for dinner ware but covering every possible pottery or porcelain use. Every plate size, every dish size, each shape and size of cup, saucer, tureen, mug, jug, ladle, footbath, garden seat and endless other shaped items required a differently engraved copperplate for each item to be printed. To this must be added well over three hundred Bat printing coppers, those for coats of arms and heraldic devices, the Pluck and Dust coppers and, although less time consuming for the engravers, the many copperplates engraved to print the outline guides used to help the paintresses of the many repetitive enamelled designs.

The hot printing process was very hard on copperplates which were rubbed with the dabber and then with the scraping knife. In consequence half the time of an engraver could be taken in cleaning, repairing and 'going through' or recutting the engravings on worn and damaged coppers and only half could be employed on new designs. During Spode's time the later practice of steel plating the coppers after they were engraved to give a longer life had not yet been introduced. The Spode factory was the largest manufacturer of printed ware in the country yet its output was only a small part of the printed wares pouring out of Staffordshire and other pottery centres in the first quarter of the nineteenth century. What exactly this meant in numbers of skilled hand engravers is difficult to imagine when decoration by water slide coloured transfer has taken much of the day to day trade now leaving the Spode Company as the sole Staffordshire manufacturer of top quality underglaze blue printing.

Very little is known about the engravers employed by the Company before 1833. Simeon Shaw in his *History of the Staffordshire Potteries*, written in 1829, reporting on the commencement of blue printing in Staffordshire, stated:

> About 1783, James Richards, John Ainsworth and Thos. Lucas, an engraver, left the service of Mr. Turner at Caughley, and engaged with the Staffordshire manufacturers; Richards and Lucas with the first Mr. Spode (hereafter mentioned); and Ainsworth with the first Mr. John Yates of Shelton.

Earlier, in a passage quoted in Chapter 2, Simeon Shaw named Mrs. Mary Broad, who had died before the 1829 publication of his book, as the first transferrer at Spode Works who was asked to give her recollections of events in 1783 or 1784. In one copy of Shaw's book, the names James Richards and Thos. Lucas are crossed through and over-written as John Rickett and John Lucock in corrections appearing to have been made many years ago. Which pair of names is correct is difficult to ascertain but no mention is made of engravers or printers for the earlier 'black printed' ware.

Llewellyn Jewitt in his book *The Ceramic Art of Great Britain* published in 1878, nearly 100 years after the event he was recording, offers a different history. Neither Richards and Lucas nor Rickett and Lucock receive mention and Spode's early engravings were said to be the work of Thomas Minton. Minton, after apprenticeship and early employment with Thomas Turner at Caughley, removed to London, where he is said to have engraved some patterns for Josiah Spode. Jewitt further states:

> From London, having married, he removed into Staffordshire in 1778 or 1779, where the rapidly increased demand for blue printed earthenware gave promise of

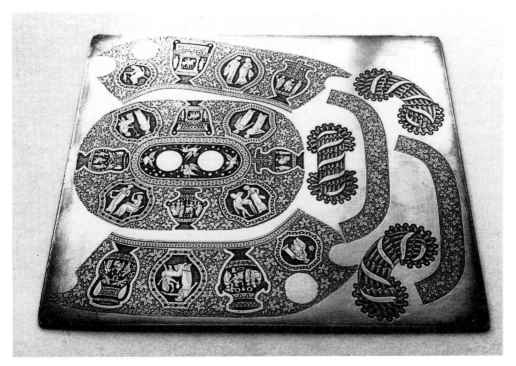

Sauce tureen and cover, 18cm overall, transfer printed with Greek P906 together with the copperplate to produce the prints for its decoration. The cover is transferred with a single main print which has to be fitted around and over the handle which in its turn is decorated with a separate transfer wrapped around it. The tureen itself needs four prints plus the two handles, all a complicated job for the cutter and transferrer, considering that they must work with thin tissue paper covered with sticky colour which if touched or misplaced is ruined — hardly unskilled mass-production!

a good opening for the skilful draughtsman and engraver he had become. On removing into Staffordshire, he set up as a master engraver at Stoke-upon-Trent, his residence and engraving shop being a block of buildings then called Bridge Houses, erected by Thomas Whieldon, the first partner of Josiah Wedgwood. Here he became very successful, one of his chief employers being Josiah Spode, for whom he engraved a tea-ware pattern called the 'Buffalo', which continued in demand for many years; the 'Broseley', so called for being first produced at the Caughley Works, the 'Willow pattern' and many others.

It is evident that the two historians, Shaw and Jewitt, are reporting two different aspects of Spode's early engravings. Shaw's account was of the employees of the Company, whereas Jewitt detailed the engravings placed with the outside engraver Thomas Minton. Neither history is in itself complete but between them they give a picture of the whole. Josiah Spode I supplemented the output of his own engraving department by placing instructions for additional engraving with an outside engraver, a practice long continued.

Additional information about Thomas Grocott, one of Spode's and Copeland and Garrett's employees whose pocket recipe notebook has survived, came to light by curious chance when in 1931 a commemorative punch bowl was purchased in a local sale and placed in Spode Museum. The punch bowl bears the inscription:

At the suggestion of Mr. Thomas Grocott, this punch bowl was manufactured from the bones collected after entertainments given by Messrs Copeland and Garrett, Stoke-on-Trent, to their workpeople on the 13th and 14th November, 1834, to commemorate their taking the establishment March, 1833. To be considered as a permanent appendage of the Wheatsheaf Inn.

As was reported in the *Staffordshire Sentinel* under the heading 'Link with the Stoke of a century ago', the entertainment was a feast for 800 workpeople at the Wheatsheaf Inn which is situated beside the Works. This report drew a comment from a Mr. William Pepper of Derby also printed in the *Sentinel*. In this Mr. Pepper stated that he was the great grandson of the Thomas Grocott at whose suggestion the bowl was manufactured and presented to the inn. He further stated that Mr. Grocott, who was from one of the oldest families in Stoke-on-Trent, was on the maternal side connected with Josiah Spode and was employed at the Spode factory as chief engraver, his work being held in high repute.

That Mr. Grocott was a person of consequence in the Company is made clear by the acceptance of his suggestion and furthered by the inclusion of his name in the inscription. No doubt he held the position of chief engraver ascribed to him by his descendant Mr. Pepper. However, from the evidence of the information contained in his notebook, detailed in Chapter 4, it seems likely that the duties of the post then included some of the responsibilities now undertaken by the art director in the design and initiation of printed decoration. The importance of his position in the Company perhaps can be judged from the list contained in his notebook of the main gate key-holders, seven in total, of which he was one and which included William Outrim, the general manager.

The Engraving Shop in 1931. The shop was situated on the top floor of the China Terrace with a view through the windows of the china ovens shown in Chapter 1. Not all the engravers worked in this part of the shop crowded together as shown; some were brought round for the photograph. Taken some seventy years ago, a hundred years after the end of the Spode family ownership, it suggests that little had changed. The traditional three-legged pottery stools were still in use. The heating was with coal stoves with the coal carried up by the apprentices as it always had been. The engraving tools and methods were unchanged and even the modern electric light now looks old-fashioned.

In 1931 sixteen engravers were employed at Spode Works. In 1810, around the heyday of Spode's printed productions, it must have been more, although evidence suggests that as many copperplates were engraved by outside engravers at that time as were engraved in the Works. Spode's Italian P710, Castle P711 and Lucano P712 all appear on Welsh pottery from Swansea, and the Italian pattern is also printed on the wares of many Staffordshire makers as is the Castle. The multi-scene pattern Indian Sporting, P904, similarly has three makers although Spode does seem to be the original and best engraved which perhaps suggests that manufacturers copied each others successful patterns. However, separate engraving establishments willing to sell their patterns to any potters proliferated in the Potteries. Sixteen such engraving establishments were listed in the *Staffordshire General Commercial Directory* of 1818 and ten years later the number had risen to twenty-eight. The smaller potteries may have relied upon them entirely for new designs although perhaps doing their own re-engraving and repairs.

The use of patterns common to many manufacturers is a marked feature of blue printed ware. It is more difficult to be certain that the Bat printed coppers with punch stipple-engraved printed design were the work of outside printers. The prints of Landscape scenes P201 to P285 contain views that appear similarly printed by other manufacturers including New Hall, Miles Mason and Chamberlain's Worcester. The position of each punched dot varies from maker to maker but the same print has been copied from an original paper print or, perhaps, direct from a rival manufacturer. A note of other manufacturers using the same pattern has been placed in the catalogue beside the appropriate pattern number in Chapter 5.

Examination of the copperplates at Spode Works shows that a number of Bat designs were engraved on the reverse of portions of reused earlier coppers. These earlier coppers, with outmoded engravings, were cut up to make the smaller sizes for Bat printing with their original reverse refaced and stipple punched with the new design. A number have parts of orientally inspired designs upon what is now the reverse. One Bat copper, P410 Sleeping Dog, is of particular interest. The back has a section of Rotunda P707 engraving which, as discussed in Chapter 7, can be dated to before 1796. This evidence suggests that many Spode Bat printing copperplates were engraved at Spode Works and not by outside engravers.

The copperplates for Bat printing are generally both smaller and of a thinner gauge than those for hot press printing, either underglaze or on-glaze Pluck and Dust. This is understandable and logical. 'Black printed' and 'Bat printing' are the same hand printing process differing only in the type of engraving and the usual colour used in employment. Neither the copper nor the print can be much larger than can be held in one hand. The copperplates were subject to very little wear. They were not rubbed by anything harder than the palm of the hand, nor were they heated thus avoiding the knocks and bangs of hurried handling that can befall a heated copperplate. Many of the original engraved Bat coppers have survived for two hundred years or so intact, little altered and in usable condition.

Amongst these are a number that are stamped with the name of the copperplate manufacturers. One firm of these copperplate makers, Benjamin Whittow, his son, and their subsequent partner and next proprietor, G. Harris, is particularly useful in that the name of the partnership and the place of business frequently changed, giving a guide to the year in which the copperplate was manufactured. Copperplates in Spode Works so marked vary in date from 1792 to 1810 or later. Care should be taken, however, in ascribing a date to the engraving as being the same year as the manufacture of the copperplate. The source of the print engraved on the copper may date well after the calculated year of the manufacture of the copperplate. Evidently copperplates were not always engraved immediately after manufacture. Nevertheless marked coppers are unusual and are of interest. The list of the copperplate makers is shown at the end of this chapter.

Many of the hot printing copperplates for underglaze blue and for on-glaze Pluck and Dust printing also survive at the Works from Spode's times. The copperplates themselves are of heavier gauge than those most used for Bat printing. This is not surprising since most of the engravings are much larger, and in any case a stouter copperplate is required to withstand the hard handling which is a normal part of the hot printing process. Many of the

A small part of the copperplate room at Spode Works. Many thousands of engraved copperplates are held in this room in alphabetical order of the name of the pattern last engraved upon them. The photograph shows a small section of the copperplates for designs starting with the letter 'I'. Since many of the early coppers with outdated designs no longer popular have been re-engraved on the reverse with later designs, it is only the second use of the copper that appears in the alphabetical list perhaps concealing a more interesting early design.

surviving coppers have been re-engraved or 'strengthened' and now transfer a stronger and darker print than they did before 1833. A possible explanation is that at some time since then, the normal supply of cobalt colour was interrupted and the substitute material produced a weaker print than formerly. Re-engraving with a deeper cut to hold more colour would redress the balance and build up the weaker colour to the appearance previously attained. Modern colour now used is much of the same strength as in Spode's day, hence the stronger and darker print. It is interesting to note that Tower pattern, P714 is still exported to America and Germany in the present stronger blue and re-engraving may only indicate a change of market, a change of taste or possibly a change of glaze.

By about 1800, or slightly later, the full techniques of line and punch engraving coupled with the imaginative use of cobalt blue were beginning to be fully understood. The first engraved coppers for underglaze printing were cut all over to the same depth and were exclusively line engraved with the graver. Punching was not used. The designs, based on Chinese art, were not only of flat appearance but were a single tone of blue. Progress was first made by varying the depth of the line-cut engraving, thus adding tone and shade to the print. Punching was then added and gave the appearance of an extra texture to the work.

One further characteristic of underglaze printing cobalt colour was understood and was increasingly used in the design of the engravings. Cobalt blue is a volatile colour which tends to spread, particularly into the lead based glazes of Spode's times, to give a slightly hazy appearance to each line or dot of a print. This can be seen when comparing even the sharpest underglaze blue print with that of an on-glaze black print. By close arrangement of cross cut lines or of punched dots which run together in the blue print, the appearance of a solid colour could almost be achieved, the shade of which could be varied by the depth of cut or dot.

Spode's Caramanian, P905, and European views of around 1810 show the joint mastery of engraving, printing and transferring of blue wares at their best. The change from the 'black printed' type of on-glaze engraving to 'Bat printing' stipple punching appears to be about 1803 with patterns 500 and 557 being stipple punched using charcoal grey colour as listed in the Colour Mixing Book illustrated in Chapter 5. Pattern 473 is engraved both by graver and punch and is printed in black and not charcoal grey. The Napoleonic prints taken from original caricatures issued in 1803, are typical 'black printed' line cut and punched and also are printed in black.

The copperplate makers

Copperplates with makers' back-stamps from three manufacturers are found at Spode Works. Only about one in twenty of the engraved Spode coppers exhibit these back-stamps, since the larger sizes of copperplates originally supplied were often cut up in the Works for use with smaller engravings. A search through trade directories and the *UK International Genealogical Index* has revealed some details of these makers.

1. Benjamin Whittow, his partners and successors — London.
Benjamin Whittow and Thomas Large were established as copperplate makers at 48, Shoe Lane, Holborn, London and insured their premises through the Sun Insurance Company in 1771. The first entry in a London trade directory was in 1776, the year that Josiah Spode I bought the present Spode Works, when they were described as Whittow and Large, copperplate makers, 48, Shoe Lane. The same entry continued to 1779.

At some time in the 1780s, Large left the partnership and Whittow continued alone at the same address. The entries in the various directories between 1790 and 1794 are confusing. The *Universal Directory* for both the years 1790 and 1791 lists the firm as Benj. Whittow at the new address of 43 Shoe Lane, yet *Kent's Directory* of 1792 and *Andrew's* of 1793 show Whittow & Son of 48, Shoe lane, the move to number 43 not being recorded until 1794. Since directories are notorious for offering out-of-date information and do not greatly figure in the

Print engraved about 1820 showing the interior view of the Copper and Brass Works at 46, 47 and 48 Shoe Lane, London. This is probably a larger works than those of Whittow, Shafe and Harlow and included the original Benjamin Whittow premises no. 48. Smaller flat plates, as used by Spode, can be seen being beaten on anvils at the rear. Judging by the numbers of workers hammering on empty vessels, copper and brass plate making was not a peaceful undertaking.

business of foretelling the future, we can safely say that the change of address took place in 1790 as the compilers of the *Universal Directory* were unlikely to have been given four years' prior notice of the move to number 43. The exact trading style of the firm must be in some doubt until 1794 when all directories show Whittow & Son at 43, Shoe Lane.

In 1798 the firm Whittow & Son moved to 31, Shoe Lane and in 1805 a new partner, George Harris, joined with the trading name changed to Whittow & Harris. Perhaps the Whittow in this partnership was the son. Finally in 1808, the Whittows died or retired and the firm traded then as G.Harris at 31, Shoe Lane until 1826 or 1827 when he removed to 4, Harp Alley, Shoe Lane. In 1828 George Harris took into partnership William Eastwood and traded variously as Harris & Eastwood and Harris & Co. until about 1835. In an 1836 directory the occupant of 4, Harp Alley is shown as William Eastwood (late Harris & Eastwood) who continued at this address until 1848 when the entries ceased. The firm under its several partners and proprietors had traded as copperplate makers for seventy-five years.

2. John Shafe — London

Born in Shoreditch, London in November 1779, Shafe first appears in *Kent's Directory* for 1804 at 40, Shoe Lane. In the following year of 1805 and until 1808, he remained at 40 Shoe Lane and was described as coppersmith and brazier and copper and brass plate maker. In 1809, as noted in *Holden's Triennial Directory,* he moved to 64, Shoe Lane and added tinplate worker to his list of trades. In *Holden's Annual London and County Directory* for the Year 1811, Shafe was described as Copperplate maker at 63, Whitechapel and in 1815 he is listed in his final address at 24, Little Moorfields. John Shafe's final appearance in a directory was in *The Post Office London Directory* of 1844–45 when he would have been aged sixty-five.

3. John Harlow — the Potteries

Unlike the wealth of London trade directories, those surviving of Staffordshire and the Potteries are few and far between. *The Staffordshire General Commercial Directory* of 1818 lists John Harlow as brazier and tinplate worker, Union Market Place, Lane End which was the earlier name for the present day Longton. *The Newcastle and General Pottery and Commercial Directory* of 1822–23 shows him as a brazier, tin and copperplate worker, Market Street, Lane End, thus confirming his activity as a copperplate maker. His move to Stoke indicated by his back-stamp J. HARLOW, STOKE must have been after 1823, a conclusion confirmed by the later style of engraving found on coppers so marked.

Based on these details Table 4 has been drawn up. All the makers' marks illustrated appear on the coppers used for underglaze printing but surprisingly this is not so of the Bat coppers. Marks 9 and 10 have not been found on these. Bat coppers with makers are individually listed in the right hand column of the table. This may be some guide to the first possible date for the engravings listed but cannot do more than this since some coppers were divided at the Works with the various sections engraved at different times.

Table 4. Copperplate makers' marks

Mark reference number	Mark	Probable dates of manufacture of the copperplates	Print reference of Bat engravings
1.		1790–91 Street number defaced. Probably used about time of removal from 48 to 43 Shoe Lane	P231
2.		1790–94 and perhaps to 1797	P404

Table 4. Cont'd.

Mark reference number	Mark	Probable dates of manufacture of the copperplates	Print reference of Bat engravings
3.	B. WHITTOW & SON N°. SHOE LANE HOLBORN LONDON	1797–98 Street number defaced. Probably used about time of removal from 43 to 31 Shoe Lane	P207, P213, P214, P337
4.	B. WHITTOW & SON N°. 31. SHOE LANE HOLBORN LONDON	1798–1804	P133, P172, P192, P253, P390, P402
5.	WHITTOW & HARRIS N°31 SHOE LANE LONDON	1805–08	P412, P418, P422
6.	G. HARRIS N°31 SHOE LANE LONDON	1808–27	P161, P162, P166, P167, P168, P342, P350, P352
7.	I. SHAFE SHOE LANE LONDON	1808–09 Street number defaced Probably used about time of removal from 40 to 64 Shoe Lane	P335, P347, P348
8.	I. SHAFE 63 WHITE-CHAPEL LONDON	1811–14	P264, P265, P331, P332, P336, P339
9.	SHAFE LITTLE MOORFIELD LONDON	1814–44	No Bat coppers so marked. Illustration from P813 Bowpot copper.
10.	J. HARLOW STOKE	After 1823	No Bat coppers so marked. Illustration from P822 Blue Rose copper.

Chapter 4

Patterns and proofs, shapes and sizes

The long and continuing establishment of a manufactory without break or interruption for many years has particular advantages for those interested in its past productions. In the case of Spode's early printed wares not only are many of the copperplates still held in the Company's copperplate storerooms but a number of record books are also still available. Of these the Pattern Books are the most illuminating, but much of interest is also contained in the Arms and Badge Books, the Proof Book, the Recipe Books, the 1820 Shape Book to which must be added Messrs Copeland and Sons Engravers Badge Crest and Letter Book dated July 28th 1868. The Pattern Books are a record of painting and gilding so that repeat and further orders could be properly and exactly matched. They are also a partial record of printing patterns, as we shall see.

Spode patterns are numbered in a simple sequence from number 1 upwards and reached about number 5300 by the end of the Spode period in 1833. The first Pattern Book does not show the earliest numbers and commences at pattern number 133 with many omissions until number 251 is reached, after which the pattern of nearly every number is illustrated. The first eight pages of this book deal exclusively with enamel-painted creamware border patterns which could be expected to have been manufactured in the eighteenth century From this it seems likely that the pattern number system had been adopted for easy reference in the Works some time before the full reordering record in the form of Pattern Books was started. It is probable that the double stimulus of the new management of Josiah Spode II in 1797 and the completion of the development of the new bone china in 1799 or 1800 would make the Pattern Books a necessity. When the first book was commenced only those earlier patterns still in production or likely to be reordered would be included. However, all subsequent examples had to be shown with the most usual presentation of the patterns in the books becoming that on a teacup or decorative bone chinaware.

The first four Pattern Books almost cover the Spode period, the last entry in the fourth book being pattern 5191. The first book consists of three smaller books bound together and ending with pattern 1023. Some of the paper used in all four books is dated by watermark. The first patterns on dated paper are 251, 281 and 322 in the first section of the first book with the date marked in the paper of 1799. However, the second section of the same book showing pattern 354 to 560 uses paper watermarked 1794 and several further instances occur where later patterns appear and are illustrated on earlier paper. Who would have thought in 1800 that a simple decision to use up old paper would have caused confusion 200 years later? Did some storeman issue his stock from the top leaving the bottom of the pile untouched for years or perhaps the draughtsman could not stand the modern paper and asked for the almost Napoleonic pre-war quality of 1794 to improve his drawings of the patterns. Whatever the reason, some caution must be used when dating patterns drawn upon watermarked paper. The paper was not always used during its year of manufacture, thus, although the introduction will never be before the year of watermark it may well be sometime later.

The introduction of new patterns or variations of existing patterns warranting a place in the Pattern Books continued at a remarkably steady rate of about 150 entries every year. As Whiter pointed out in his book, from this it is possible to obtain an approximate year for the origination of design by dividing the pattern number by 150 and adding the quotient to the date of 1800. Thus pattern 1222, a number found on bone china with a gold banded edge and Bat printed with Animals and Sprigs in black would be first introduced about 1808. An approximate origination date can be found for every numbered pattern in the same way but this may not be the date of manufacture of every piece bearing that number or with that design. Some patterns, including Bat printed decoration, were very popular and continued in production for many years.

In about 1822, a second and additional series of pattern numbers was introduced for simple and inexpensive designs of underglaze decoration.

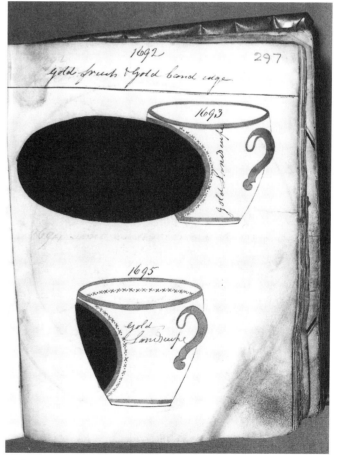

Two pages from the second Pattern Book. Pattern 1191 of 1807 is illustrated with a drabware antique jar. This is the first pattern mentioning 'Animals' and refers to prints P401 to P422. For an example of the ware see illustration S66. Patterns 1692, 1693 and 1695 give written instructions and illustrations of gold bat printing. The dark areas on the cups indicate cobalt blue panels to take the gold Bat printing.

Again the numbering was a straightforward consecutive sequence commencing with no.1 but with the capital letter B placed before each number. Patterns and numbered variations were added at the rate of about fifty per year reaching between B350 and B400 by 1833. In 1822, when this series commenced, a number of additional colours able to withstand the high temperature glost firing had been developed and could be used underglaze. The designs included in this B pattern series rather than in the main pattern series, were all underglaze and of a simple country style designed to compete with the less expensive range of earthenware shapes and decoration using the new underglaze colours both printed and hand decorated.

As already briefly stated, the Pattern Books are a record for the decorators of all painting and gilding undertaken in their department so that repeat orders will exactly match the original design The books record all free-hand painted patterns, infill painting of printed outline patterns and additional hand decoration on fully printed patterns. Special orders and matchings of the products of other factories were not included nor were the most sumptuously painted pieces, probably on the grounds of excessive expense in producing the Pattern Book copy and the little likelihood of exact repeat business.

On-glaze and underglaze printed patterns were treated very differently from each other. On-glaze printing, both Bat and Pluck and Dust are recorded by their gilded or colour-painted edge or border decoration, further by the colour of their prints and, in some cases, by the body of the ware upon which the print is placed. Additional painting on the print and the use of coloured grounds and borders are also recorded and separately numbered. To clarify these statements, some variations listed in the Pattern Books of the second Bat printed pattern 500 consisting of small flower and leaf sprigs illustrated in the catalogue of Bat prints P100 to P131 are described as follows:

Pattern 500   Slight black sprigs with gold edge
Pattern 523   French brown printed sprigs with gold edge same as 500
Pattern 2393 Black sprigs same as 500 with Chocolate edge
Pattern2947   Rose colour 500 sprigs, leaves.   Washed over in green enamel

As can be seen, each variation rates a separate entry and pattern number. Landscape views prints P201 to P285, first used on the very well-known pattern 557, appear over the years printed in colours including black, red, brown and gold, with variously gilded or painted edges with decorative bands and borders. Each variation is numbered separately. Pluck and Dust on-glaze prints are similarly treated An early design, Vine Border P522, first appears on pattern 1030 printed in red with a red edge. This debut is followed immediately with variations in colour of print and edge by patterns 1031, 1032, 1033, 1045, 1047 and 1048. A difficulty arises with on-glaze prints in that the prints themselves, in many cases, do not appear in the Pattern Books, which show the gilding or other decoration with the printing space left blank, or with a short written description. This is understandable perhaps since the Pattern Books were a record for the decorators and not the printers and would have been compiled within the decorating department. Sometimes even the assistance of a written description of the printing is omitted from the Pattern Books and the list of Bat and Pluck and Dust printing pattern numbers included in Chapters 5 and 6 cannot always give an accurate description. Where doubt occurs, it is so marked. Where information in the Pattern Books is lacking but marked examples of the pattern are known the description has been added.

A very different approach was made in recording underglaze printing. Underglaze blue printed patterns, without further added decoration, with very few exceptions are not included in the Pattern Books. This printing process, started in Spode Works in 1784, preceded the first known Pattern Book by some fifteen years and must have been well established long before the Works numbering system was introduced for the creamware border patterns. No attempt seems to have been made to include blue-printed patterns in this system and they have always remained known by names not numbers. The copperplates themselves act as their own pattern book and true record of the design. However, the addition of hand colouring to an underglaze blue-printed design rated an immediate entry to ensure that repeat painting applied by the decorators matched exactly that previously supplied. A partial exception to this was gilding, particularly on teawares. Many, but by no means all, are not entered in the Pattern Books especially the simpler gilded edges, although the ware must have passed through the decorating department to be gilded. When further high-temperature colours were developed for underglaze printing, the designs with additional hand decoration continued to be entered with a number. However, in the B series Pattern Books, unadorned underglaze printing in colours other than blue sometimes, but not always, was shown with a pattern number.

This 'hit and miss' method of entering underglaze designs in the Pattern Books might be termed 'miss and only sometimes hit'. Obviously it is some help in dating the origination of a design to find an over-painted blue print numbered and illustrated. It is likely that the first variation would not long follow the introduction of the plain print. By no means all plain blue prints were further decorated, and conversely, far from every print over-painted was produced in plain blue. It is not possible to tell exactly how many blue-printed patterns were produced between 1784 and 1833. 'Unknown' patterns still occasionally appear to the delight of those that 'find' them and to the continuous interest of those that hope to 'find' the next.

Spode Pattern Books give a guide to another aspect of the Company, that of the forcefulness and enterprise of the management and its eventual decline. Omitting the B series of patterns from consideration, about 150 new patterns were added each year. This total was made up of entirely new patterns and

A page from the fourth Pattern Book. Patterns 1942 and 1943 are variations in colour of Pembroke Bat printed flower sprays on Persian shape cups and saucer. Pattern 4944 is a Bat print of Birds in Branches with print P472 shown. All are of the years 1832/3. Notice the change of style and decoration in the years intervening between the two Pattern Books.

of variations of existing patterns. The first three Pattern Books cover the period from 1800 to 1827, the period of the management of Josiah Spode II. Book 4, patterns 4080 to 5191, continues first under the management of Josiah Spode III and then, from 1829, the trustees.

In this Pattern Book the introduction of new patterns sharply declines and the numbers are made up with more and more variations of existing patterns. Examination of the list of Bat printed pattern numbers in Chapter 5 shows a marked increase in these variations where every likely and unlikely combination is duly entered. The same is true of painted wares and of printed wares infilled with painted colours. The pressure from the top had gone. The 'quota' of new entries and new numbers was made up in the easy way without too much thought and care. Decline is evident. Perhaps William Taylor Copeland's purchase of the Works in 1833 was a necessity to protect his London business and his livelihood from the lowering standards of wares that were being sent to him to sell.

A leather-bound book, marked on the spine Arms Book, is the first existing record of Arms and Badges supplied to the customer's special order. This book contains 116 pages, the paper watermarked J.WHATMAN 1831. Some, but not all, of the Arms and Badges with dates ranging from 1834 to 1852 are in random order. A number of the Arms shown have been found on ware marked Spode, first supplied before 1833. Judging by the disordered arrangement of the dates and the entry of Spode prints, it seems likely that this book superseded earlier records in an endeavour by the new management of Copeland and Garrett to tidy up a previous system. Of the existing prints, perhaps Arms and Badges thought likely to be reordered were included and those thought moribund were omitted.

Some 120 years ago, about the period of the final withdrawal of Bat printing from production at Spode Works, prints from the bat copperplates and other fine engravings were proofed into the back of the Engraving Shop Badge and Proof Book. Exactly why this should have been done is not clear. Perhaps the firm wished to retain a record should this form of printing return to fashion. Proof of only about half the known Bat prints appear in this form. Examination of these proof prints shows some of likely origin after 1833 but some, in subject-matter, style and execution, fit Spode's earlier prints and yet are proofed copperplates that no longer exist. These prints, some of which have been noted on early wares or are illustrated in the Pattern Books are included in the catalogue of Bat prints shown in Chapter 5.

The two surviving main Recipe Books were both compiled after the withdrawal of the Spode family from the Works. The larger of the two, a leather-bound volume with a brass clasp and lock, contains 606 pages, size approximately 12.5cm x 20cm and is labelled 'Manufactured by B. Mathews 370 Strand – two doors from Exeter Hall'. The recipes are written in the same clear hand throughout. It is evident from the contents of the book that an endeavour was made to bring together all past recipes for manufacture of bodies, glazes, slips, dips, inks, oils and every item or process used in the Works. Not only are innumerable recipes and processes shown with lists of materials and their uses, but the results of costings and other experiments are included with records stretching back well into the times of the Spodes' ownership.

Pages 370 to 375 tell us that there were many different bodies for felspar

Bat prints proofed into the back of the engraving shop Badge and Proof Book. Prints from P200, P300 and P400 series are shown. The scarcely legible print of P359 used in our first edition has been superseded by a clearer print on a small plate in this edition.

porcelain. Body no.10 was chosen for the first introduction of the ware in November 1821, marked with an impressed open cross. Body no. 17, not surprisingly, came later on 15th September 1832 and is marked with an impressed F. An experiment recorded on page 476, was made in 1825 to find the cost of oil and blue colour for printing table plates in Filigree, P818 The printing mixture tested is now known as plate blue and is still used for printing Italian P710 pattern. The calculated cost of 2d. per dozen plates for colour can be compared with the recommended charge in the Staffordshire Potteries price list of 4s.0d. per dozen for printed table plates, of which 2s.3d. was allowed for printing. That the costs worked out in 1825 were worth re-recording some years later as still being of value tells us much of the stability of the currency.

Pages 559 to 564 of this book list 'Articles used in printing and why they were added' with a summary included on page 565 which is illustrated. What fairy-tale names they are. The description of the use of item 6, Oil of Swallows reads 'is a good drying oil and makes the colour fasten to bear rubbing'. You cannot doubt that it did but how was Oil of Swallows prepared and what from? Did the poor swallows survive and what about the horse of item 22? Nor can the Balsam of Capivi be a fragrant, languorous, mysterious eastern princess as the name suggests, it disappointingly turns out to serve 'much the same purpose as Beeswax to make the colour draw out of the engraving'. As for lampblack, it is

Page 476 of the larger Recipe Book giving details of the underglaze costing experiment of 1825.

Page 565 of the same book, listing twenty-two of the possible twenty-nine ingredients of printing oil. Those listed but not shown on this page are sugar of lead, white lead, red lead, litharge, spirits of vitriol, linseed oil and rape oil. The most important item from the complete list is boiled linseed oil.

dismissed as 'is good for nothing but sometimes used to make the oil look black'. It still does.

The second Recipe Book, also leather bound, is smaller than the first both in its size and in its content. The pages are 9.5cm x 16cm but only the first 66 pages have been used with the majority untouched. The paper is watermarked J. WHATMAN 1837, the same supplier as the Arms and Badge Book but six years later in date. The handwriting, except for the last few pages, is the same as that in the larger Recipe Book. It is not clear why two books were used but this appears to have remained in use to a later date than the first. The recipe on page 66 for cream colour glaze is dated 1858, the latest date in the book, and yet page 14 shows a cream colour glaze no.4 of March 1826. Many of the recipes are not dated but the years 1820, 1822 and 1830, all in the Spode period, appear amongst those so marked. Perhaps this smaller book includes earlier recipes found to be missing from the larger book in its completion

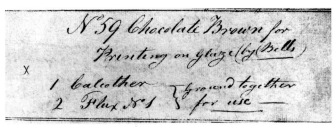

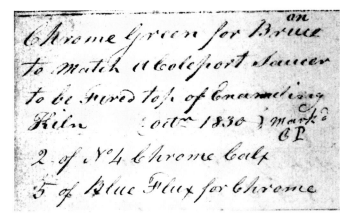

Two recipes for colours for the on-glaze printers Bell and Bruce from the colour shop Mixing Book. The second, dated October 1830, is to match a Coalport saucer. The position in the enamel kiln needed to obtain a true colour match is also specified.

together with the subsequent additions of the later years. An illustration from this book will be found in Chapter 5.

A further notebook size 9cm x 24.5cm, marked on the board cover 'No.1' and with the paper watermarked GILLING & ALLFORD 1816, contains recipes for colour mixing for use in the colour shop. In it the names of Bruce and Bell, the printers, are frequently shown with the recipes of colours made for their use. Further reference is made to this in Chapter 6.

The final surviving book used during the Spode period containing recipes is the personal notebook of Thomas Grocott whose senior position at the factory was discussed in Chapter 3. The paper is watermarked RUSE & TURNERS 1820 and written inside the back cover is Thos. Grocott, Stoke-upon-Trent, Jany 1825. The date of origination of a number of recipes is shown, the earliest being 1817 and the latest 1839. Perhaps Mr. Grocott entered all recipes that affected his work from 1825 onwards, including, when he needed, those already in use. Listed in the book are a number of different bodies and, most interestingly, recipes for a great variety of blues, thus confounding those who grandly claim to recognise instantly the colour of 'Spode' blue. Amongst those entered, each with a different formula, are:

Common blue for printing	Net blue
Common blue for china	Arms & Crest blue
New pattern blue (Filigree)	Peacock blue
Plate blue	Arcade blue
Frog blue	America blue
Broseley blue for china	South America blue
Pale Broseley blue	Sunflower blue

Some connect directly to underglaze blue printing; others are more difficult to place.

The Spode factory did not produce a catalogue of shapes in the manner of those issued by Wedgwood, Leeds, Castleford or the Whiteheads. All these shapes catalogues were based on the various styles of English creamware made during the seventeenth and early eighteenth century. It is true that Spode I made creamware in common with most Staffordshire manufacturers but his

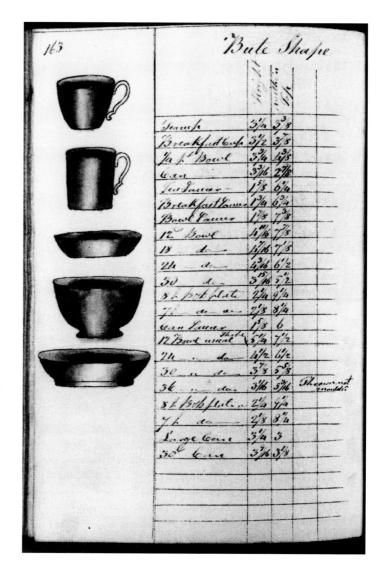

Page 163 of the 1820 Shape Book. *The surprise from this list of Bute shaped teawares is the number of different sizes of tea bowl and coffee can that were made. Six sizes of bowl are listed and three of can, shown as can, large can and 30s can. The seemingly haphazard variation in Spode can sizes was a deliberate customers' choice and not a deviation in manufacture as is sometimes supposed. The two common Bute shapes of saucer are illustrated. The upper being the teacup saucer with a recessed foot rim, and the lower being for tea bowls and having an applied foot rim. Also listed, but not illustrated, is the more unusual can saucer, a smaller and more angular version of the teacup saucer.*

main production, judging by the antique remains left to us, soon turned to underglaze blue printed pearlware which continued as the staple production of the factory and has held its popularity to this day. With displays of wares held at Stoke and in London and samples carried by travelling salesmen, perhaps the shapes were subservient to the patterns printed upon them. Whatever the reason, no Shape Book for customers was ever issued. The best-known book, Josiah Spode II's 1820 Shape Book, is a handbook record of shapes and sizes for throwers and turners and perhaps for warehouse and sales staff.

Two copies of this book are still extant, that still at the Works and a copy now held in the Henry Francis du Pont Winterthur Museum in America. This second copy may well have been that used at the London warehouse. It is identical to the first and written and drawn by the same hand. The entries made together with thumbnail sketches of the shapes are in no particular order, contain much information useful only in manufacture and obviously were never intended to be shown to a customer. However, the books could form a link between warehouse and Works for shapes and sizes, as well as being a record of the various manufacturing requirements in the factory. Bone china shapes in use in 1820 and 1821 are recorded and then only those that were thrown and turned. With very minor exceptions, pressed or cast wares were not included, thus precluding many of the more interesting items found particularly in blue-printed earthenware.

As the items listed were all in manufacture in 1820 or 1821 obviously later innovations do not appear, nor did a number of earlier forms which by then had dropped out of fashion and production. No catalogue can do more than show the pieces available at the time of compilation. As can be seen from the illustration on page 163 showing Bute Shapes, the Shape Book is not easy to follow or compare with other catalogues. Many of the items shown were not used for printed ware, nor does the book cover much of blue printing, as earthenware, including dinner services, is not shown. The shapes in the 1820 Shape Book used for printed ware are particularly noted in the illustrated sections of this book. Spode archives include two other pocket-books containing very similar information as that in the 1820 Shape Book. The books are heavily stained with white clay and give every indication of serving a similar purpose for the clay departments as the 1820 book did for throwers and turners.

A further shapes record still survives. It is the smallest of the four, size 10cm x 16.5cm with the paper watermarked JOHN HAYS 1810. The owner's name and the date are written inside the front cover, T. SHAW 3rd May 1817, a little earlier than the better known book. Again it contains the sizes, or measures as they are more technically called, for throwers and turners. Page 178, the next to last, is dated 18th May 1818, so it would seem that the book took a year to complete. The little sketches are in pen and wash, the writing is very small and again no moulded forms are shown. However, the wares are not confined to bone china and include many domestic and utilitarian shapes with their proper names and descriptions.

The range is enormous with such diverse and interesting items as: handled leech jars with pierced covers, drinking horns, char pans, wine funnels, pickle jars hooped and plain, union buckets, saucepans for the Emperor of Russia, lemon drainers, handled milk sieves, lizard jars and stoppers, beehives, tea tasters and suckling pots. Since many such items can be found decorated with underglaze blue prints, three pages from this book are included with corresponding blue-printed pieces in the illustrations of shapes of underglaze printed wares at the end of Chapter 7.

A further document in the Spode records, now held at Keele University Library and can be seen there, is a printed three-page leaflet headed 'Staffordshire Potteries – Prices current of earthenware 1814' and with a subtitle stating 'Revised and Enlarged December 1st, 1843 and January 26th, 1846 in Public Meetings of Manufactures'. The title tells us that agreement was first reached in 1814 and it seems likely that Spode, one of the chief manufacturers of earthenware in Staffordshire, would have been a party if not a prime mover. The year 1814 was a year of cut-throat competition with export potential still limited by the Napoleonic Wars. The agreement must have been made in an endeavour to lift prices in much the same way as the earlier saltglaze manufacturers' agreement. That it was similarly unenforceable is likely as can be guessed from the fourth line: 'Whatever rate of Discount is taken from this

List of Prices, Five Pounds per cent is expressly considered in the same for items of Breakage.' The manufacturers agreed the prices but not the discounts, leaving the true price open for separate negotiation. However, the agreed prices must have been of some value as the list was still in use over thirty years later.

The prices shown are obviously those of 1846 and not of 1814, although they may not have varied greatly as wages and prices changed but slowly in those times. The main interest lies in the relationship between the costing of the plain undecorated ware and that of the printed ware. Printed ware, on average, was two and a half times more expensive than plain ware although, like every price list, there seems no rhyme nor reason for some of the prices when printed ware is four times more expensive than plain. It is a pity that illustrations were not included but could not be expected in a trade list. Who can be certain that they have never met a 'Beef Steak Dish, in three parts', an expensive printed item at 10s.0d? or a 'Hash Dish, in two parts' at 8s.0d. The toy dinner sets of about sixty pieces at 8s.0d. per set would have been a fine investment considering the present price of a single dinner plate.

Perhaps some explanation should be given on the sizes shown in this list. It was Dr Plott in 1686 who first described the Staffordshire potters system of sizing holloware. A pint capacity was counted as 12 to a dozen written '12s'. A smaller number indicated a larger capacity and conversely a higher number indicated a smaller vessel. Flatware was always measured in inches. In Spode's time competition was seriously disordering the holloware system. Agreements on prices were always based on this sizing system yet manufacturers competed by enlarging the capacity of their vessels. Spode's '12s' pint jug was said to hold three half-pints yet would have been charged at '12s' prices.

This disarray continued and worsened. At the beginning of the twentieth century Copeland's catalogue, of necessity, included an explanatory page of sizes and capacities. From this we learn that Jugs, barrel '2s' held 11 pints and yet Jugs, Dutch '2s' could only manage 7. Jugs, hooped tankard, did not have a '2s' size but the capacity of the 6 quarts size was 13 pints. The 4 quarts jug more sensibly held 8 pints, yet reason departed with 3 quarts holding 6½ pints and the 2 quart size having a capacity of 5 pints. A hundred years had not improved the system.

The final record in which is traced the subsequent history of a number of the copperplates engraved during the Spode period is a book dated 28th July 1868 and entitled 'Messrs Copeland & Sons Engravers Badge Crest and Letter Book'. On its pages (size 22cm x 28cm) are shown part of various patterns listing the number of copperplates and the year upon which they were brought up from the copperplate store The record started in 1868 and first included 32 double sided pages of obsolete badges and crests followed by 103 double sided pages of miscellaneous patterns. By no means all of these patterns were engraved on copperplates during the Spode period nor were all engraved for underglaze printing. Evidently the book was compiled to keep some record of the copperplates that were being taken out of service with the engraving on one side being removed by planishing, as described in Chapter 3, and thus being made ready to be re-engraved with a new pattern.

Few pages show the complete copperplate pattern but just sufficient of each is shown squashed haphazardly on the pages yet making a clear record of the

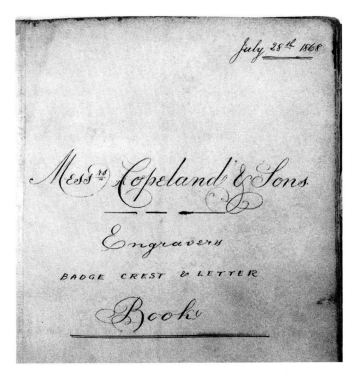

The cover heading of the 1868 Copeland Crest and Letter Book and an entry in the book showing a dish of Buffalo P616 marked 30 plates 1873 is shown here. With Buffalo being made by a number of manufacturers, this gives a very clear picture of Spode's version, which can be used to check unmarked ware.

designs that had been removed. It is not clear whether all the patterns shown in the book were planished but it does seem likely as many of the remaining Spode copperplates in the copperplate store are engraved on both sides with differing patterns. Written against each pattern illustration is a note giving the date, the pattern name and the number of plates to be planished. On one page against an illustration of much of a copper showing Italian P710 is written 'Italian' 81 plates landscape same in all brought up Jan/72. Fitted below are part of two sections of a design named as Ceylon and dated Jan 72 with 30 plates crossed through and planished added in a different hand. On the same date Jan 1872, no less than 45 copperplates of Net P620 were added plus 51 coppers of India P623 and 29 coppers of Athenaeum, a later pattern, plus 48 coppers of Blue Rose P822. In March 1872, just three months later, 50 copperplates named as Jassamine now known as Jasmine P820 were added. The juniors in the engraving department must have been heartily sick of continuously rubbing down the unwanted engravings with the three grades of wet stone used being Middle Brook, Tam o' Shanter and Water of Ayr, the last being the finest finishing grade. In 1873 the quantity of engraved plates to be refaced by planishing included more Spode engraved copperplates but the quantities of each pattern was reduced making the total work less of a burden. In the two years 1872 and 1873 some 32 different patterns engraved during the Spode years were reduced in numbers held or entirely removed from the available range.

In the later years of the eighteenth century earthenware manufacture had been dominated by Josiah Wedgwood who died in January 1795 aged sixty-four. After his death the factory, the largest in Europe, was left to his son Josiah

Wedgwood II who placed the business in the hands of Thomas Byerly, his cousin. The latter had recently been assistant to the elder Wedgwood and had, in 1795, retired to live the life of a country gentleman. By 1804 it had become obvious that Byerly was unable to manage the business at a profit and Josiah II was forced to return and take over with Byerly becoming manager of the London showroom. Some idea of Spode's activities can be found in Wedgwood's correspondence between their London showroom and the Wedgwood Works at Etruria, Stoke-on-Trent.

From London 24th July 1807 — To succeed in the Country trade we must not be niggardly in our sizes — the best makers act otherwise e.g. Spode's pint jug holds three half pints.

From a dealer's order to Wedgwood in 1810 — In consequence of the great delay (of Wedgwood fulfilling previous orders) we were obliged to apply to Spode & Co.

From London 18th May 1811 — Mr. Spode's prices of blue printed are so low that Mr. Bateman (the chief Wedgwood traveller) can get no orders for blue ware. — Mr. Spode has imitated our Water Lily and Corinth for the purpose of saying to the dealers — here are the very same patterns at much lower a price.

From London Feb 22nd 1812 — A lady in our rooms a few days ago stated that she had seen Mr. Spode's new blue pattern of the bridge at Rome over the Tiber, and she thought it very handsome.

From London April 15th 1812 — Mr. Spode's Rome plates are charged 5/- (25p) per dozen wholesale .

Spodes were competitors indeed with better patterns at much lower prices. Josiah Wedgwood's decision to turn his back on underglaze blue printing cost his successors the lead in blue-printed which they were unable to capture.

Chapter 5

On-glaze glue Bat printing

Perhaps before meeting the materials and men and listing the catalogue of prints and shapes of the glue bat process, it would be as well to enlarge upon Mr Battam's 1851 description, in itself made over 150 years ago. In this he refers simply and without further detail to 'a preparation of glue being run upon flat dishes about a quarter of an inch thick'. In these days of two part epoxy resins and of instant glues that can leave you stuck to the object for repair, the simple word glue may not bring to mind, as it would in 1851, the composition of the transfer medium used for glue Bat printing. The glue to which he refers is the residual substance, after removal of intractable solids, obtained from stewing skins, tendons, ligaments and bones of animals. When warm it is an amber fluid and in cooling passes through stages of soft to stiff jelly. After further evaporation of its water content it dries to a hard, rather brittle cement. It was the traditional glue for furniture but always had the drawback that in damp conditions it was liable to reabsorb water and return to a more fluid state thus weakening the joints. In its stiff jelly form it has a very flat smooth shiny surface ideal for holding minute quantities of oil without spreading or smudging.

For bat printing the glue was boiled up in a jug standing in a saucepan of water. When it became liquid it was poured into glazed pans so that, on cooling, it formed sheets of stiff jelly about 3mm thick. When ready for use as bat transfers it was not as hard as the little separate twisty bits of yesterday's children's party jelly stuck fast to the dish, but was nearer the consistency of the main left-over body of the same jelly now not so wobbly as it was at first serving, stiffer but still flexible. Being more glutinous, the bats were of greater elasticity and less easily split than children's jelly.

After use bats could be wiped clean with a damp soft sponge and having dried slightly, becoming tacky, could be reused. Similarly, clean bats could be stored overnight if piled face to face six or eight high on a damp plate and covered by a second plate. After two or three days the bats became too stiff for proper use and required reboiling with the addition of further glue mixture. After boiling the glue, the printer's last duty at night was refilling the pans so that the warm liquid glue could set before the next day's work. It is not clear whether the reuse and storage of bats rather than immediate reboiling was the normal practice at Spode Works. However, reuse may be one of the causes of difference in strength of prints from the same copperplate which is noticeable in glue bat printing. Another cause of variation in density of print was the humidity of the weather. On a damp and humid day, strong, clear transfers would result whereas a dry day would give rise to weaker prints.

Recipe no. 35 in the larger Recipe Book gives the ingredients for bats as: '6lbs Best Glue and 1 quart of Old Ale to which is added while it boils 3 pennyworth of Ising Glass well melted'. It concludes: 'Should the oil pour out wavy add a little more Old Ale and stir well among it which will remedy this defect'. Surely old ale is more usually thought the cause than the remedy for 'waviness'. However, in Josiah Wedgwood's Common Place Book, 1786–94, there is a copy of a recipe for bats for printing on the glaze stated to be from 'the late George Barnett's Pocketbook'. In this it gives the ingredients as 2oz isinglass, 8 of glue, ½ pint French Brandy. 'Waviness' must have been even worse at Etruria.

The bats were pliable, of some elasticity and easily cut to size. These qualities allowed them to be pressed around shaped ware and make a firm contact without slip or creep that would smudge the impression. However, the very elasticity that permitted the bat to conform to shapes without tears or folds did cause difficulty in distortion of the printed design. Illustrated are three transferred prints from the same copperplate, P341, The Beggar at the Gate. The first shows the print transferred to a flat sheet, the second to a porringer shape teacup and the third to a moulded cream jug.

The effects of the stretch of the bat required to conform to the shapes of the holloware can clearly be seen in the distortion of the gate. The more uneven

P341: *the Beggar at the gate.*

P341: *on porringer shape teacup.*

P341: *on moulded cream jug.*

P340: *on a moulded cream jug.*   P340: *on a flat surface without distortion.*

the shape to which the transfer was fitted the greater the stretch that was needed, hence further distortion of the print. As can be seen the top of the print on the jug has been wiped away above the line of the moulding as it would seem that the second change of plain was impossible to transfer satisfactorily with the glue bat process. The illustration of print P340, printed flat and on the reverse of the same jug, shows how a different design can hide stretch distortion, although careful comparison reveals that it is still present. This stretch can be useful in deciding whether a glue bat or tissue paper has been used as the transfer medium. Using a glue bat two prints from the same copper are rarely exactly the same shape as is far more likely with the non-stretch transfer paper.

A necessity for successful printing on the glaze, whether using the black printed line engraved ware or the later developed bat printed stipple punched ware, was to fasten the very small quantities of colour used to the surface of the glaze so firmly as to resist scratching and wear, a hazard to this decoration particularly on a saucer. The colours were basically the same enamels as were used for hand painting on the glaze. To prepare these a metallic oxide, the colouring agent, was mixed with ingredients of the glassy glaze itself, mostly ground calcined flint and lead. The object was to produce a coloured material compatible to the glaze and which, when fired to melting point, would fuse firmly to the glazed surface. To this coloured glaze mixture was added a flux. This last description does not imply, as a historian might suppose, a low state of health in medieval times brought about by over-indulgence the night before. In a ceramic context, a flux is a substance when mixed with another lowers the melting point of the latter. Borax was commonly used. The addition of the flux allowed the colour mixture to melt at a lower temperature than the already applied glaze which would be softened only sufficiently to ensure fusion yet remained undamaged. To obtain a consistent material the metallic oxide or oxides, the glaze ingredients and flux were well mixed together and were then fired until becoming a molten liquid. On cooling and hardening the mass was 'finely ground' as stated by Mr. Battam in his brief account, to make the fine powdery dust to colour good on-glaze printing.

In the eighteenth century, the wares most chosen to decorate with 'black printed' glue Bat decoration were principally the alehouse types of wares, mugs, jugs and bowls, printed mainly with subjects that might be expected to appeal to the male users of the vessels. This continued in the nineteenth century with prints in various colours, some with added enamelled decoration, and included Spode's range of Napoleonic satyrs based on London prints of 1803.

However, with the spread of plainer teawares and larger cups and saucers, their bodies better able to withstand boiling water without cracking, glue bat printing proved the ideal method for an inexpensive range of decoration. At Spode, from about 1803, Bat printed teawares were available using the Old Oval shape teapots, cream jugs, sugar boxes and slop basins supported by Bute shape cups, saucers and coffee cans produced in Spode's newly developed bone china. These were duly entered in the Pattern Books, the first pattern being 473 a range of flowers engraved using both punch and graver and printed in the 'intense black' preferred in earlier productions. This was followed by patterns 500 and 557 with the engravings produced only in stipple punching and printed in the charcoal grey adopted by Spode for glue bat printed tea wares.

Although John Sadler listed the use of six or seven colours for glue bat printing by 1766, no such early record exists for Spode. The Pattern Books list the use of various colours with the most frequent colour description being 'black' used first with pattern 500 and 557 and then in subsequent patterns. Henceforth, this term denotes Spode's new softer black, best described as charcoal grey and not the 'intense black used in the eighteenth century and still occasionally used for glue bat printing in the nineteenth. The probable dates of introduction of the colours for bat printing, calculated from the information in the Pattern Books, is as follows: Black (charcoal grey) and French brown 1803, blue 1804, chocolate brown 1810, gold 1811, red 1817 (although it may have been earlier on pattern 557), purple 1818, rose 1819, green 1821 and between 1827 and the end of the Spode period in 1833, olive drab, light brown, chestnut brown and possibly pale grey. A number of these colours were used much earlier for hand enamelling and for Pluck and Dust printing. After printing, the colours (with the exception of blue) were fired in the enamel kiln at temperatures between 700 and 800^{0}C. The proper temperature varied from colour to colour, but all were well below the glost oven firing temperature of about 1100^{0}C. Generally, the designs are most obviously printed on the glaze and are sharp and clear and very slightly raised. However, the firing temperature was critical. Underfiring tended to leave the print standing too proud, not thoroughly hardened, and susceptible to damage. When overfired, the colour sank into the softened glaze and the design, spreading a little, lost its sharpness. Underfired pieces could be, and often were, returned to the kiln to be refired at slightly higher temperature to correct the fault. No such remedy was possible for overfiring.

Blue on-glaze bat prints, however, are very different. A close inspection of blue-printed bat designs poses the question as to whether it is on-glaze or underglaze. The prints themselves are always hazy as against the clarity of other colours. The stipple dots are no longer separate but have run together even in the finest print. The glaze is nearly always flat and smooth with none of the slightly raised effect of other colours. The difference lies in the nature of the cobalt blue. When dusted or printed cobalt blue is an uninteresting and dull purple colour. Its translucent lustrous blue tones do not develop until higher temperatures than those of the enamel kiln are reached and it must be fired in the glost ovens. Secondly, cobalt blue is of a very volatile nature. When so fired it permeates the glaze, spreading slightly in all directions. Hence the hazy, run-together look and the penetration of the colour into the glaze. The blue colour finished in-glaze rather than on-glaze has much of the appearance of underglaze printing in which, of course, the blue has come forward into the glaze in the same manner. The exact temperature of firing in the glost oven was critical. Too high damaged the glaze and smudged the print, whereas too low did not allow the true colour to develop properly. An over-heavy glaze which allowed deeper penetration of the blue could also add to the haziness of the print. Finally, the glue bat printing technique was not designed for blue printing as was the underglaze method, and the contrast in tones is more muted with prints from bat copperplates. It is not surprising, therefore, that with the occasional exception, blue on-glaze bat prints remain second best to blue underglaze printing.

Spode's use of gold for on-glaze bat printing commenced in 1810 or 1811. The very act seems to have been an infringement of Peter Warburton's patent granted in 1810 and used by The New Hall Company. Of the three methods of printing named in this patent, the first was normal glue Bat printing using powdered gold instead of enamel. The copperplates for printing Landscapes and Classical Humanity, Fruit and Animals were used unchanged. Perhaps Spode considered Warburton's patent unenforceable since glue bat printing was well established over fifty years before 1810 and there was no novelty in powdered gold. However, Spode gold bat printing has rarely been found marked with Spode's name until after the expiry of the patent although nine patterns are shown in the Pattern Books, all probably of the year 1811. A single example marked in red with Spode's name and the pattern number 1693 has recently been noted but otherwise only the pattern number is shown and Spode's name is omitted. Since 1693 was the first of several pattern numbers used by Spode for gold Bat printing it would seem likely that, after objection from the New Hall company of appearance of the Spode name, an agreement may have been reached by Spode to be allowed to manufacture unmarked on-glaze gold printed ware perhaps on the payment of a fee although no trace of such an arrangement can be found nor is there any evidence of an endeavour to enforce the patent rights.

The series of Spode's gold bat prints produced first in 1811 were transferred directly on to white bone china or were placed upon panels or wide borders of rich cobalt blue already underglaze printed upon the bone china and subsequently glazed and passed through the glost oven before receiving the on-glaze gold print. A separate copperplate was used to produce the cobalt panels engraved with closely shaded lines deeply textured to carry much colour, which relied, with every success, on the volatile nature of the cobalt to even out the print within the glaze and produce panels of a dark lustrous even cobalt blue. The very fine nature of bat copperplates was not really suitable for gold dusting. On the white ware the deposit of oil was insufficient to hold enough gold to give the contrast obtained with the charcoal grey for which the copperplates were designed. The gold on cobalt blue was more successful, giving a better contrast and a richer tone. Both suffered from their inability to stand up to wear owing to the small quantity and soft nature of the metal used. A tea service in felspar porcelain, printed in gold with flowers and border, is marked with printed mark no. 41 in puce and 3743 written in red. It appears to be the first Spode marked service made after the expiry of Warburton's patent. A new flower design, P142, had been more heavily engraved on the copperplate than the original designs used in 1810 or 1811 and produced a firmer and clearer gold print than was possible from the earlier copperplates. Sometime either just before or just after the change of ownership in 1833, the factory adopted the Pluck and Dust

Pattern 500 with plain banded edge, shown on Bute teacup and saucer.

Pattern 557 with band and line gilding, Bute coffee can and saucer.

Pattern 1922 with gilded dontil edge shown on 18cm plate.

method of gold printing. The deposit of oil by this method was more lavish than that deposited by the glue bat printing method thus increasing the weight of gold dust on the ware with marked improvement of the product.

Bat printed tea wares are usually finished by the addition of coloured or gilded edges or borders. These vary from a simple banded edge to very elaborate gilded design as seen on patterns 558 and 2435. Without an edge decoration, Bat printed tea wares have a slightly naked, unclothed look. A plain enamel edge improves the appearance greatly, but even the simplest gilded decoration enhances both the ware and the printed decoration by adding life and warmth. Gilding was a more expensive edge finish than plain enamel yet, assessed by the quantity of each now remaining to us, Spode's customers must have adjudged the extra gilding cost as money well spent. The three most popular gilded decorations used on Bat printed tearwares were the three most simple: a plain banded edge, a band and line and a dontil edge illustrated here on patterns 500, 557 and 1922.

Bat prints overpainted in enamel colours, as was practised at a number of factories, was not undertaken by Spode to any great extent. The rare Napoleonic prints P380 to P394, of 1803 appear in plain 'black printed' versions and are over-painted in enamels in a manner superior to all their competitors. Of the later tearwares probably the most attractive is pattern 2947, of 1819, found both on bone china and on earthenware. The flower sprays and sprigs are Bat printed in a rose colour with the foliage overpainted in a green enamel, the whole set off in a gilt banded edge. On the other hand, over-painting Bat prints in enamel colours was the principal aid to reproduction of enamelled badges, crests and monograms. A light dusting of a neutral printing colour did not interfere with the polychrome enamels and was enough to ensure a constant shape for the crests on the largest dinner services and, no doubt, upon the subsequent replacement pieces. The Arms and Badge Books show innumerable proofed examples of these Bat prints extending into the 1880s.

Very little is known about the Bat printers at Spode Works. Only two families are recorded by name, those of Bruce and Bell. The first, a George Bruce, was apparently the senior, perhaps in charge of the department. His name appears in both Pattern Books and Recipe Books and it is likely that his family followed him in the employ of the Company. The first mention of his name is in the Pattern Book on pattern 2435 showing the gilded border design and the words 'Printed by Bruce' written in the space for the decoration. This can be seen in the illustration of the page of the Pattern Book together with an 18cm diameter bone china dessert plate printed with The Sailor's Farewell P350 set within the gilded border shown in the Pattern Book. The plate would have been printed, perhaps by Bruce, about 1816. A further named entry in the Pattern Book occurs on a later pattern 7084 which can be dated to about 1844. Entries naming 'Bruce' occur in the Arms Books up to 1886, the last being an ornate initial 'W' supplied on tableware on 9 April, 1886. The Arms Book entry is marked 'Printed by Bruce in gold and burnished'. The customer, a Captain Webb but not the Channel swimmer, was marine superintendent of the London, Brighton and South Coast Railway at Newhaven.

In the Recipe Books there are three recipes for mixed colours, two for purple and one for rose, in which it is stated that the colours were made for Bruce for printing. His name also appears in a recipe for a special slip. Further reference is made in the *Newcastle and General Pottery and Commercial Directory* of 1822–23 in which George Bruce printer, is shown as living in King Street (now Consort Street) opposite the Works. In the agreement of the sale of the Works and houses by the executors of Josiah Spode III to William Taylor Copeland dated 12 October 1832, Bruce was listed as a tenant living at Cliff Bank at an annual rent of £6. 10s. 0d.

It is inconceivable that the Bruce mentioned about 1816 and again in 1886, some seventy years later, were one and the same man. The later entries must surely have been made about another man, perhaps the son of the first as tradition has it in the Works. The name of Bruce went even further; Mrs. Kate Bruce is listed in the 1907 *Sentinel Directory* as living at 6 King Street. She was then believed to be about eighty years of age and was thought to be the widow of a Bruce, a printer at the Works, and herself lately employed there, the last of a long association.

Two members of the Bell family are recorded in employment as printers in the Works. The elder, Richard Bell, is mentioned in a colour match recipe as being the printer of an on-glaze Dresden sprigs in a black-brown colour to match that used for pattern 3767 — Union Sprays. Both Richard Bell and George Bell, thought to be his son, are entered as printers in the *Newcastle and General Pottery and Commercial Directory* of 1822–23 with Richard living at Cliff Bank and George at Honeywall its extension and both close by the Works. George Bell is also listed as a tenant in the sale agreement between Josiah Spode III's executors and William Taylor Copeland in 1832. His rent was

Page from the Second Pattern Book showing designs introduced in 1816. As can be seen pattern 2435 is marked 'Printed by Bruce'. Humanity P300 series prints have been found with ware marked with this number. Also shown on this page is the next pattern 2436, which is the last variation of the Pluck and Dust design P525 Convolvulus Border.

Recipe from the Colour Mixing Book giving the formula for mixing the black colour powder for the popular Bat patterns 500, 557 etc. no doubt including pattern 2435. Notice that the mixture was three parts of flux to two of colour which in itself was equal parts of dark yellow and dark blue to give, after enamel firing, the well known charcoal black of Spode's Bat printing.

Plate of pattern 2435 with Print P350 in black.

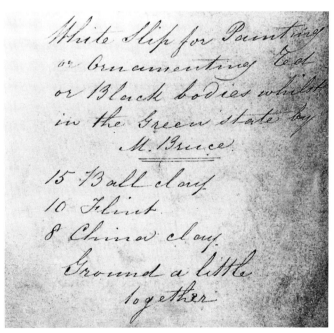

A recipe for white slip from the Second Recipe Book. This is the white slip that was painted on the decoration panels of the revived Astbury-Jackfield ware before Bat printing, see illustrations S33, S34 and S69. The reference, in this case, is to M. Bruce rather than plain Bruce as was usually made when referring to George Bruce. Perhaps M. Bruce refers to a woman, the wife or an offspring of George Bruce.

Page of the Second Pattern Book showing pattern 2435 illustrating only the gilding and further described as 'Printed by Bruce'. The 18cm diameter bone china dessert plate is decorated with The Sailor's Farewell P350 from the Contemporary Humanity series, no doubt Bat printed by Bruce. It is marked SPODE and the pattern number 2435 both in red.

Pluck and Dust printed ware in iron red. From back to front. Rectangular bone china dessert dish, Bamboo P501 print with elaborate border and gilding, pattern 1185 – marked with rare Prince of Wales feather mark of 1806. Circular plate with Red Birds first print P504, pattern 1615. New Oval sugar box with Vine Border P522 and gilding, pattern 1045. Coffee can with Oak Border P523 and gilding, pattern 1050. New shape tea cup and saucer printed in Bamboo P501 in the first Pluck and Dust pattern 581.

£5.5s.0d. per year, rather less than that of Mr. Bruce, suggesting a smaller house. The 1841 census shows Richard Bell as being aged seventy but does not list an employment, not surprising perhaps considering his age. On the other hand George Bell, with age given as about fifty, was recorded as printer (pottery). These sparse facts are all that can be found of the men themselves but their work is still with us and is a lasting epitaph of which many would be proud.

A large majority of Spode Bat prints will be found decorating bone china tea wares. This is in marked contrast to the ale mugs and jugs often chosen by many potters for similar black printed decoration in the eighteenth century and include Spode's black printed Napoleonic mugs and jugs based on the outpourings of the London print shops in 1803. Whilst a number of Spode's complete or partially complete tea services with stipple engraved designs still exist, only one has been recorded that can be dated with any degree of confidence. This is the Hester Savory service of which forty-six pieces remain. The teapot is missing but the Old Oval shape sugar box with cover and the cream jug together with the slop basin and the larger bread and butter plate survive with the numbers made up with Bute shape teacups, coffee cans and saucers. Only the cream jug, slop basin and bread and butter plate are marked in gold with the pattern number 557 alone. The landscapes are printed in what is described in the Colour Mixing Book as 'Pale Black for printing patterns 500, 557 etc.' being 1 part Calcined Umber (dark yellow), 1 part Blue Calx (dark blue) and 3 parts Flux No.1 ground together for use. Although the name 'black' appears to have been retained as a general description in the Works with 'Intense black' being used to describe the earlier true black shade, the colour used on Spode's teawares is better described as charcoal or charcoal grey.

Before describing the pieces further, it would be as well to establish the antecedents of this service. Hester Savory, the reputed and likely first owner after whom the service is named, was the eldest child of Joseph Savory of Cheapside, London, a goldsmith and a Quaker. She was born in May 1777 and on 1 July 1802 married Charles Dudley, a merchant. She died of a fever on 9 February 1803 and lies buried in Bunhill Fields. Prior to her marriage she lived in Pentonville with her family where she was frequently seen by Charles Lamb, the poet and essayist, who lodged with his sister in the same street. That she was extremely beautiful is without doubt, but it is through Lamb that this beauty will remain with us. In 1803, in a letter to his friend Manning in Paris, Lamb wrote:

> I send you some verses I have made on the death of a young Quaker you may have heard me speak of as being in love with while I lived at Pentonville, though I had never spoken to her in my life. She died about a month since.

The poem reads

Hester

When maidens such as Hester die
Their place you may not well supply
Though ye among a thousand try
With vain endeavour.

A month or more has she been dead
Yet cannot I by force be led
To think upon the wormy bed
    and her together.

A springy motion in her gait,
A rising step did indicate
Of pride and joy no common rate
    That flushed her spirit.

I know not by what name beside
I shall it call if 'twas not pride
It was a joy to that allied
    She did inherit.

Her parents held the Quaker rule
Which does the human spirit cool
But she was trained in Nature's school
    Nature had blest her.

A waking eye, a prying mind
A heart that stirs is hard to bind
A Hawk's keen eye ye cannot blind
    Ye could not Hester.

My sprightly neighbour gone before
To that unknown and silent shore
Shall we not meet as heretofore
    Some summer morning?

When from thy cheerful eyes a ray
Hath struck a bliss upon the day
A bliss that would not go away
    A sweet forewarning.

Charles Dudley remained a widower for twenty years and then remarried. At some point, not clear in the family history but perhaps on the death of Dudley, the ownership of the service devolved from the Dudley family to that of Savory, to a niece of Hester Savory (a daughter of her brother) and thence through the line of the same brother to Mrs. Moore of Tonbridge finally passing out of the family in 1982.

An examination of the service gives every indication of an early date for manufacture. The major pieces are in Old Oval shape not favoured after the introduction of the New Oval shape about 1805. The glaze on the pieces is not as perfect as was later achieved, particularly on the backs of the saucers and on the bases of the cups and cans. Although Leonard Whiter has suggested that 1803 was the probable likely introductory year for pattern 557, it could well be

Restrained elegance of about 1810. New Oval bone china teaware in Spode's most popular Bat printing pattern 557, here with P400 Animals, on a mahogany tray of the period.

a year or two earlier. Family tradition places it in the ownership of Hester Dudley née Savory with likely purchase for her marriage in July 1802. The plain shape of Bute cups and cans potted in the new bone china and decorated with simple Bat printed landscape designs in charcoal grey could well meet Quaker taste for austerity and simplicity yet the added band and line gilding lifted the ware to an acceptable level for afternoon drawing room tea.

Dinner and dessert wares in bone china were also decorated by Bat printing as were the very occasional services in earthenware. Generally in ornamental and decorative bone china, only the smaller items such as match pots and footed beakers received Bat printed decoration and the larger and more expensive designs were reserved for hand enamelling. More utilitarian items such as punch bowls and jugs were made Bat decorated but are only infrequently found.

The process, being an inexpensive form of decoration, was used at times, but by no means always, on seconds or slightly substandard wares. Seconds are not always marked as this was an additional cost in manufacture. This is particularly true of the later felspar porcelain. The full felspar marks 40, 40a, 40b, 41 and 42 are all in themselves Bat prints and their use would entail the same cost as a normal print on a teacup or saucer. The moulded cream jug illustrated on page 74 as an example of stretching of the Bats and distortion in the prints is of the felspar body. It has three small fire cracks which reduces it to seconds quality.

Earthenware Garden Seat 48cm high with the shape exactly copying earlier Chinese examples. However, the decoration in underglaze blue showing fragments of the Roman Empire is taken from the Caramanian designs P905–1 A Triumphal Arch of Tripoli in Barbary and P905-3a Antique fragments at Limisso. Compare the bold underglaze blue printing used here on a large piece of earthenware with that used by On-glaze Bat printing shown on page 86 opposite.

It is decorated with two Bat prints and a simple blue edge. To print the full felspar mark would have added a third to the decorating cost. It is not surprising to find that it is unmarked or that best felspar porcelain cups and saucers usually have simple painted marks with the full Bat printed mark used only on the larger pieces.

Apart from bone china and felspar porcelain, the body most chosen for Bat decoration was drabware. Spode's was a dry body of a colour between oatmeal and ochre but perhaps best described by the name of the ware. The body was enhanced by a lustrous lead glaze and very often set off by a gilded edge. It was used for tea and dinner ware, both full size and in the toy sizes, and for a range of useful and ornamental shapes. Though occasionally seen painted in enamel colours and with Pluck and Dust printing with only moderate success, it is usually found with no further decoration than gilded edges or with additional decoration of Bat prints in charcoal grey. The colour of the ware, brightened by the gilded edge, was ideal for Bat printing and the combination of crisp potting and precise printing is most attractive.

The last class of ware upon which Spode Bat printing can be found is a very interesting group which appears to have been specifically designed to be decorated by this process. It is not common and pieces rarely appear. Perhaps it did not meet the taste of the times in which it was produced, probably the second decade of the nineteenth century. A close examination shows the body to be redware of a refined type of the common pottery body used for flowerpots and innumerable items throughout the centuries. This body is covered with a black or chocolate-brown dip in the manner of Jackfield or Astbury wares of the preceding century. The shapes were designed with a panel or reserve for decoration with a raised rim or edge around it. This reserve and the interior of holloware were covered in a white slip by Mr. Bruce or perhaps in his department. The recipe for this slip is the lower on page 46 of the smaller Recipe Book. The recipe refers to red or black bodies, but the few pieces seen are all of the cheaper redware body. The term used in the recipe 'whilst in the green state' was, and still is, the Potters' description for ware that after moulding or throwing has been dried in the drying room but has yet to be fired in the kilns. After biscuit firing, the ware was glazed with a pearlware glaze, giving a bluish tinge to the white slip and then Bat printed in the decoration panel. The final embellishment was to gild the edge of the vessel and the rim around the decoration panel. The range of wares found with printed decoration on this ware includes cups, saucers and cans, mugs, jugs and bulb pots. Illustrations of the cup and saucer can be seen at S33 and S34.

The plain style of this revived Astbury-Jackfield ware makes it unlikely that production continued after about 1825, although the recipe for the slip appears copied into a later book. By 1825 fashion had changed and the London shape teacup, having already ousted the simpler Bute shape from popularity, was in its turn being superseded by more ornate styles. The angular cup shape fitted with Spode's Bute handle found in this ware does not appear to have been used on any other body, although the recipe suggests other ornamentation beside printing may yet be found.

A decision seems to have been taken at Spode Works regarding the printed decoration to be used on the new bone china. The art form used for on-glaze Bat printing was entirely European and that for underglaze blue printing was purely Chinese in origin. These followed the tradition built up within the industry in the eighteenth century when on-glaze black printing, with very few exceptions, copied contemporary engravings and prints of the European art form. On the other hand, underglaze blue printed ware mirrored the Chinese blue-painted porcelain and was the English potters' successful attempt to oust Chinese imports from the lucrative British market for dinner wares. The third and later printing method, Pluck and Dust, having two different applications, was divided and designs printed by this method derive from both European and Oriental art.

From examination of the Pattern Books and Bat printed ware it is possible to trace the history in the nineteenth century of this printing process. The first pattern number referring to on-glaze printed ware is number 473 followed closely by pattern number 500. Both were decorated with flowers with pattern 473 engraved with a mixture of line and stipple punch work and printed in the traditional black of the eighteenth century black printing, However, pattern 500, which obviously followed it closely in date, was the first to use the new charcoal grey, especially prepared for the stipple punched flower sprays of this pattern and the landscapes of pattern 557 and used for later patterns. This softer charcoal look for use with stipple punched engravings was still termed black in the Pattern Books with the original black from the eighteenth century now termed as intense black.

A difficulty does arise in exactly pin pointing the first year of production of any pattern since this information is not included in the Pattern Books, Leonard Whiter, in his book *Spode,* suggests that Josiah Spode II began the Spode numbered pattern system after his return to the Works in 1797. However, the extant copy of the first Pattern Book offers a very incomplete list of early pattern numbers. The first entry is of pattern 133 and proper continuity does not appear until pattern 307 has been reached although an occasional number or numbers have been omitted subsequently. It would appear that the simple numbering system may have been adopted before 1797 and that Josiah Spode II may have only insisted that a proper record was kept. The first years of the nineteenth century with the production of the Old Oval tea ware with Bute shape cups, cans and saucers all in bone china would appear to fit with the introduction of the first Pattern Book with pattern 473 being the first printed pattern shown. This was printed with flowers in intense black from punched and line engraved copperplates with the pieces band and line gilded. It was followed by pattern 500 with similar flower sprigs stipple punched and printed in the new charcoal grey known from then as black, with simple gilded edges.

No division into Landscapes and Humanities, as used in this book, was made in Spode's Pattern Books. The earliest Landscape pattern is number 557 with plain landscape views appearing in our catalogue as the P200 series of prints. Yet intermingled with these and under the same pattern number 557 appear the classical humanity prints P301 to P317. They are a startling contrast to the 'Landscapes' of the P200 series yet no distinction is made in the Pattern Books and both appear on cups and saucers found in tea ware services. Similarly, pattern 557 appears to have been used for the introduction of the P400 Animal series with Bute tewares marked with 557 in red. However, the bald description 'Landscapes' in the Pattern Books for 557 suggests that the Animals were not engraved and in use for the initial designs for this popular pattern and were probably added to the 557 tewares about 1807–8 at the same time as appearing on the drabware pattern 1191.

Further slight confusion occurs in the Pattern Books, again with the description 'Landscapes'. In the new series of prints engraved about 1812–13 and introduced on pattern 1922, the human form dominated the designs rather than being a minor element of a general view as was usual in most of the earlier landscapes. These designs have been included in our Classical and Contemporary Humanity P300 series as P331 to P359 and not lumped in as more 'Landscapes' as the Pattern Books suggest.

In 1827, the Pembroke shape of tea ware was introduced in a both plain and a more popular embossed form. With the latter, smooth decoration panels were enclosed by the raised area of flower design embossment. The saucers had three decorative panels all designed not to be obscured by the cups which themselves had two panels of a similar size. One of the decorating methods chosen for this new shape was Bat printing. The existing Bat prints, designed for a single application in the centre of a saucer or opposite the handle on a cup, would not fit these smaller decoration panels and new designs therefore had to be engraved. The first of these, landscape views with additional small separate floral sprigs, was ready in 1829, pattern 4406 being the introduction of the new designs. Earlier prints of Landscapes were used on the larger tea ware

1. Gold bat printed bone china ware. New Oval Teapot with cover and stand and 18cm dessert plate all printed in pattern 1703 with print P238 showing on the teapot and P275 on the dish. The cream jug is in pattern 693 with print P262. None are marked with Spode's name.

pieces of teapot, cream jug, sugar box and bowl, thus the new service was originated by the addition of a number of small landscapes.

This was followed in the same year on pattern 4433 with a further new series of designs.

P112   *Four versions of this small spray have so far been found, printed from various states of different coppers.*

P119   *Four versions of the same size engraving are shown, the last P119–4 being a print from the present copperplate. Additional shading and flowers can be seen in the later versions.*

P121   *A print from the earlier state of the copperplate is shown at P121–1, with the present-state print being P121–2.*

2 and 3. *Gold Bat print on blue ground in centre of plate marked with the name of Spode and pattern number 1693 and showing print no. P303. Perhaps claimed by New Hall as an infringement of Peter Warburton's patent granted in 1810 and thus leading to disappearance of the Spode name on gold Bat printed ware until the termination of patent rights fourteen years later.*

4. *24cm Spode drabware shell dish Bat printed in gold with Fruit P187. Pattern 1692 unmarked.*

5. *Octagon shape Spode felspar cream jug Bat printed in gold with P142–1 and added gilding. Printed Spode felspar mark no. 41 in puce and pattern number 3743 in red, a production after the termination of the patent.*

Birds in Garden Landscapes, P440 to P451 followed, again fitting the new Pembroke shape and again with supporting floral sprigs. For this pattern, with no existing prints from which to draw, a more extensive range was engraved and was used for both tea and dessert wares. A further series of new designs for the Pembroke shape was produced in 1829–30. Again, similar small supporting sprigs were used, but this time the main decoration was larger Flower Sprays. The earliest Pattern Book illustration of these sprays on a Pembroke teacup is pattern 4601. Later patterns also show the same and some additional sprays decorating different shapes of cup and dessert plates with a total of forty-five variations of colour, gilding, enamelling and background colour shown before the end of the Spode period in 1833.

The final Spode Bat printing introduction was a second series of Birds, P460 to P476. With these background scenery was not included and the birds were perched on a branch or amongst a spray of flowers. This was ushered in with a flurry of new pattern numbers, the first being 4944, printed on a cup of '4643' shape with the birds placed both inside and outside the cups. Twelve variations of the first series 'Birds in Garden Landscapes' and nineteen of the second, 'Birds on Branches' were produced before the end of the Spode management in 1833.

The profusion of variations of the Bird prints and the Pembroke Flower Sprays would lead a collector to believe examples of these printed wares crowd every antique shop and antiques fair. This is not so, both Birds series being particularly hard to find yet Landscapes on Pembroke-shaped ware offered with only four variations of colour and gilding, are far more common. The Birds in particular do not seem to have met contemporary public taste and the production of many of these and of the Flower Sprays were perhaps vain attempts to sell the unsaleable.

A number of Bat prints were not included in the system of numbered patterns. The most noticeable of these are Spode's reproductions on both bone china and pottery mugs and jugs of some fifteen Napoleonic cartoons produced by the London print sellers during the Great Invasion Scare of 1803. Josiah Spode II, since his return to Stoke, commanded the Pottery Troop of Volunteers with the rank of Captain. The Troop consisted of some seventy volunteers mounted and uniformed at their own expense. This, no doubt, accounted for his interest in the production of the Bat printed Napoleonic wares of which four of the original copper plates are still held at Spode Works. Prints from three of these were illustrated in the first edition of this book published in 1983 but at that time no ware had been noted printed with designs taken from the copper plates. None of the mugs and jugs since found and illustrated as P380 to P393 are marked with Spode's name but a pair of barrel-shaped creamware jugs, both with the gilt inscription under the spout reading *I.Topham 1804,* included a print from two of the copperplates held at Spode Works, BRITANNIA *Blowing up the Corsican Bottle Conjurer* and *A* STOPPAGE *to a* STRIDE *over the* GLOBE, appearing on the smaller vessel and two further cartoons appearing on the larger. The prints follow the traditions of the eighteenth century black printing with the copperplates both line engraved and stippled punched and printed in intense black used for black printing rather than the new charcoal grey favoured by Spode for his newly introduced range of Old Oval shape teawares with Bute cups, cans and saucers.

A further confirmation that this range of transfer printed Napoleonic cartoons was undoubtedly manufactured by Spode can be demonstrated by the brick red banding lined with black used on the above prints which matches a similar finish on a tea service of a Spode shape decorated with small sprigs, P131, taken from another copperplate still at Spode Works. Details of the fifteen known Spode Napoleonic prints appear in colour in the Catalogue of Bat prints.

This catalogue has been updated to include all the designs appearing in the first edition plus all the additional prints that have been traced in the last twenty years. With the exception of the Napoleonic prints added in colour, the Bat catalogue has been retained as black and white prints since by far the greatest number appear on printed ware in that form. The catalogue includes references and illustrations of original prints and notes on the artists, engravers and print sellers where these are known. The brief outline of the possible sources of the four categories of the Bat printed ware are as follows —

1. Flowers P100 series. Jean Pillement 1727–1808. French Court, worked in Paris and in London where his work was published by Robert Sayer, the best known being *The Ladies' Amusement*. Flower sprays and sprigs may well have been adapted from *Small Bouquets of Flowers* published by Robert Sayer in 1787.

2. Landscapes P200 series. As well as being used by Spode, a number of these prints appeared on rival potters' wares copied from the same original source prints. Since the majority of the copperplates were stipple punched without use of the graver, an exact copy was not practicable and was not attempted. A close inspection of the rival potters' prints will always show differences in the placing and strength of the punched indentations. The name of the known rival manufacturer is shown after the print number below the illustration.

3. Classical and Contemporary Humanity P300 series. The additional item appearing in this section include the fifteen Napoleonic prints already mentioned plus Spode's reproduction of Admiral Lord Nelson and the battle plan of the Battle of Trafalgar printed on a Bute cup and saucer.

4. Animals, Birds, Sporting subjects and Armorial prints P400 series. Although few new prints can be included in this section, more information regarding the origination of several prints have been included in the catalogue.

Catalogue of Bat prints

Illustrations are from prints taken from the original Spode copperplates still held in the Works or prints on ware of Spode manufacture. The illustrated prints are divided by subject with the appropriate pattern numbers listed at the end of each section. Not all prints were included in the list of patterns, indeed Spode's mugs and jugs decorated with printed Napoleonic cartoons do not carry the Spode name nor a pattern number and other designs were similarly treated.

P100 series Flowers and Fruit

The first Bat printed pattern, 473, which was copied from the earlier painted pattern 343, was printed in the eighteenth century black from designs engraved on the copperplates using both the burin and the punch. This survivor of the eighteenth century practice was closely followed by pattern 500 using the new softer charcoal black and taken from copperplates engraved by stipple punching alone. The use of flower sprigs and sprays as printed decoration continued throughout the Spode period with the full range of early designs probably built up over a number of years. These were followed by newer styles from 1817 with the final Pembroke shape sprays appearing in 1830.

The forerunner of the very distinctive Fruit prints was the painted pattern 581. The Bat printed ware itself was not produced until 1810 or 1811, with the last version appearing twenty years later about 1830.

P100

P100 to P131   The prints listed under this heading are basically stipple engraved, heightened by some line work. The smaller motifs, although engraved in groups on a single copperplate, were used separately. The designs are of eighteenth century and probably derive from the drawings of Jean Pillement whose work greatly influenced the decoration of eighteenth and nineteenth century English porcelain. The prints are found on patterns 473, 500, 523, 1222 with Animal prints, 2393 and finally on 2947 in 1819. The production of pattern 500 continued throughout the period and these early prints can be found interspersed with the later Pembroke sprigs on bone china teawares. This evidence of long and varied use is borne out by the state of the copperplates, which show many signs of re-engraving and repair. Leaves have been added and removed as has shading and tones. Besides these alterations on the state of the coppers, designs are also found in slightly varying sizes and altered minor detail. Sizes vary from the largest spray P126–1, size 8.5cm x 7cm to the smallest sprig under 1cm square.

P101

P102

P103

P104

P105

P106

P107

P108

P109

P110

P111

P112 Four versions of this small spray have so far been found, printed from various states of different coppers.

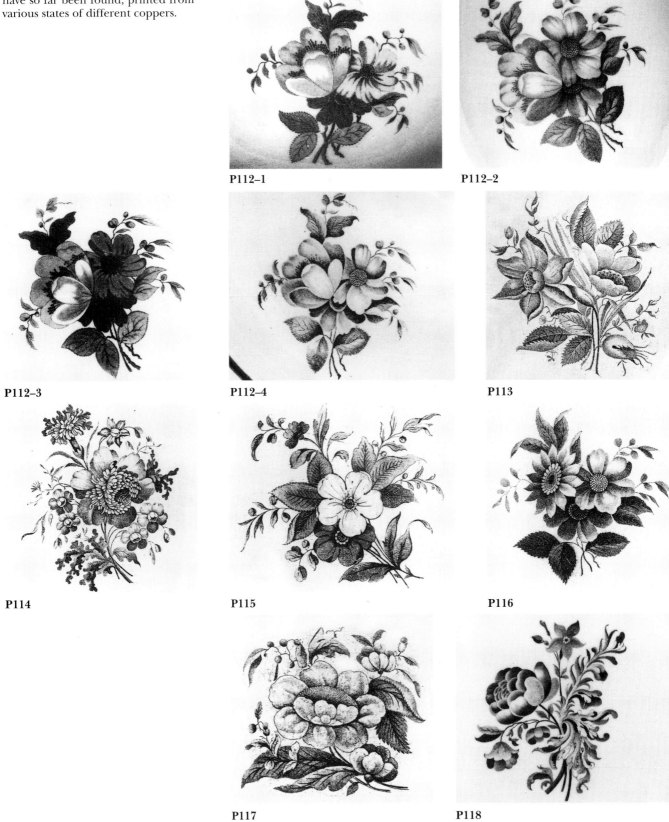

P112–1

P112–2

P112–3

P112–4

P113

P114

P115

P116

P117

P118

P119–1

P119–2

P119 Four versions of the same size engraving are shown, the last P119–4 being a print from the present copperplate. Additional shading and flowers in the later versions can be seen.

P121 A print from the earlier state of the copperplate is shown at P121–1, with the present-state print being P121–2.

P119–3

P119–4

P120

P121–1

P121–2

P122

P123

P124

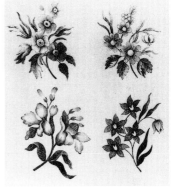

P125

Catalogue of Bat prints

P126 This spray of flowers was engraved in three sizes. P126–1 shows the largest print and the slightly simpler medium size illustrated with P126–2. P126-3 and 4 show two states of the smallest print.

P127 Again the largest size, P127–1, is the more intricate. P127-2 and P127–3 are two states of the smaller copper.

P126–1

P126–2

P126–3

P126–4

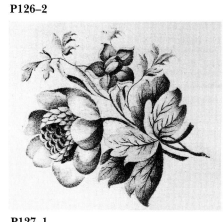

P127–1

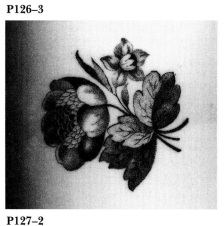

P127–2

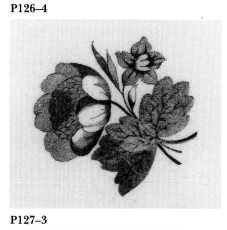

P127–3

P128

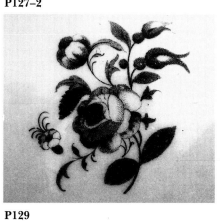

P129

P130

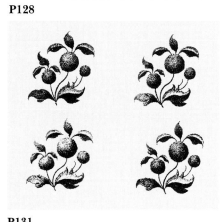

P131

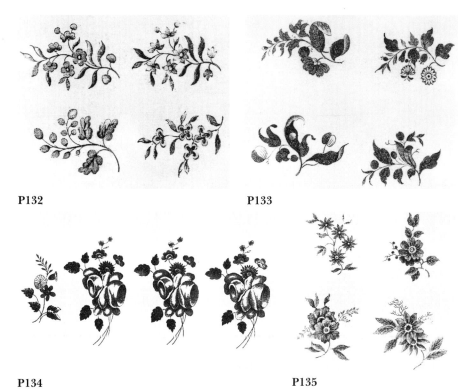

P132

P133

P132, P133 and P134 These small sprigs were likely to have been used for supporting decoration. The copperplate of P133 has part of the copperplate maker's mark 4 on the back which suggests early manufacture, perhaps for pattern 500.

P135 These sprigs are found both on pattern 500 decorated pieces particularly of London shape and, most commonly, on embossed Pembroke shape tea wares. In both cases they are supporting sprigs only and are generally referred to as 'Pembroke Sprigs'.

P136 This design was introduced in 1817 on four patterns 2569, 2570, 2571 and 2572 to decorate teawares. A New Oval teapot and stand is illustrated in the shape section S20 and S21. The teapot decoration is made up of joined sections of P136–1 and the teapot stand of P136–2.

P134

P135

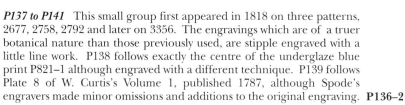

P136–1

P137 to P141 This small group first appeared in 1818 on three patterns, 2677, 2758, 2792 and later on 3356. The engravings which are of a truer botanical nature than those previously used, are stipple engraved with a little line work. P138 follows exactly the centre of the underglaze blue print P821–1 although engraved with a different technique. P139 follows Plate 8 of W. Curtis's Volume 1, published 1787, although Spode's engravers made minor omissions and additions to the original engraving. **P136–2**

P137

P138

P139

P140

P141

P142 The main flower spray, P142–1 appears on the London shape teacups illustrating patterns, 3669, 3670, 3743, 3763 and 3764 in the Pattern Books. The style of engraving, a mixture of line and stipple, could be used either as a plain print or part enamelled with colour. P142–2 illustrates the small sprigs that were used inside the cups. The engravings date from 1824. This centre, differently engraved for underglaze blue printing, was used in pattern P836 within a border of flowers on dessert plates.

P143 This is one of several sizes of this design

of Union prints. The only illustration of these prints shown in the Pattern Books is 3767 of 1825. However, similar sprigs were used, differently engraved, for underglaze blue transfers.

P144 This has a factory name of 'Black Basket'. The engraving is designed for a part enamel finish, as is P142, although it is possible that a printed only version was issued. It appears in the Pattern Books on patterns 3828 and 3885 of 1825. P144–1 and P144–2 show the two sizes of copperplate still existing and P144–3 the sprigs used with the main basket decoration.

P142–1

P142–2

P143

P144–1

P144–2

P144–3

P145 A different basket design of about the same period which seems to have been engraved for Bat printing without over-enamelling. It is not entered in the Pattern Book which perhaps supports this view. A piece of ware printed with the design has not been recorded.

P146 and P147 These odd little views of perhaps Oriental inspiration and of the late 1820s or early 1830s are extremely hard to find. They have a marked similarity to the P400 series 'Birds in Garden Landscapes' and are of like date.

P148 to P160 These flower sprays and sprigs were introduced about 1830 for the new Pembroke teawares and similar more decorative shapes. As can be seen, the sprays have a more open and loose look than those used earlier in the century which were based on eighteenth century designs. The long list of patterns using these prints is shown in Table 5.1 of Spode Flower and Fruit patterns listed at the end of this section. The use of the prints continued well after the end of the Spode period in 1833.

P145

P146

P147

P148

P149

P150

P151

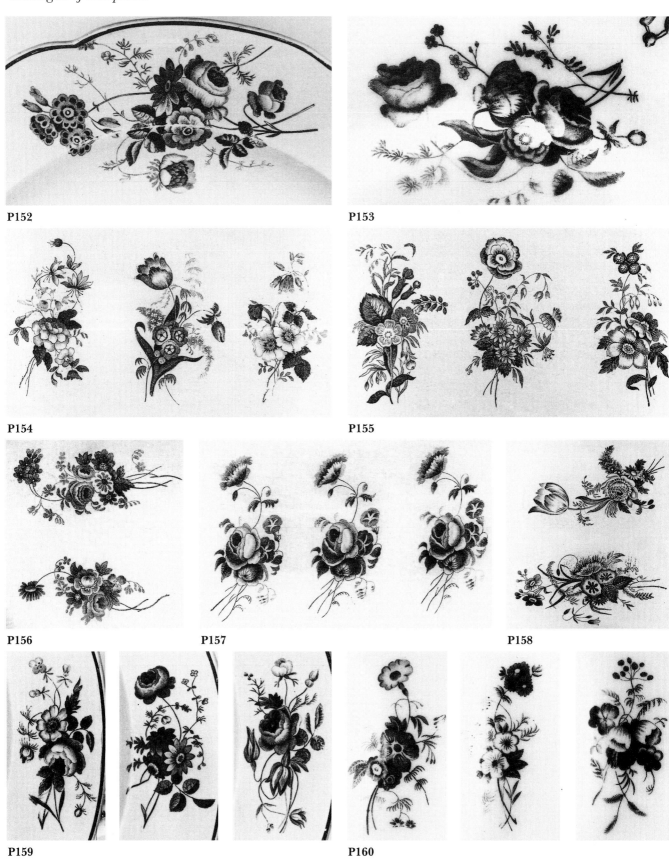

P152

P153

P154

P155

P156

P157

P158

P159

P160

P161

P161 to P195 The source for the design of this extremely decorative range of Fruits is not known. They appeared on eleven patterns between 1810 and 1830 and were brought back into use since. In 1937 they were introduced as the 'Chatham' design and continued with this name until 1980 although the actual printing was no longer by the Bat method. In their original form the copperplates were entirely stipple engraved and the band and line gilding and chocolate-brown print of pattern 1516 probably shows them at their best. Their popularity, almost continuous use and later adaptation for more advanced printing techniques have resulted in uneven wear. Some copperplates now produce very pale prints and have been 'repaired' with line engraving. The prints on Spode period wares will be found to be of an even stipple nor will the names M. Edge and H. Hamley appear on earlier wares, being added later to please customers for the 'Chatham' design in the twentieth century.

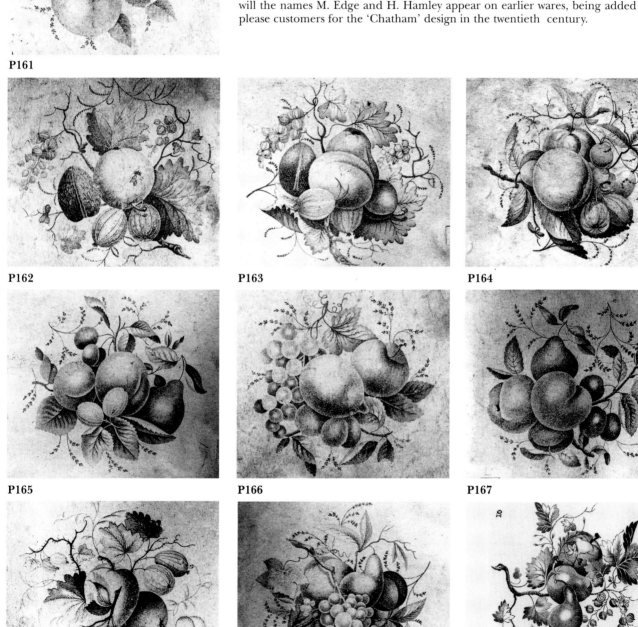

P162   **P163**   **P164**

P165   **P166**   **P167**

P168   **P169**   **P170**

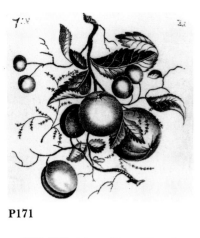

P171

P172

P173

P174

P175

P176

P177

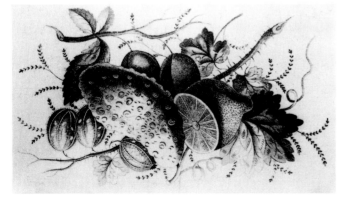

P178

P179

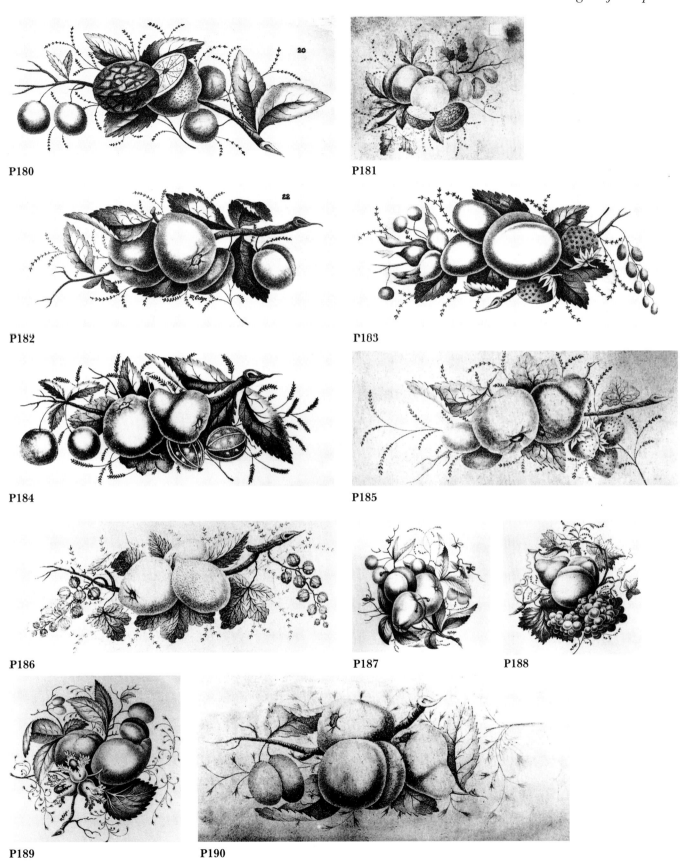

P180

P181

P182

P183

P184

P185

P186

P187

P188

P189

P190

P191

P192

P193

P194

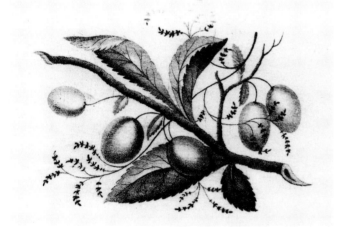

P195

P197

P198

Copperplate makers' marks are stamped on the reverse of the following P100 series Flowers and Fruit coppers.

Mark no.4   Prints P133, P172 and P192.
Mark no.6   Prints P161, P162, P166, P167 and P168.

Table 5.1   Spode patterns decorated with Bat printed Flowers and Fruit P100 series

Pattern number	Probable date of introduction	Description and colour of prints	References of the prints usually found on the pattern
473	1802/3	Intense black sprigs with band and line gilding	P100 to P131 & P198
500	1803	Slight black sprigs with gold edge	P100 to P131
523	1803	French-brown printed sprigs with gold edge, same as 500	P100 to P131
1222	1808	Animals and sprigs with gold band edge (see also P300 and P400 series)	P100 to P131
1513	1810	Black printed fruits with band and line gilding	P161 to P195
1515	1810	Black printed fruits with gilding on blue band	P161 to P195
1516	1810	Chocolate-brown printed fruit with band and line gilding	P161 to P195
1676	1811	Printed black sprigs washed green gold edge	P100 to P131
1677	1811	Similar but with beaded edge	P100 to P131
1686	1811	Embossed dessert ware, white & gold fruits and gold line	P161 to P195
1691	1811	Three groups of gold fruit on blue ground	P161 to P195
1692	1811	Gold fruits on gold band edge	P161 to P195
1696	1811	Three groups of gold fruit on blue panel on embossed ware	P161 to P196
1700	1811	Gold fruit on blue panels	P161 to P196
2393	1815–16	Black sprigs (as 500) with chocolate edge	P100 to P131
2569	1817	Border sprays in black	P136
2570	1817	Border sprays in red	P136
2571	1817	Border sprays overpainted in green	P136
2572	1817	Border sprays overpainted in three colours	P136
2677	1818	Geranium centre	P137 to P141
2758	1818	Purple flower gold band edge (Illustrated in Pattern Book with P140)	P137 to P141
2792	1818	Purple flower with pink edge	P137 to P141
2947	1819	Pattern 500 sprigs printed in rose with green painted leaves	P100 to P131
3056	1820	Bat fruit overpainted in full colour	P161 to P196
3269	1821	Bat fruit washed in green	P161 to P196
3356	1822	Flower sprays in brown on green ground	P139
3669	1824	Flower sprays and sprigs in blue	P142
3670	1824	Same flower spray and sprigs in blue with blue edge	P142
3743	1824	Same flower spray and sprigs in gold with gold edge	P142
3763	1825	Same flower spray and sprigs in blue with gold edge	P142
3764	1825	Same flower spray and sprigs in green with gold edge	P142
3767	1825	Union sprays in brown or blue	P143
3828	1825	'Black basket' and sprays overpainted in full colour	P144
3885	1825	'Black basket' finished in green or blue	P144
4407	1829	Black 500 later sprays and sprig washed over in green	P100 to P135
4585	1829	Fruit in purple brown on pink ground	P161 to P195
Pattern nos. as listed	From 1829	Open flower sprays and sprigs used in forty-five versions of colour, ground, enamel and gilding on the following pattern numbers — 4594, 4601, 4606, 4609, 4624, 4625, 4627, 4628, 4656, 4682, 4689, 4754, 4755, 4797, 4801, 4804, 4805, 4814, 4815, 4843, 4851, 4852, 4853, 4854, 4855, 4856, 4857, 4858, 4859, 4866, 4879, 4882, 4942, 4943, 4961, 5024, 5025, 5027, 5056, 5058, 5059, 5083, 5157, 5175, 5197.	P148 to P160

P200 series Landscapes

Shown in this section are views of landscapes in which the human and animal forms play only a supporting or subsidiary role or are entirely omitted. Where either dominate, they are listed in the appropriate P300 and P400 series. Landscapes are probably the most popular and long-lived of Spode's Bat prints. It is difficult to date the origination of every landscape print but to give some assistance, those prints found on the Hester Savory service have been marked (HS) after the print number, thus P202 (HS). Some of these prints, probably first appearing before 1803, were still in use in 1833 and can be found on tea and dessert wares of that period.

In some instances very similar prints can be found in the wares of rival manufacturers obviously copied from the same source prints as were used by Spode. The rival manufacturers are named in brackets placed after Spode's print number and include New Hall, Miles Mason, Chamberlain's Worcester, Wedgwood and Ralph Wedgwood.

Prints of Spode's landscape views fall into loose groups of related subjects, and, to simplify identification, the catalogue has been divided into these groups in the following order: Ruins — Country Scenes — Cottages — Notable Buildings — Prints for Pembroke shape wares — Bridges and Rivers. The groups merge from one to the next with prints that contain elements of the neighbouring group, and indeed there are a few romantic landscapes showing every heading in a single print which defy certain classification. The order in which they are illustrated is not necessarily that in which they were originated. Commenced before 1803, it seems probable that the series, other than the Pembroke prints, was completed by 1812, since in that year a new series of 'Humanity Landscapes' was introduced on pattern 1922.

Only one copperplate contains a hidden date of 1811. However, the print itself follows an eighteenth century design on a plate attributed to Ralph Wedgwood and dated 1786. Research has found a number of drawings and engraving upon which Spode's landscapes were based. As would be expected, some of the grander buildings can now be named, but the humble cottages and country scenes remain anonymous, perhaps composed from an amalgamation of several items from original prints. The sizes of Spode prints vary very considerably with the largest, for teapots, being 18cm x 8cm. The most usual shape is a square or a circle of about 8.5cm designed for cups and saucers, although a rectangular form was designed for the same use perhaps by different engravers. The variety of sizes betoken a wider range than tea wares and handsome dessert services can be found decorated with these prints as can other interesting pieces.

Ruins P201 to P215

These engravings are more likely to be romantic landscapes rather than true presentations of actual views. This is borne out by P205 in which the ruin is placed upon the seashore in open mountainous country. It is shown by George Holmes, the Dublin artist, in a view of Askeyton, a town in the county of Limerick, as standing by the river in the town itself. Holmes' drawing, engraved by Walker, was published as print no.182 in the *Copperplate Magazine.* The ruin in Spode's engraving closely follows that of Holmes but is transported from town to country. Other prints may have a similar basis of reality, but others must surely be products of romantic imagination.

P201

P202 (HS)

P203

P204 (HS)

P205

P206

P207

P208 (HS)

P209

P210

P211 (HS)

P212 (HS)

P213

P214

P215

Country Scenes P216 to P234

This classification covers views that defy a more definite description and show a general picture, if a little romantic, of the English countryside in the early nineteenth century. The small prints, P224 and P225, are normally found as a pair on teapot and sugar box covers and P226 was designed for a teapot. It is P227, which is of most interest. The exact source has not been traced but a creamware plate included, in other printing, the date 1786 and a second version is known on a Wedgwood circular creamware tureen of the early nineteenth century. In both of these a road or lane runs in front of the cottage and not the river shown in the Spode engraving. The cottage, cowherd and trees are similarly placed which points to a single source of origin. In contrast to normal Spode practice, the copperplate is engraved with the initials I.K. and the date 1811. The fact that they are minute and hidden in the bank to the left of the cows may account for their first and continued existence.

P216

P217

P218 (HS)

P219 (HS)

P220

P221 (HS)

P222 (HS)

P223 (HS)

P224 (HS)

P225 (HS)

P226

P227 On right — Print from existing copperplate. Below — Enlargement, in negative, showing position of initials and date in bank to the left of the cattle. Below right — The initials and date taken from the copperplate in its present condition. The line between the letter K and the date is a scratch.

P227

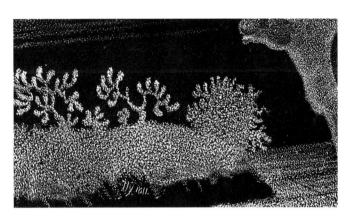

P228

P229

P230 (HS)

P231

P232

P233

Bridges and Rivers P235 to P249

These prints using a bridge or a river as their main theme may well have been based on original drawings produced in a series. The exact source has proved elusive. Prints P238 and P239, both of which contain a river, decorate each side of a new oval teapot although the views may be romantic imagery rather than based on actuality. Print P243, however, shows Llangollen Bridge — over the river Dee. New Hall's version of the same unknown original is named on some prints of the view. See p. 114.

P234 (HS)

P235

P236

P237

P238

P239

P240

P241 (HS)

P242

P243

P244 (HS)

P245 (HS)

P246

P247

P248 (HS)

P249

Cottages P250 to P263
The country cottage is the centre-piece for these prints but no original source has been traced. The series, with few exceptions, is well executed in stipple engraving.

P250

P251

P252

P253

P254 (HS)

P255

P256 (HS)

P257 (HS)

P258 (HS)

P259

P260 (HS)

P261 (HS)

P262 (HS)

P263

Notable Buildings P264 to P277 and P284

The origins of a number of Spode's engravings have been traced in this group of prints. Spode's copies vary from their originals in very different degrees. Some, such as P268 Bisham Abbey, follow closely the source drawing with minor repositioning to reduce the size of the print. Others evidence only the basis of their origins and have been freely adapted, as can be seen in P277 West Wycombe Park. With both these views the original print is shown. Generally the alterations made in Spode's representations fall between the two examples.

P264 and P265   These two views of Dunrobin probably fit a teapot, but the only print so far seen is on a mug S55. Dunrobin Castle has a connection with the Potteries which may account for the appearance of its name on the copperplates. It is the ancestral Scottish home of the Dukes of Sutherland. Their English seat, now demolished, would have been on the bounds of the modern city of Stoke-on-Trent. It was Trentham Hall from which they were driven by the evil smelling effluent carried from the Potteries to their ornamental waters. A later Duchess, 'Meddlesome Millie', perhaps continuing the connection with the industry, was responsible for speeding up legislation to ban the use of lead in ceramic glazes, the chief cause of lead poisoning or 'potter's rot'.

P266 and P267   These prints, that seem to pair, are of teapot size. P266 is illustrated at S4 (page 158) on a 20.5cm. saucer-shaped plate, which it fits rather ill, being too long and narrow. The view is of West Clandon Place, Surrey the seat of Lord Onslow, from an original print engraved Medland published in January 1793 in the *Copperplate Magazine*.   The name of the building and the source of the print P267 have not come to light.

P264

P265

P266

P267

P268, P269 and P270 These three prints are excellently stipple engraved. P268 shows Bisham Abbey in Oxfordshire, with the original drawing by Richard Corbould also illustrated. This was published in *Copperplate Magazine* in 1792 engraved by Ellis. Richard Corbould, 1757–1831, a Londoner, was a competent book illustrator. His son Henry, also an artist, and another son, George, was an engraver. It was he who engraved the print after Richard Westall, RA, copied by Spode for P335. P269 is a view of Sherborne Castle, Oxfordshire also taken from a drawing by Richard Corbould in 1792. Finally, print P270 shows Kirkudbright, Scotland depicted in the same year in a drawing by Alexander Reid and copied by the Spode engraver. Alexander Reid, the Scottish artist and miniature painter, has his studio in Dumfries. He is best known for his miniature of Robert Burns who averred 'it was the best likeness ever taken'.

P268

Bisham Abbey, original print.

P269

P270

P271 to P275 This small group of ancient buildings is engraved in a similar style to the three previous engravings. The castellated towers illustrated in P271 and P274 cannot yet be named. However, the artist for P271 could well be Richard Corbould. When comparing the horse and rider for the original illustration for Bisham Abbey, P268, with the horse and rider in this print, P271, the marked similarity gives cause for the deduction. Print P272 is of Conway Castle. The model for this engraving is a drawing by John Nixon, 1760–1818, a clever amateur artist who is best known for his work in the series of 'Views of the Seats of English Nobility and Gentry' which were engraved by William Watts. Print P273 is a view of Rivalx Abbey, Yorkshire, which was the spelling used on the original print published in 1792 in the *Copperplate Magazine*. The drawing for this print was the work of Francis Nicholson, 1753–1844, a landscape painter from Yorkshire who exhibited at the Royal Academy in 1789 and, in 1804, became a founder member of the Water Colour Society. The castle in P275 is thought to be Bothwell in Lanarkshire but the original print or drawing used by Spode has not been found.

P271

P272

P273

P274 (HS)

P275

P276 and P277 This pair of early prints, used on the Hestor Savory service, probably for the reason of their smaller size, are found on the later Pembroke shapes as well as on earlier wares. The origin of P276 has not been found, but P277 is a view of West Wycombe Park, Buckinghamshire. The engraving by Ellis after the original drawing, again by Richard Corbould, is illustrated here. Spode's engraver has taken very considerable liberties with the original, which was published in 1793, but sufficient is left to justify the continued use of the name for the view.

P276 (HS)

P277 (HS)

Original print of West Wycombe Park.

P278 to P282 These small prints all fit the Pembroke shape embossed tea wares first appearing on pattern 4406 in 1829. However, P281 and P282 have been used to decorate the cover of a pattern 557 bone china sauce tureen with a stand of the shape frequently supplied as part of dessert services. This does suggest that decorating the Pembroke embossed teawares was not the first use made of these prints. Print P281 was been taken from a steel engraving marked *Tombleson del R. Sands Sculp* part of a series designed by William Tombleson and named as *Island near Henley*. Long since known as Temple Island, it is the starting point for races at Henley Regatta.

P278

P279

P280

P281

P282

P283   This print was not included in the first edition and is the missing teapot side pairing with P207.

P284   The print is named below the building in script as 'Lindertis' which was, until it was demolished in 1955, in Tayside, Scotland. It was built in 1813 by Archibald Elliot for Sir Thomas Munro.

P283

P284

P285

P285   This unmarked bone china saucer came from a pattern 557 part service containing two saucers with this print.

Table 5.2   Spode patterns decorated with Bat printed Landscapes P200 series

Pattern number	Probable date of introduction	Description and colour of prints	References of the prints usually found on the pattern
557	1803 or a little earlier	Landscapes in black and, most rarely, in iron-red, with band and line gilding (see also P300 and P400)	P201 to P285
558	1803 or a little earlier	Landscapes as 557 but with elaborate gilding	P201 to P285
613	1803	Landscapes in blue	P201 to P285
1179	1807	In black on drabware	P201 to P285
1301	1808	In black with elaborate gilding	P201 to P285
1302	1808	In black with varied elaborate gilding	P201 to P285
1803	1808	In black with varied elaborate gilding	P201 to P285
1304	1808	In black with varied elaborate gilding	P201 to P285
1693	1811	Gold landscapes on blue panel	P201 to P285
1695	1811	Gold landscapes on blue panel with added gilding	P201 to P285
1697	1811	Gold landscapes on blue panel with egg and tongue gilding	P201 to P285
1703	1811	Gold landscapes with gilding	P201 to P285
2012	1813	As 557 with added gilded line inside cups & cans	P201 to P285
2037	1813	Black landscapes with dontil and feather gilding	P201 to P285
2112	1814	In chocolate with dontil gilding	P201 to P285
2150	1814	In blue with gold edge	P201 to P285
2211	1814	As 557 (black) with foreign edge	P201 to P285
2212	1814	As 557 (black) with red edge	P201 to P285
2328	1815	In black – cup with internal gilding	P201 to P285
2355	1815	In black with green edge	P201 to P285
2742 2744 2745 to 2750	1818	The Pattern Book description of this series of Patterns is 'Purple Landscape' with various gilded and painted borders. Without seeing an actual example it is not possible to tell whether P200 or P300 series prints were used, although P300 prints seem more likely	Pattern 2742 has been noted with P300 series prints.
3297	1821	Landscapes in green	P201 to P285
4406	1829	Prints on Pembroke shape in black with gilded edges	P276 to P282 and earlier prints
4445	1829	Prints on Pembroke shape in black on a pink ground	P276 to P282 and earlier prints
4492	1829	Prints on Pembroke shape in black on white reserve with gold and blue	P276 to P282 and earlier prints
4619	1830	Prints on Pembroke shape in black on buff ground	P276 to P282 and earlier prints

P300 Series Classical and Contemporary Humanity. The division of Spode Bat prints into this category, as opposed to P200 Landscapes, is decided by the prominence of the human form. If the central theme of the composition is of mankind rather than of geographical features or buildings, the print is included in this category. Spode made no such differentiation. The scenes for the ubiquitous pattern 557 and for the later pattern 1922 are both termed 'Landscapes' in Spode's Pattern Books despite the basic difference in emphasis of the views. Prints P301–1. P301–2, P302 and P303 of Classical and P360 of Contemporary Humanity appear on pattern 557 incongruously interspersed amongst the more usual Landscape views. They are, almost certainly, of earlier date than that first marketed on pattern 1922 in 1812, which are also included in this Humanity section.

In addition to the prints from these well known patterns and a further few also illustrated in the Pattern Books, there remain a number of printed Humanity designs found on Spode's copperplates and these are listed here. In addition, the range of Napoleonic prints has been extended from the three copperplates shown in the first edition to some 15 designs all found on Spode wares although none are entered in the Pattern Books nor are the wares marked with Spode's name.

Classical Humanity P301–1, P301–2, P302 and P303
These four prints, two of the same scene differently presented, appear on the first Landscape pattern 557. They were used indiscriminately intermingled with British landscape views, to our eyes an unlikely fit with, say, a view of Conway Castle. In P301 the dress of mother and child hardly seem likely to withstand the rigours of an English summer nor is Cupid in P302 a frequent transmogrified visitor to the British countryside. In P303 is the dress of the lady that which a simple shepherd would expect to find? A lady? An earlier Lady Chatterley perhaps. However, the prints really reflect the art of the times and would not appear so odd in the early nineteenth century. The Bartolozzi print 'Rural Felicity' shown as the source of P308, is a typical example of the romanticised view of the countryside to which these prints belong.

P301–1

P301–2

P302

P303

P304 to P310 The infants and cherubs depicted in these prints are in the style of the rural, classic, romantic art of the late eighteenth century. Prints P304 to P307 depicting a single cherub are lightly stippled and have the appearance of the same engraver and the same artist. They are likely to have been used in a set. Prints 308 and P309 of infant musicians and dancers are after Bartolozzi P308 being almost a direct copy of his 'Rural Felicity' published in London in 1789. Bartolozzi was an early exponent of stipple engraving and his print is a mixture of line and stipple. However, the two Spode copperplates are engraved differently; P308 is fine line work and P309 is stipple engraved. P310 is also stipple engraved, although the infant revellers are not so finely drawn as those in the two previous prints. It is taken from 'The Wine Harvest' engraved by Bartolozzi in 1766.

P304

P305

P306

P307

P308

Engraving by Francesco Bartolozzi

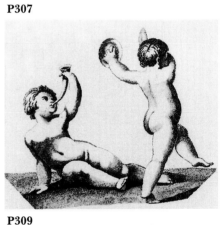

P309

P310

P311

P311 and P312 Print P311 shows a band of cherubs besporting themselves on clouds. The print was first used on pattern 2643 in 1817 where the cherubs and clouds are overpainted on a sumptuous beaded *déjeuner* service, a cup from which is illustrated in the Pattern Book. The sectionalised prints are laid closely together to produce an almost continuous border. This print also appears in combination with P312 on patterns 3658 and 3665 issued in 1824. On these patterns print P312, which it is tempting to name 'Miss Christmas' or 'Helping Father', appears on the outside of a London shape teacup in the Pattern Book with a single section of P311 placed on the inside of the cup. Two slightly smaller versions of P312 were engraved varying only in minor detail, and the lower line of P311 also occurs on a separate copper.

P312

P313

P313 to P317 Prints P313, P314 and P315 of scantily clad females in the classical style have a close affinity to the similar females in P301, P302 and P303. The lower numbered prints are invariably found with band and line gilding on pattern 557 tea wares, yet these ladies are placed most often on the later pattern 1922 with a gilded dontil edge. Neither classical set fits happily with British Landscapes and Contemporary Humanity prints which form the major part of pattern 557 or 1922 as can be seen. Their separation into two groups on different patterns seems odd when viewed 195 years later. Prints P316 and P317 of heavenly charioteers are even further from the main theme of pattern 1922 shown in prints P331 to P359, yet the allegorical scenes are found mixed with contemporary presentations in the tea services of those times.

P314

P315

P316

P317

Contemporary Humanity

P331 to P359 These prints of Contemporary Humanity are found intermingled with the Classical Humanity prints P313 to P317, with both first seen on pattern 1922. It is clear that the prints were designed in the first place for tea ware. The engravings include two large prints P331 and P332 for the sides of a New Oval teapot, two smaller prints P333 and P334 for the decoration of the teapot and sugar box covers with two further larger prints for the saucer-shaped bread and butter plates. The general prints are in two forms: rectangular used for sugar boxes and creamers as well as cups and saucers and square prints mostly found on cups and saucers. Prints P331 and P332 were both taken from a portrait-shaped original and have been elongated to a landscape design by Spode's engravers to fit the sides of the teapots. The original for Print P331 was taken from a small volume entitled 'The Farmer's Boy', a rural poem by Robert Bloomfield containing four small portrait engravings entitled 'Spring', 'Summer', 'Autumn' and 'Winter'. Spode

used three of these but omitted the last 'Winter'. 'Spring' formed the basis of P331 with the man and his horse copied with the print reshaped by removal of the upper foliage and additional sections added both to the right and left of the figure to make up a suitable landscape shape for the teapot. The second teapot side, P332, was taken from an engraving by William Finedon, after a water colour by Richard Westall RA, used to illustrate a poem by William Cowper entitled 'Retirement'. Again the shape of the original print had to be changed from portrait to landscape by removal of the background and adding to the length by an island of tiny trees, doubtless, especially cultivated for Spode by the Japanese masters of the bonsai art. A copy of the original page is shown here. Prints P333 and P334 are almost certainly after Westall. Similar drawings of a man and a dog appear in a number of his book illustrations including a print 'The Woodcutter' in which a man and a dog very closely resemble Spode's prints, of which one is also a woodcutter.

P331

P332

RETIREMENT.

...or with ill-fashion'd hook
To draw th' incautious minnow from the brook
Are life's prime pleasures in his simple view.

P331, P332, P333 and P334 This set was designed to fit a New Oval teapot or similar vessel with the two larger prints, size 16 cm approx. x 8 cm, on the body and an impression from P333 and P334 on each side of the cover. The original source of P332 was a water colour by Richard Westall, RA. An engraving by James Heath based on this was issued separately and a further engraving, this time by William Finden, was included in Sharpe's *Poets* first published in June 1810. The print is used to illustrate the poem 'Retirement' by William Cowper. The page from Sharpe's *Poets* is shown here. Prints P333 and P334 are almost certainly also after Westall. Similar drawings of a man and a dog appear in a number of his book illustrations including a print 'The Woodcutter' in which a man and a dog very closely resemble Spode's prints, of which one is also of a woodcutter.

P333

P334

P335 and P336 This pair appear to have been designed to fit the two sizes of Spode's saucer-shaped bread and butter plates used with the New Oval shape tea service with Bute shape cups, saucers and cans. The larger, P335, is also after a Richard Westall original and again is used in Sharpe's *Poets* with a Cowper poem, this time 'The Task'. Spode's presentation follows exactly the book engraving which is printed with the following verse:

That call the unwanted villager abroad
With all her little ones, a sportive train
To gather king-cups in the yellow mead

The same design was used by Flight, Barr and Barr at Worcester decorated in full colour. Print P336 is the second taken from Robert Bloomfield's 'The Farmer's Boy' with the central figure a reversed copy of the print 'Autumn' with the trees somewhat altered.

P335

P336

P337

P337 to P346 This series was designed to decorate both cups and saucers and other small items of a tea service, cream jug, sugar box and slop basin. The copperplates are almost entirely stipple engraved and of excellent workmanship and a credit to their engravers. The illustration in the Pattern Book of pattern 1922, the first upon which the series was used, is of a Bute teacup decorated with print P337. Only a single source has been noted, that for P346. It is the frontispiece of a series of twelve small volumes entitled:

ELEGANT EXTRACTS
From the most elegant Prose writers.
London

The books were published by John Sharpe and Hector Maclean and the original print for P346 was drawn by Rd Cook and engraved by J. Pye and C. Heath. Of the twenty-four illustrations contained in this series of books this was the only print used by Spode.

P338

P339

P340

P341

P342

P343

P344

P345

P346

P347, P348 and P349 The first two prints were engraved on two left-hand quarters of a divided copperplate centrally back-stamped by John Shafe when he was at Shoe Lane, London. The right hand half of the back-stamp cannot be traced in the copperplate stores. The mother and child shown in P348 was also printed by the New Hall Company but without the supporting landscapes, as were the children in P349.

P347

P348

P349

P350 to P359 The square format, also used for Contemporary Humanity, particularly on cups and saucers, varies a good deal in quality, style and content. They are all unnamed although P350 could obviously be called the 'The Sailor's Farewell' and P355 'The Tea Party'. P357 is the third print taken from Robert Bloomfield's 'The Farmer's Boy' entitled 'Summer' with the farmer's boy hearing and viewing a rising lark, only just discernible in the engraving.

P350

P351

P352

P353

P354

P355

P356   P357   P358

P359   P360   P361

P360 and P361 Print P360 differs in style from those preceding it. It has been noted transferred on to a rather splendid bone china coffee pot marked SPODE in red with the pattern number 557. Perhaps the few chickens in the foreground and the inclusion of the cat added it to the Spode 'Animals' prints, if so, it is like no other. P361 is again an odd man out with the print taken from the copperplate held in Spode's museum store although the print has not been seen on Spode marked wares. A similar design has been noted on an unmarked London shape cup and saucer showing the boy and the begging dog although a woman has been added standing behind the dog.

P362 This print is probably taken from the mezzotint illustrated which, in its turn, was copied from an oil painting by James Northcote RA. Spode's print is reversed and the gentlemen — the Reverend Theodore Dixon Hoste and his friend William Asheton — bear little resemblance to those in an original painting of 1802 entitled 'Grouse Shooting in the Forest of Bowland'. This particular scene was well liked by Staffordshire potters and can be found applied to sprig decorated mugs amongst scenes of drinking and coursing.

P362

Mezzotint after James Northcote, RA.

P363

P364

P365

P363 This print is placed in the centre of a 23.3cm bone china dessert plate with standard P102 sprigs transferred on the rim within a gold band edge. The P102 sprigs set within a gold banded edge is the normal description of pattern 1222 which usually contains P400 animal prints as the centre motif. It is true that the sheep lying beside the shepherd are 'Animals' yet the shepherd dominates the scene. Thus it must be categorised as *Contemporary Humanity.*

P364 and P365 This pair of prints, known respectively as 'Kneeling Man' and 'Sleeping Maiden' here decorate an elaborately gilded porter mug. They are both receiving a heavenly visitation although exactly why is not clear. The third print on this mug, opposite the handle, is print P349 showing the musical children known by some as 'The boy with the dustbin lid'. An example of a similar but plainer mug joins P364 and P365 to a third winged apparition more obviously doing his duty in P302.

P366 and P367 A pair of plump, well dressed children decorate two sides of a jug and are depicted chasing and endeavouring to catch a butterfly in their hats. That they are successful can be seen in the second print when the small girl achieves the impossible in holding a captured butterfly still and unmoving by grasping a single wing of the insect. The third print decorating this jug opposite the handle is P101–2 showing a mother and her even younger child.

P366

P367

P368 and 369

P368 and P369 The first print showing the bust of Admiral Viscount Nelson was copied from one of the forty portraits painted of Nelson by Lemuel Francis Abbot whose early portraits are said to be the best ever painted. This is borne out in a letter from Lady Nelson to her husband on July 3rd 1798: 'I am now writing opposite your portrait. The likeness is great. I am well satisfied by Abbot.' Such was the demand for portraits of Nelson after his victory of the Nile that the London print shops produced rival engravings many using one of Abbot's paintings as the model for their print. One of these, George Riley, published, in March 1779, a print with a copy of an Abbot head of Nelson supported by naval embellishments in a similar manner to the engravers at Spode. However, Spode's head of Nelson follows more nearly the original Abbot painting for Lady Nelson now hanging in Downing Street. The saucer used with Spode's cups shows Nelson's battle plan for his final victory at Trafalgar. Nelson abandoned the Admiralty fighting instructions of forming a line of battle parallel to that of the opposing fleet in favour of attacking in two columns. The object was to break through the enemy line and overwhelm the enemy centre and rear before their vanguard could tack about to help them. In this he succeeded, although it cost him his life.

P380 to P394 Three copperplates engraved with different Napoleonic cartoons had been found in Spode Works before the publication in 1983 of the first edition of *Spode Printed Ware* and were illustrated in the catalogue as P390, P391 and P392. At that time no ware was known decorated with prints from these copperplates. Subsequently a London Salesroom offered a pair of barrel-shaped earthenware jugs, the smaller of which was decorated with prints taken from the copperplates P390 and P391 and included the gilt inscription 'I.Topham 1804'. Some fifteen different cartoons have now been identified as being used by Spode transferred to a range of mugs and jugs although none are marked with Spode's name. The cartoons already numbered as P390, P391 and P392 in the first edition retain these numbers in this edition but can no longer appear as the first of the Napoleonic prints due to the great increase in prints needing to be numbered and illustrated. However, the plain barrel shaped jug that connected Napoleonic prints to Spode is illustrated here and details of Josiah Spode II's connection to the Pottery Volunteers and his production in 1803 of some fifteen cartoons of the Great Invasion Scare are discussed on page 143 in this chapter. The original prints were published in London from various print shops in 1803.

P380   John Bull giving Boney a Pull.
Illustration P380–1 shows an earthenware Dutch jug printed with the Napoleonic cartoon placed amongst a tea bowl, coffee can and saucer decorated with black sprigs from a copperplate still at Spode Works and finished with the same brick red banding lined in intense black around the foot and handles as is the jug.

The matching mug P380–2 is transferred with the same print in which Napoleon cries 'Ah! Misericordi Ah! Misericord! Jean Bool! Jean Bull! Hanging not good for Frenchman.' To this John Bull replies 'I shan't Measure the Cord you Foutre! I am sure it is long enough to hang a Dozen such fellows as you.' P380–3 shows the original print published by Ackermann on 7th August 1803.

P380–1

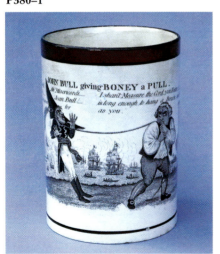

P380–2

P380–3

P381–1

P381–2

P381   THE BONE of CONTENTION or the English Bulldog and the Corsican Monkey.

P381–1   shows an earthenware barrel-shaped jug printed with the cartoon with the brick red band and black lines already seen. This was published by Fores on 14th June 1803 during the short-lived Peace of Amiens and illustrates one of the causes of the resumption of hostilities later that year. The British Bulldog, standing holding a large bone marked 'MALTA', breaks both wind and water to the detriment of Napoleon's invasion fleet and growls: 'There Monkey that for you'. The Corsican Monkey can only reply: 'Eh you Bull Dog, vat you carry off that bone for, I vas coming to take dat for myself. I vas good mind to lick you but for dem Dam Tooths'.

P381–2   illustrates the same print but transferred in black to a bone china Dutch jug with a gilded rim and handle introducing a new finish to Spode's range of Napoleonic wares.

P381–3   shows Fores' original cartoon.

P381–3

131

P382   THE KING of BROBDINGNAG and GULLIVER.

P382–1   A bone china jug of hooped barrel shape is transferred in intense black with this caricature based on Swift's *Gulliver's Voyage to Brobdingnag* with George III appearing as the huge King and dwarfing Napoleon as Grildrig. A bone china jug with an intense black print and gilded rim and handle follow the style of decoration used in P382–2. The original satire, P382–2, was drawn and etched by Gillray and published by Hannah Humphrey on 26th June 1803. It included the following soliloquy from the King which was not included by Spode:

My little friend Grildrig, you have made a most admirable Panegyric upon
yourself and Country, but from what I can gather from your own relation
and the answers I have with much pains wringed and extorted from you, I cannot
but conclude you to be one of the most pernicious, little odious reptiles that
nature ever suffered to crawl upon the surface of the earth.

King George is depicted in military uniform and is wearing a bagwig. After seeing the cartoon, he was reported to have said 'Quite wrong, quite wrong, no bag in uniform'.

P382–1

P382–2

P383–1

P383   A COCK and BULL STORY

P383–1   The satire, reproduced by Spode on a small earthenware mug printed in black with the familiar brick red banded edge, differs only in that the black line normally painted below the cartoon has been omitted through lack of space. The cockerel with the head of Napoleon, spurred and ready to fight, turns and faces across the Channel a bull with a typical John Bull head with features perhaps borrowed from George III, although he would not have been pleased to hear this suggestion. They threaten each other in awful doggerel. The cock boasts:

> Cock adudle doo. I shall soon come over to you.
> I'll fight true game & Crow my Fame
> And make you all look Blue.

To which he receives this shattering riposte:

> You impertinent Cock, I'll have you to know
> On this side of the Brook, you never shall crow
> And if you are not quick and give up your Jaw
> I'll teach you the nature of English Club Law.

P383–2   shows the original satire drawn and published by Piercy Roberts.

P383–2

P384 – THE END OF BONAPARTE.

P384–1 shows the now familiar earthenware barrel shaped jug with a black print and black outlined brick red banded neck. Napoleon is in a popular position much favoured by John Bull who sinks to his knees speaking just a single word 'AMEN'. Behind is a multi-national cheering body proclaiming in a most curious hotchpotch of European languages their approval of the proceedings. Even the rungs of the ladder leading up to the gallows are worded with Napoleon's alleged crimes namely — Ingratitude to Barras — Alexandria Massacre — El Arish 5000 Turks — Jaffa Soup 500 sick — Switzerland enslaved — Hanover pillaged, no doubt given a few more years after 1803 the list of crimes could have been greatly increased.

P384–2 is a print of the broadsheet published by John Babcock of Paternoster Row on 10th August 1803 under the title *THE APOTHEOSIS OF BONAPARTE*. The print was renamed by Spode, possibly to help the simple-minded drinking public who might well have been puzzled by the word Apotheosis.

P384–1

P384–2

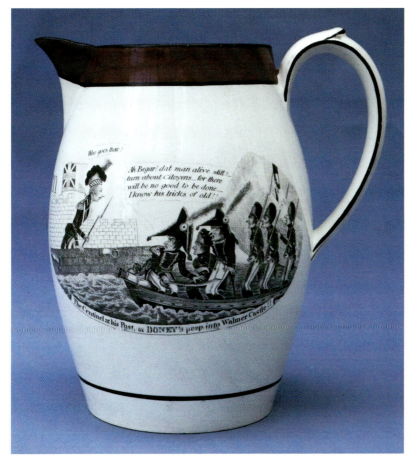

P385–1

P385 *The Centinel at his Post, or BONEY'S peep into Walmer Castle.*

P385–1 is of a cartoon on the larger earthenware jug of the pair named and dated 'I.Topham 1804'. The tall figure on the left is that of William Pitt, dressed in the uniform of the Cinque Port Volunteers, who challenges the approaching craft with 'Who goes there?' Napoleon, leading his trembling troops in the gunboat, recognises Pitt and exclaims, 'Ah — begar — dat man alive still — turn about Citoyens — for there will be no good to be done — I know his tricks of old!!'

When superseded as Prime Minister by Addington in 1801, Pitt, as Lord Warden of the Cinque Ports, withdrew from London to live at Walmer Castle. On resumption of war, he was gazetted Colonel of the Cinque Port Volunteers and raised three battalions each of forty officers and one thousand men. He took his military duties seriously and fully intended to lead his regiment against an attempted French invasion which was hourly expected.

P385–2 shows the original satire published by Fores on 22nd October, 1803.

P385–2

P386–1

P386–2

P386   *An Old PERFORMER playing on a New INSTRUMENT or one of the 42nd Touching the Invincible.*

P386-1   Transfer printed on the reverse of the last jug shows a Highlander of the 42nd (Royal Highland) Regiment, later to become the Black Watch, playing a surprised looking 'Corsican' bagpipe. The 42nd Regiment took a prominent part in the British victory over the French outside Alexandria later being awarded the battle honour of 'Egypt with Sphinx'. The verse of the tune being involuntarily aired by the bagpipe reads:

> God save great George our King
> He fell in love with Egypt once, because it was
> the high road
> To India for himself and friends to travel by a nigh road
> And after making mighty fuss and fighting day and
> night there
> T'was monstrous ungenteel of us who would not let
> him stay there.

P386–2 shows the same cartoon transferred in black on to a bone china mug with a plain gilded border and a gilded handle.

P386–3 is the original London print although the tune for the bagpipe is limited to the title line and the verse, of minimal literary merit, appears to have been added at the Spode factory.

P386–3

P387–2

P387–1

P387–1 is shown transfer printed and fully over enamelled on a bone china, low Dutch jug with a gilded rim and handle. Napoleon is depicted manacled, reversed on his horse and led in triumph through the streets of London escorted by Light Horse Volunteers.

P387-2 in an enlargement of the chargers ridden by the Volunteers, it can be seen that Bonaparte was certainly getting a horse laugh.

P387   THE GRAND TRIUMPHAL ENTRY of the CHIEF CONSUL into LONDON.

P387–3   shows the original cartoon published by Fores on 1st October, 1803.   The bystanders' remarks, not included in Spode's copy, regarding the Bull Hanker and Candle Ends refer to Wyndham. He was much opposed to arming a mass of Volunteers and Militia at the expense of the Regular Army, which was perhaps the unintentional consequence of the policy of the Addington Government. This view obviously was not shared by James Williams, chief caricaturist for Fores.

P387–3

P388–1,2 and 3 show a ribbed bone china barrel shaped jug with gilded rim and handle transferred in black and over-enamelled in full colour taken in three positions to show the full print. The original satire by Lee was published by James Asperne on 27th August 1803 and was priced at three pence plain or at £1.15s.0d. per 100. Josiah Spode duly invested three pence and his copperplate engraver copied the original print in every detail except the title. In Asperne's publication the title ceased after the wording 'the little Corsican Monkey'. The additional wording 'as he may probably appear at the above Receptacle of Foreign Curiosities on or before Christmas' was added by Spode, as can be seen on the illustrated jug. As Christmas, after Christmas came and went without the slightest chance of Napoleon's downfall, if judged by the rarity of the transfer, Spode may have wished that this sale inhibiting addition had not been made. Exeter Change was situated in the Strand on the site of the London home of the Cecil family rebuilt in the late 17th century as an exhibition and shopping centre. By the end of the 18th century the three floors were occupied by Gilbert Pidcock to house his menagerie despite the noise and smell pervading the whole of the Strand. Pidcock died in 1810 and the menagerie was taken by Polito who continued there until 1817 to be followed by Cross until 1828 when the 'Change was pulled down to allow the Strand to be widened'. Asperne's print and through it Spode's transfer, are likely to be the only surviving portraits of the first proprietor of the menagerie, Gilbert Pidcock.

P388–1

P388 PIDCOCK'S GRAND MENAGERIE, EXETER CHANGE *with an exact representation of BONAPARTE, the little Corsican Monkey as he may probably appear at the above Receptacle of Foreign Curiosities on or before Christmas.*

P388–2

P388–3

P389–1 Spode's presentation of this cartoon transferred to a plain circular bone china mug with gilt rim and handle is well enamelled in a wide range of colours. As can be seen, Napoleon stands before the premises of S.W. Fores, the print publisher's second shop, No. 50, Piccadilly, shown with its window dressed with views of London's major buildings, Boney's playthings, which are guarded by an overweight John Bull flamboyantly dressed in London Volunteer regimentals. The weeping Boney pleads:

> Pray Mr. Bull let me have some of the Toys if 'tis only that little one in the corner.
> With some sense, his pointing finger indicates the Bank of England.
> Regrettably the hardhearted John Bull refuses to please the 'child' and declares
> I tell you — you sha'nt touch one of them — so blubber away and be d—d.

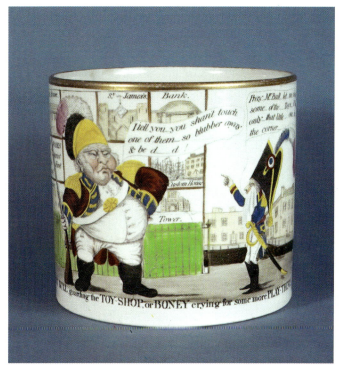

P389–1

P389   JOHN BULL guarding the TOY-SHOP or BONEY crying for some more PLAYTHINGS.

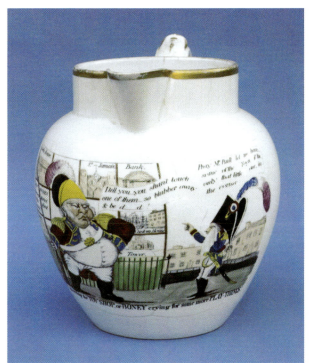

P389–2

P389–3

P389–2 shows the same print but transferred to a low Dutch jug and *P389–3* is the original print published by Fores on 29th October, 1803.

P390–1 illustrates one of the two prints taken from the copperplate shown in the first edition of *Spode Printed Ware* transferred to the smaller of the pair of earthenware jugs named and dated 'I.Topham 1804'. The print, coupled with the brick red band finished with black lining and the similar banding around the base of the jug and on the handle, marked the ware as Spode and led the way to the further discoveries of Spode's Napoleonic prints. In this print, made in intense black used throughout this series, Napoleon questions John Bull with,

Ah, who dares to interrupt me in my progress?

To this he receives the reply,

Why 'tis I, little Johnny Bull, protecting a little spot
that I clap my hand on and d—n me if you come any further
thats all.

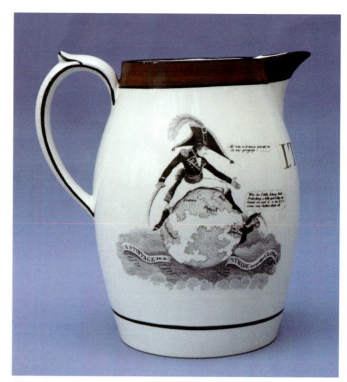

P390–1

A STOPPAGE to s STRIDE over the GLOBE

P390 *A STOPPAGE to a STRIDE over the GLOBE.*

P390–2 is the original cartoon by Piercy Roberts showing the changes Spode made to keep Napoleon dressed in the Spode style and the adoption of the Spode style of lettering used in the series.

P390–2

P391 **BRITANNIA Blowing up the CORSICAN Bottle Conjurer.**

P391–1 is transferred with a print in Intense black taken from Spode's copperplate showing Britannia seated inside a short bulbous bottle having speared Bonaparte to shoot him out of the neck amidst a cloud of gas and foam. The title of the satire appears on a long ribbon passing behind the neck of the bottle and behind the Spirit label. This label reads:

BRITISH SPIRITS
composed of
True Liberty. Courage
LOYALTY & RELIGION

The copperplate used in this transfer remains in the Works and was illustrated in the first edition of *Spode Printed Ware*. The transfer-printed jug is that decorated with P390–1, the smaller of the two named and dated jugs.

Print P391–2 is of the original cartoon engraved by Isaac Cruikshank and published by Ackermann on 17th August 1803. As can be seen, Spode much reduced the height of his reproduction to a more manageable shape to fit on to his productions of mugs and particularly of jugs.

The infamous first appearance of a Bottle Conjurer can be traced to the year 1749. The January edition of the *Gentleman's Magazine* reported thus:

…A person advertised that he would, at the Theatre in the Haymarket, play on a common walking cane the music of every instrument now used to surprising perfection, that he would, on the stage, get into a tavern quart bottle, without equivocation; and while there, sing several songs, and suffer any spectator to handle the bottle; that, if any spectator should come mask'd, he would, if requested, declare who they were; that in a private room, he would produce the representation of any person dead, which the party requesting it could converse some minutes as if alive…

On the date set, 16th January, 1749, the theatre was crowded with the gullible who waited in vain for the spectacle to begin. With patience exhausted and further incensed by a cry 'That for double prices, the conjurer will go into a pint bottle', those attending left in an uproar carrying much of the theatre fittings with them which they burnt in the street.

P391–1

P391–2

P392   NATIONAL Contrasts or BULKY & BONEY.

P392–1 shows a rather damaged hooped bone china barrel jug transferred with the satire in intense black with the brick red banded rim and black lining finish. Contrast this with

P392–2 a print taken from the third surviving copperplate at Spode Works, and it will be found that the title differs with 'and' written in full between 'Bulky and Boney' in place of the ampersand used on the all black example in ***P392–1***. This is not the only difference with the black areas shown in the first example being left uncoloured on the second.

P392–1

P392–3a,b show a fully enamelled example obviously printed from the extant copperplate at Spode Works. The original by Piercy Roberts was a penny plain example and the twopenny coloured appears to be a Spode adaptation to enable them to also offer an all coloured example. Of the four other fully enamelled examples that have been noted no all black examples have yet been seen. They may not have ever existed but the possibility must remain.

P392–2

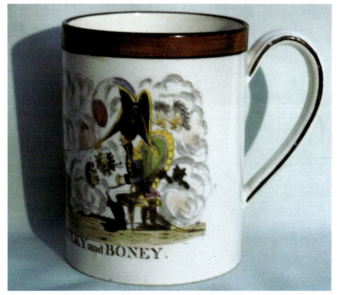

P392–3a

P392–3b

P393 A SENATUS CONSULTUM on BONAPARTE
*making his Will, before his Invasion of England &
Conquest of the World.*

This appears on a bone china Dutch jug with gilded
rim finish. The rather far-fetched title of 'Senatus
Consultum' is taken from the form of decree of the
Roman Senate, represented in the print by Beelzebub
with two demons in attendance, in which advice was
given to a magistrate, here being Napoleon himself.

Bonaparte speaks first:

My Old Friend, I am puzzled about naming my
Successor. Pray let me know my fate before I go to
conquer England.

The Devil replies:

Don't trouble yourself about your Successor, there it is
settled — The English are waiting for you, so am I,
there is your fate.

P393

With these happy words, he points to two ethereal messages, if such a description can apply to
pronouncements from Hades, naming Napoleon's successors with the words 'BOURBONS
RESTORED' and his fate as 'DEATH, Bonaparte, DEATH'. It is unusual for an English satire
to even mention the Bourbons, the enemies of England for so many years before the French
Revolution. With his second prediction, the Devil must be on a winner since death is the
inevitable conclusion of life.

With this print one difficulty remains. The contents and wording have every appearance of
a satire published during the Great Invasion Scare of 1803 which subsided in 1805 with the
withdrawal of the last major units from the French invasion camps. This contention is
somewhat confounded by the date of 19th September 1808 which is very clearly printed on a
Fores satire of the same title featuring the same scene and wording as that found on the Spode
jug although rather more sketchily drawn. The origins of all the other Spode prints can be
dated to 1803 and it seems most unlikely that Spode would have bothered to bring out, at
considerable engraving cost, a further transfer five years later centred on the 1803 invasion
scare when he had already offered no less than thirteen different prints covering the same
subject any of which could be re-used at no additional expense. It appears more likely that the
surviving Fores prints of 1808 were updated reissues by Fores of a print first issued in 1803
which, by the minimal additional expense of changing the numeral 3 of 1803 on the
copperplate to the 8 of 1808, could be given the appearance of a new issue.

P394   *JOHN BULL extinguishing a Firebrand.*

P394

With the type of humour that must have made it an instant success in every ale house in Britain, the final Napoleonic satire from Spode Works also remains somewhat a mystery. Napoleon retains his Consular uniform not yet attaining the glories of Emperor yet the style of lettering is not that used on the fourteen other Spode examples already illustrated. The only example of this cartoon yet discovered is printed on an earthenware wall tile clearly marked on its reverse 'Copeland & Garrett late Spode' which firmly fixes the date of manufacture of the tile between 1833 and 1847 and this transfer of the cartoon to the same date or possibly even later. With the copperplate still housed in Spode Works and the original printed satire from which the Spode copy was taken still to be traced, a date during the Great Invasion Scare of 1803 when the other Spode copperplates were engraved seems the most likely. This view is reinforced by the appearance of a very similar cartoon by Piercy Roberts of 1803 entitled 'John Bull Drowning an Enemy' using the same method of overcoming Bonaparte but shielding the source of the flow from the delicate eyes of the beholder.

Copperplate makers' marks appear on the following
P300 series Humanity coppers.

Mark no.3   Print P337
Mark no.4   Print P390
Mark no 6   Prints P342, P350, P352
Mark no.7   Prints P335, P347, P348
Mark no.8   Prints P331, P332, P336, P339.

Table 5.3   Spode patterns decorated with Bat printed Classical and Contemporary Humanity P300 series

Pattern number	Probable date of introduction	Description and colour of prints	References of the prints usually found on the pattern
557	1803 or a little earlier	In black with band and line gilding (see also P200 and P400 series)	P301, P302, P303 and P360
1222	1808	Black with gold band edge (See also P100 & P400 series)	P363
1693	1811	Gold printing on a cobalt blue panel	P301, P302 and P303
1922	1812–1813	In black with gilded dontil edge	P313 to P317 and P331 to P359
2208	1814	In black with black edge	P313 to P317 and P331 to P359
2209	1814	In blue with blue edge	P313 to P317 and P331 to P359
2210	1814	In intense black with rose colour edge	P313 to P317 and P331 to P359
2435	1816	Pattern Book marked 'Printed by Bruce'. In black with elaborate gilded border	P313 to P317 and P331 to P359
2643	1817	Cherubs on clouds overpainted in colour	P311
2742	1818	Pattern Book description reads only 'Purple Landscapes' Examples of ware have been noted with P300 series prints Gilded dontil edge	P313 to P317 and P331 to P359
2744 2745 2746 2747 2748 2749 2750.	1818	These patterns are described, as is 2742, as being printed with 'Purple Landscapes' with various gilded and painted borders Without seeing an example it is not possible to be sure whether P200 or P300 series were used	Probably P300 series prints, but judged only from examples of pattern 2742
3649	1824	Pattern Book illustrates cup with Contemporary figure outside and small flower spray inside P348	P331 to P359 and perhaps P313 to P317
3658	1824	Chariots and cherubs with plain edge in brown or perhaps blue	P311 and P312
3665	1824	Chariots and cherubs with gilded edge	P311 and P312
3851	1825	As pattern 1922 but in rose colour	P313 to P317 And P331 to P359

P400 series Animals, Birds, Sporting subjects and Armorial bat prints

The first engravings in this series, P401 to P422, were taken from a number of sources including the works of the well-known artists and engravers George Morland, Samuel Howitt and Robert Pollard. However, three prints were taken from *Buffon's Natural History* originally published in France in ten volumes with the English translation printed and published by J.S. Barr of Covent Garden on December 30th 1791, under the general heading of *Barr's Buffon*. Similarly a single print from Church's *Cabinet of Quadrupeds,* published in 1805, was used by Spode although rival potters used many more. The Pattern Books record nine patterns with the prints simply described as 'Animals' but only two print colours are included being black and gold and a shard has been found showing an animal in red.

It does seem likely that the first coppers were ready at Spode in 1807/8 and that the early set was completed soon after. The transfers are most commonly found in black on pattern 557 bone china tea wares followed by pattern 1222 used in conjunction with P100 series flower sprigs on a wide variety of bone china shapes. Pattern 1191 is not only the first pattern upon which the name 'Animals' is shown in the Pattern Books, but the drabware vase illustrating the pattern is one of the only two examples of this ware appearing in the Books.

Besides bone china and drabware, prints are also found on Revived Astbury-Jackfield wares and on earthenware. The later series of bird prints *Birds in Garden Landscapes* numbered from P440 onwards, was introduced from 1829 and are in complete contrast in style to the earlier designs. These were followed in 1831/32 by a second series of bird prints *Birds on Branches,* numbered from P460, in which the sketchy backgrounds are omitted and the birds perch in a cluster of flowers. Only one Armorial service is known where the device was transferred in plain Bat printing without the addition of enamel colouring. This is illustrated at the end of the section.

P401 and P402   These two prints of dead game can be found on the signed works of Samuel Howitt although that does not necessarily mean that he was responsible for the origination of the design. Both Spode's copperplates are stipple punched and in the case of P402 the image has been reversed and is now a mirror of Howitt's engraving.

P401

P402

P403

P404

Original Howitt engraving used for P404

P403 and P404 These two transfers from Spode's copperplates are straight copies of Howitt's prints as can be seen from the illustration. Howitt has put his own name on the dog collar but Spode has omitted it.

P405 The two rabbits, here decorating a Spode bone china saucer, are taken from John Church's two volume *Cabinet of Quadrupeds* engraved by James Tookey from drawings by Julius Ibbotson. This was published by Darton and Harvey, Gracechurch Street, London in 1805. The two volumes contained 84 prints of which 38 have been found transferred to ceramics mostly printed in underglaze blue on earthenware. The two rabbits are the only animals taken from this series by Spode.

P406 This Spode copperplate of a ram and ewe derives from two Illustrations in *Buffon's Natural History* translated from the French and printed and published by J.S.Barr of Bridges Street, Covent Garden in 1792. The English version of 1792 shows the pair of sheep as separate engravings with the ewe marked on its flank with a large capital letter 'E'. As can be seen, this is not repeated on Spode's copperplate and the two animals have been brought together as a pair engraved on a single copper.

P405

P406

P407 This very odd subject for decoration of tea ware hardly fits the European scenes of the remainder of the set but it was used indiscriminately with them. It was taken from volume 22 of the 1804 edition of *The Sporting Magazine* with the print named as 'Leopards devouring a horse'.

P407

P408 and P409 The two original prints of this pair of Stag and Hind appear in the 1792 English translation of Barr's *Buffon*. The original prints were line engraved whereas Spode's copperplates were stipple engraved and give a smoother and more gentle look. The earlier state of Spode's engraving of the Stag can be seen in a print on a tea cup compared with a print from the final state on a saucer. The additional clumps of grass in the foreground are particularly noticeable in the final state.

P408   P409

Final state of copperplate to print P408

Earlier state

P410

P411

P410 and P411 In the first print the dog has a particularly smug and self-satisfied look. The scene is engraved on the reverse of a cut-up portion of an original Rotunda P707 copperplate from the eighteenth century. The source of P411 is an engraving after Samuel Howitt published by Orme in June 1809 and shown here. Howitt had used the same animal in the same attitude in a pheasant shooting scene in Orme's publication in 1807 of *British Field Sports* but the closeness of the copy points to the 1809 issue as being Spode's model.

Engraving after Samuel Howitt (Source of P411)

P412

P413

P412 and P413 Two further English scenes. The cow is uncommon and the copper is no longer at the Works.

P414–1

P414–2

P414–3

P414 and P415 Two versions of P414 can be found — P414–1 with the greyhounds pursuing a fox and P414–2 with the same two greyhounds now chasing a hare. A close examination of the copperplate explains this. The faint outline of the fox's tail can be seen above and to the left of that of the hare and the fox's brush is still just discernible. The fox has been removed by knocking up and burnishing and the hare has been engraved in his place. But who objected? Did some irate master of foxhounds appear whip in hand? Or perhaps the proud owner of greyhounds was angered by the fox, a quarry spurned by his well-trained animals. The original engraving of the two greyhounds closely following a fox appeared in *The Sporting Magazine Volume 38* of 1806. P415, another transfer showing two greyhounds was often used as a pair on Spode wares with P414. It was copied from an aquatint by Robert Pollard issued in 1804 and shown here when Pollard was still at Spa Fields. Spode's copy follows the original very closely except the usual change of engraving to stipple engraving.

P415

Aquatint by Robert Pollard, source of P415.

P416 and P417 These two prints are larger than those used on saucers and will be found most frequently on the two sizes of Spode's saucer shaped bread and butter plates used with the Old Oval and the New Oval teaware services. Both copperplates were in the Works collection although the smaller with three cows can no longer be seen. Spode's stipple engraving, P417 was copied from a mezzotint engraving of 1800 by W.Ward after George Morland's original painting 'The Last Litter' As can be seen, Spode considerably simplified Morland's picture so that the design could fit a circular form.

P416

P417

The Last Litter **after George Morland.**

P418

P418 to P422 These five prints have all been found on bone china teapots of the New Oval shape although they do appear on other shapes of Spode wares. Print 418 is the most unusual and in the last twenty years only two examples have been noted with the usual prints on Spode 'Animals' teapots being P421 and P422. Print 422 is a simplified version of George Morland's painting of 1792 'Morning or the Benevolent Sportsman' which hangs in the Fitzwilliam Museum, Cambridge. The pair of prints P419 and P420 decorate the teapot cover and do a similar duty for the cover of the sugar box. The source of P421 has not been found.

P419

P420

P421

P422

Morning or the Benevolent Sportsman **by George Morland.**

P435

P436

P435 and P436 These two prints, with the birds engraved in stipple in the style of the first quarter of the nineteenth century, have no matching designs although P435 is proofed into the back of the engraving shop Badge and Proof Book amidst proofs of P200 and P300 series of prints. The border design of P436 could well be expected to appear in gilding although no piece from either copper has been found.

P440 to P451 Birds in Garden Landscapes. These prints, introduced in 1829, were engraved to fit the new Embossed Pembroke shaped tea wares. The engravings could not be further in style, nor regrettably in quality, from the earlier prints in the P400 series. A number of copperplates have been re-engraved and slightly altered since 1829 and earlier prints may not exactly match the illustrations. They were

supported by undistinguished flower sprigs in a similar manner to the other Bat prints used on Pembroke shape wares. Sizes vary from 10cm x 5.5cm for the largest to 4cm x 2.5cm for the smallest. Despite sixteen variations of colour, gilding, overpainting and background colours produced before 1833, printed examples are extremely rare and, in consequence, it cannot be certain that the illustrations cover all the original designs. The smaller prints are engraved in groups on the copperplates which would have been charged with oil with the transfer tissue divided after stripping from the copperplate to allow each section to be used separately on transfer to the ware. Print P448 shows a pair of small flower sprigs for use with the birds although similar small sprigs in P100 series would also have been used.

P440

P441

P442

P443

P444

P445

P446

P447

P448

P449

P450

P460 to P476   Birds on Branches. This, the last Spode Bat printing series issued in 1831/32, is shown in the Pattern Books decorating the later tea ware shape named by Leonard Whiter as '4643' shape, this being its first appearance in the Pattern Books. The birds are drawn to a smaller scale than the branches and flowers in which they perch almost as though they were added to the Pembroke shape P100 flower sprays as an afterthought. Again the printed ware is very scarce although twenty-two variations were almost immediately offered for sale, some richly gilded with various coloured backgrounds giving a very opulent appearance. Many of the prints were engraved upon the copperplates in the groups shown in the illustrations. In this they followed the systems adopted for the first small P100 series flower sprigs and also used in the Birds in Garden Landscapes. The very small designs of P460, P461, P462 and P474 were used inside the rim of teacups with the slightly larger prints P471 and P472 decorating the outside.

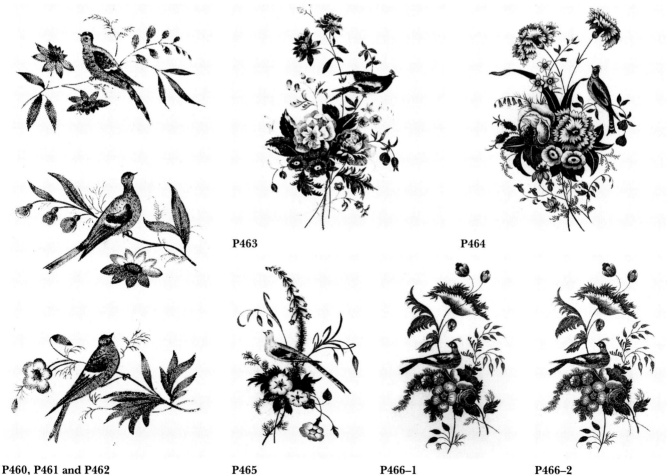

P460, P461 and P462   **P465**   **P466–1**   **P466–2**

P463   **P464**

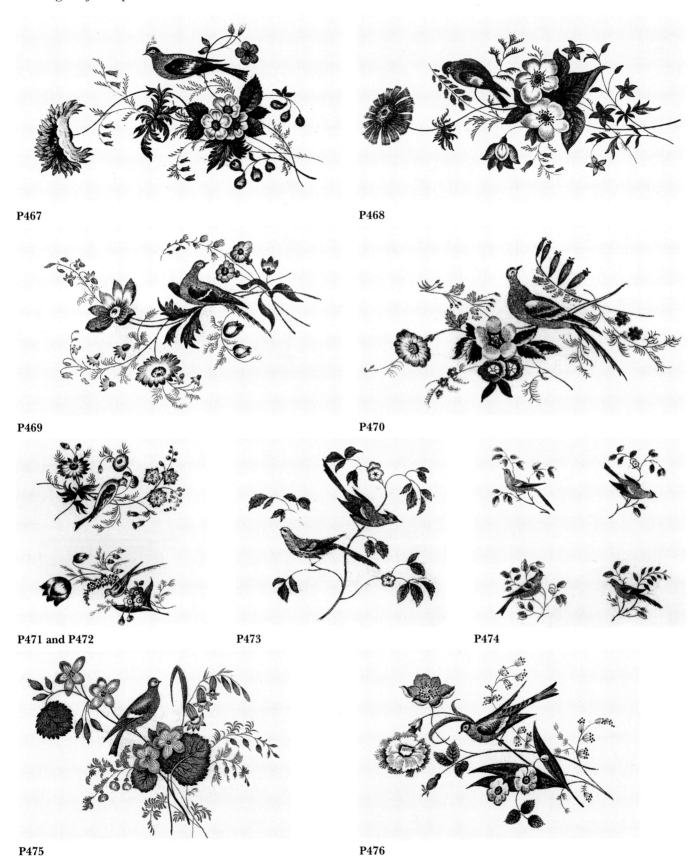

P467

P468

P469

P470

P471 and P472

P473

P474

P475

P476

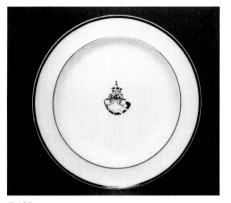

Armorial Bat prints The only heraldic device so far seen in plain Bat printing without further decoration is that of the Corporation of Ripon, P490, printed in black on a fine creamware service. However, Bat printing was much used as a basis for fully decorated Coats of Arms, the fine print giving the painters and paintresses the necessary unobtrusive guidance for matching repetition. The illustration of such decoration shows a fully enamelled Coat of Arms of Captain Faith surrounded by a border decorated with prints P152 and P159.

P490

Copperplate makers' trademarks are stamped on the backs of the following P400 series coppers:

Mark no.2   Print P404
Mark no.4   Print P402
Mark no.5   Prints P412, P418 and P422

Table 5.4   Spode patterns decorated with Animals, Birds, Sporting subjects and Armorial prints P400 series

Pattern number	Probable date of introduction	Description and colour of prints	References of the prints usually found on the pattern
557	1807–8	Probable year for Animals P400 series on this pattern. Printed in black with band and line gilding	P401 to P422
1191	1807–8	Animals in black on drabware gold edge	P401 to P422
1222	1808	Animals and Flower sprigs in black, gold band edge (see also P100 series)	P401 to P422
1483	1809	Animals in black with elaborate gilding on cobalt border	P401 to P422
1485	1809	As 1483 but variation in gilding	P401 to P422
1486	1809	As 1483 but variation in gilding	P401 to P422
1688	1811	Animals in gold with band and line gilded border	P401 to P422
1699	1811	Animals in gold on cobalt blue panels	P401 to P422
1701	1811	Animals in gold with gold banded edge	P401 to P422
Pattern nos. as listed	1829–33	Birds in Garden Landscapes with variations in colours, over enamelling, gilding and background colours on the following pattern numbers: 4433 4441 4555 4560 4568 4589 4590 4591 4597 4634 4658 4880 4885 4975 5000 5169	P440 to P451
Pattern nos. as listed	1832 and 1833	Birds in Branches with variations in colours, over-enamelling, gilding and background colours in the following pattern numbers: 4944 4945 4946 4947 4948 4949 4950 4951 4952 4953 4954 4956 4958 4959 4960 4965 4967 4972 5001 5019 5082 5084	P460 to P476

Shapes of wares decorated with Bat prints

The illustrations of the wares decorated with Bat prints have been arranged under two headings, firstly tea wares and secondly pieces for all other uses. In quantity the majority of Spode's Bat printed wares fall into the first category, indeed Bute teacups, coffee cans and saucers probably outnumber the total of every other Bat printed shape. In the second category falls a very wide range of wares in various bodies that greatly add to the pleasure of collecting Spode Bat prints.

Tea wares

Most teacup shapes were manufactured in three sizes: Teacup, Norfolk and breakfast cup. The smallest and the largest are named after the meal of their intended use, but the derivation of the name used for the middle size is obscure. Perhaps the inhabitants of the county of Norfolk breakfasted in a delicate manner or were lavish with afternoon tea. The geography of Spode's tea ware in any case is confusing; Bute, London and Pembroke are shapes, yet Norfolk is a size. The full standard tea service in the most commonly found Bat printed shape of New Oval with Bute cups and cans consisted of a teapot with cover and stand, sugar box with cover, cream jug, slop basin, 21cm saucer-shaped bread and butter plate and a similar plate but 18cm, twelve teacups, twelve coffee cans and twelve saucers; a total of forty-five pieces. With the later designs of tea ware a taller cup was provided in place of the coffee can and the stand for the teapot was not always supplied, but otherwise the service remained the same. Before about 1822 with the introduction of the Gadroon shape, normal saucers were flat inside without any form of well. Cups and cans skate about in a most alarming fashion and great care has to be taken in their use.

It will be noticed that a single saucer was made to do duty for the teacup and the coffee can or later cup, and that individual tea plates were not supplied. However, plates corresponding to the modern tea plate in size do exist and regularly appear. Norfolk-size sets have been found with such a plate with every cup and saucer and it is possible that the two larger sizes could be obtained or were supplied with plates for breakfast use. Eating toast without a plate would have been a messy business. Two other additional matching items obtainable to order but not included in the standard service were coffee and a small round, sweep-neck teapot holding two cups of tea. With some manufacturers the latter would have been part of a cabaret set supplied on a tray with two cups and other small pieces. Spode, as far as can be ascertained, did not make such a set and the little teapot is usually found as a second teapot of a service, sometimes being called an afternoon pot. Bat printed coffee pots are very rare and an afternoon pot decorated by Bat printing has yet to be recorded, although underglaze blue printed examples are known as well as those with the more frequently seen enamelled decoration.

S1

S1 and S2 Illustrated in S1 is pattern no.473, the first Bat printed decoration shown in the Pattern Books probably of the period 1802–3. All of bone china, the major pieces are of the Old Oval tea ware shape with Bute cups and saucers all decorated with Flower sprays P100 series stipple engraved with some added line engraving. The decoration is coloured with intense black rather than the charcoal grey which was to be the favoured colour for the new century. Pattern no.473 marks the first appearance of band and line gilding, although this was shortly also to be used with the printed landscape pattern no. 557. The only marked piece in the 473 service is the cream jug

impressed SPODE. Compare this jug with that illustrated in S2 in pattern 500 transferred in charcoal grey from an all stipple engraved copperplate on a bone china New Oval jug from the same mould as that in S1. The simplified transferring and reduction in gilding to a plain edge band reduced the cost sufficiently to make pattern 473 a rarity and pattern 500 the norm for flower decorated Bat printed wares.

S3 Bute coffee can and saucer. Bone china, pattern 1516. P100 series Fruits in chocolate brown with band and line gilding.

S2

S3

S4

S5

S6

S7

S4 Saucer-shaped bread and butter plates, the larger 21cm diameter and the smaller 18cm. Although often referred to as saucer dishes, they are termed bread and butter plates or 'B & B's' at the Works. One of each size was included in the standard Old Oval and New Oval tea services.

S5 Bute shape cup and saucer in bone china printed with P100 series Flowers in charcoal grey with chocolate-brown edge, pattern 2393. This would have been a less expensive finish than the gilded edge of pattern 500.

S6 Old Oval teapot in bone china transferred with print P126–1 the largest of the flower prints. Compare the gilding of

this teapot in pattern 500 with the teapot appearing in S1 in the earlier pattern 473 with band and line gilding.

S7 These pieces are from the Hester Savory service details of which are given earlier in the chapter. The elegance without ostentation of Spode's first printed tea wares was wholly in keeping with the traditions of the Quakers amongst whom were the Savorys.

S8 and S9 Compare the shapes of the Old Oval slop basin S8 with that of the New Oval shape S9 both in pattern 557 with band and line gilding. The Old Oval is slightly smaller being 15cm in diameter as against 16cm for the New Oval with a more open throwing.

S8

S9

S10

S11

S10 and S11 Old Oval sugar box printed with P200 series Landscapes and elaborate gilding of pattern 558 is shown at S10. Compare with the New Oval sugar box, S11, with band and line gilding of pattern 557. Band and line gilding proved far more popular than the elaborate 558.

S12 The Common shape tea bowl and saucer in bone china, saucer 13cm in diameter. Printed in intense black and black edge in pattern 2208 with the colour especially formulated for this pattern and pattern 2210. The recipe for this intense black is shown in the Colour Recipe Book formulated for printing pattern 2208.

S13 and S14 The plain Bute shaped tea cups, coffee cans and saucers were common to many manufacturers with Spode examples only differing in the shape of handle with its very obvious kink or kick. Similar handles were made by a number of minor potters but the Spode shape is more definite than that of his rivals. S13 shows a can and a saucer in pattern 557 decorated with P200 series Landscapes. S14 illustrates the three sizes of cup available in the Bute shape from left to right: teacup, Norfolk and breakfast cup with a capacity ratio of 1: 1.5: 2. The breakfast cup holds nearly half a pint.

S15 Saucer-shaped bread and butter plate in bone china, 21cm diameter, pattern no.557 decorated in charcoal grey with P417, 'The Last Litter' after George Morland.

S12

S13

S14

S15

159

S16

S17

S18

S16 New Oval teapot and saucer-shaped bread and butter plate in bone china. Transferred in chocolate brown with P100 Fruits and with band and line gilding, pattern 1516 of 1810.

S17 New Oval teapot and stand in bone china. Teapot overall 27cm, pattern 557, Bat printed in charcoal grey with series P200 prints.

S18 Josiah Spode invoiced Stephen Tempest on 15th July 1813 for a number of bone china items. Details, taken from a transcript in the Spode MSS, are as follows:

To Josiah Spode, Potter and English Porcelain Manufacturer

			£	s	d
30 China porringer handled bowls and 30 saucers No.1922 dark black and edge	1/6d		4.	10	0
18 China Cans	-do-	9d		13	6
18 " Can saucers	-do-	8d		12	0
36 " Muffins 7in	-do-	1/6d	2.	14	6
12 " 8½in Dessert Plates	3/-		1.	16	0
5 " Bowls	-do-		11	6	
2 " 24s Dutch Jugs	-do-	3/-		6	0

S18 Shows a Porringer cup and saucer Bat printed in pattern 1922 with P300 series Humanity prints as shown in the first item of the invoice.

S19 In this illustration are shown on the left a Bute teacup and saucer and on the right a tea bowl and saucer. Both these saucers measure between 13cm and 14cm in diameter, of rounded form but differing in the foot rim. The Bute saucer is recessed and the tea bowl saucer has a raised foot rim. Between these two stands a coffee can with a different saucer. It is a little smaller, 13cm in diameter, with angled sides and a recessed foot rim. This is the can saucer of item three in the invoice to Stephen Tempest supplied when cans formed a separate item. Its shape and size certainly suits the can which sits within it most happily and the size and shape is listed in the notebooks of the turners and throwers.

S19

S20

S21

S22

S20 and S21 Joined up sections of P136 have been used to form wide and continuous bands and borders in black on a New Oval bone china teapot and stand, S20, and on a plate S21. P136–1 has been used on the teapot with P136–2 used on the teapot stand and plate giving a most attractive decoration far better than would have been expected from the copperplates.

S22 A plate of chalcedony body in typical orange colour transfer printed with the early print of the greyhounds chasing a fox, P414–1, with the rim enhanced by a bold edge of plain gilding. This coloured body was little used by Spode and examples are very difficult to find.

S23

S24

S23 New oval cream jug in bone china, 18.5cm overall, pattern 1703, printed in gold with series P200 Landscapes.

S24 Bute teacup and saucer in bone china printed with pattern 1922 with P300 series Humanity prints in charcoal grey with gilded dontil edge.

S25–1

S25–2

S25 Vase shaped coffee-pot in bone china transferred with P335 and P336 from the Contemporary Humanity series. The 1820 Shape Book shows this coffee-pot as being made in five sizes and being supplied with a stand. In Bat printing the shape is extremely rare and a pot complete with stand has not been noted.

S26 Saucer-shaped bread and butter plate in bone china, 20.5cm diameter, pattern number 557, transferred in charcoal grey with print P227. This print is from the copperplate with the hidden date of 1811 and the initials I.K.

S27, S28 and S29 London shape tea ware was not often decorated by Bat printing and examples are unusual. S27 is the London shape slop basin which closely follows the cup shape although is larger. Here it is printed with P200 series Landscapes without further decoration. The London shape coffee cup, S28, in pattern 500 has a gilded edge in contrast to the teacup and saucer, S29, which, as the slop basin, are without edge decoration, giving a naked look to the ware.

S26

S27

S28

S29

S30 Octagon shape cream jug. Felspar porcelain, 13.5cm overall, Bat printed in charcoal grey with P300 Contemporary Humanity and with blue edge. No pattern number is shown. The piece has a number of fire cracks making it a 'Second', hence the inexpensive blue edge rather than gilding.

S31 Cream jug in bone china pattern 2792 introduced in 1818. The pattern of Bat printing in purple used the botanical prints P137 to P141 with a pink/red edge. The geranium used here is a Bat printed version of the centre of the underglaze blue printed pattern Geranium P821–1, also first issued in 1818.

S30

S31

S33

S32 Two Bute shape tea saucers decorated with the same Landscape print P242. The upper drabware saucer is well printed in charcoal grey but the bone china lower saucer is printed in blue with very poor definition.

S33 and S34 Revised Astbury type cup and saucer, S33, with a redware body coated in dark-brown and white slip and printed with P200 Landscapes. The very distinctive angular shape of the cup fitted with the standard Spode Bute handle can be seen at S34.

S32

S34

S35

S36

S37

S35 and S36 Embossed Pembroke shape cups and saucers were designed with a well in the saucer and with the decoration so arranged as not to be obscured by the cup. The arrangement of a single print placed opposite the handle on a cup was superseded, and two main prints were placed one on each side of the cup were supported by flower sprigs placed both inside and outside the cup. Three main prints were used on the saucer each separated by small flower sprigs. S35 is printed in charcoal grey in pattern 4406 using a special smaller range of P200 landscapes. S36 is transferred with the flower sprays in green and the sprigs in gold in pattern 4628.

S37 Etruscan shape Milk Jug in felspar porcelain printed in gold with P142 flower spray and sprigs in pattern 3743 with printed Spode mark no 41. This is the first pattern using gold printing regularly marked with Spode's name.

S38 Sugar box in Embossed Pembroke shape, bone china, pattern number 4606 printed with P200 series landscapes in charcoal grey. Pattern 4606 was introduced in 1829 yet the print on the front of this piece P277, West Wycombe Park, was in use in 1803 on the Hester Savory service.

S39 Octagonal teapot stand in bone china in pattern 4609 with charcoal grey Bat printed flowers on an ivory ground, a production of the 1830s. Compare these flower sprays with the earlier type shown on illustrations S2, S5 and S6.

S38

S39

S40 The shape of this cup and saucer was named by Leonard Whiter as '5146' being the first entry in the Pattern Books showing the shape of the cup. The decoration shown here is in pattern 4972 with the printed designs being from Spode's last Bat print series P400 'Birds in Branches' of 1831–32.

S40

Uses other than tea wares.

Bat printing was used for decoration of ceramic pieces of varied bodies and a wide range of uses from creamware dinner services to bone china chamber-pots. Examples of pieces in this very wide category are surprisingly rare even though many are of handsome appearance.

The first six illustrations show the most usual shapes of dessert comports and dishes. The oval comports S41 and S42 gave way, probably in the 1820s, to the later oval shape of S45 and S46. Shell dishes were also a usual part of dessert services and can be expected to be found with Bat printed decoration.

S41

S41 Oval dessert comport in bone china 27cm long pattern 500. Transferred in charcoal grey with P100 series Flower Sprays and banded gilding. This piece is marked with the very rare Prince of Wales mark no. 39 which probably dates it to 1806.

S42 Pair of oval dessert comports in bone china in similar shape to S41 decorated with pattern 1922. This is not the earliest production of P414; the original fox has been changed to a hare.

S42

S43

S43 Bone china teacup, coffee cup and saucer in the unusual Bell shape decorated with P200 series Landscapes with the coffee cup showing P254.

S44 Square low comport in bone china, 21.5cm, band and line gilded pattern 557 printed with P247 in charcoal grey.

S44

S45

S46

S47

S48

S45 and S46 Standard comport shape superseding the plain oval shape shown in S41 and S42. The low form is shown in S45 and the footed example in S46. Both are in bone china and 37cm long overall. S45 is transferred with P200 series landscapes with band and line gilding of pattern 557 and S46 is in pattern 500 with flowers and sprigs of P100 series.

S47 and S48 Part of a creamware dinner service transferred with the badge of the Corporation of Ripon, P490, is shown at S47. The cover dish is particularly handsome and is slightly deeper than its bone china counterpart decorated with P100 Flowers in S48. It is unusual to find Bat printing on creamware and doubly so crested as is the Ripon service.

S49

S50

S49 Circular cover dish in bone china, 23cm diameter, printed in charcoal grey with P100 Flowers pattern 500. An uncommon shape.

S50 Dessert plate in bone china, 19.5cm diameter, Bat printed in blue with Union Sprays P143. A recipe in the *Colour Match Book* for a black-brown colour states it was for Richard Bell for printing pattern 3767, which is shown in the *Pattern Book* printed with the same Union Sprays. It seems possible that Bell might have printed this plate also.

166

S51

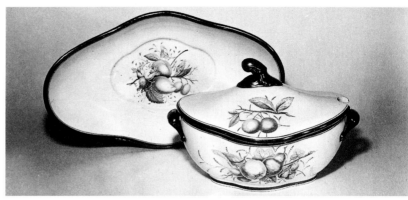

S52

S51 Small dessert plate in bone china, pattern 557 printed in charcoal grey with P252. A very satisfactory combination of restrained decoration and fine bone china.

S52 Sauce tureen, cover and stand in earthenware printed in charcoal grey with P100 Fruits. The tureen is a shape usually supplied for dessert ware.

S53 Rectangular cover dish in bone china 24cm x 20cm printed with P200 series Landscapes in charcoal grey, pattern 557. Both the prints shown appear on the Hester Savory service although the cover dish is a later production. The shape is also found in stone china with an example noted printed in underglaze blue with Grasshopper P621.

S53

S54

S55

S56 Old shape egg hoop in bone china, pattern 557, transferred in charcoal grey with P200 series Landscapes.

S54 Beehive in bone china, 12cm high overall, printed in charcoal grey with P100 Flowers pattern 500. These were made in three sizes for honey or jam.

S55 Porter mug decorated with Dunrobin Castle P265, in charcoal grey but with the name of the castle, which is included on the copperplate, omitted on the mug. The initials MG are gilded as is the dontil edge.

S56

S57–1

S58

S57–2

S57 and S58 These two pieces are examples of decoration with pattern 1222 with the main prints from the P400 Animals series supported by early P100 Flower sprays and sprigs. S57 shows two views of an Ice Pail in bone china with the two main prints being P421 and P422, the two prints often found on Animals teapots. Although Spode made one shape of a single ice pail, most were of double construction with a raised and drop-in liner and a cover with a ring handle. This example may have been originally fitted with such a liner and cover. The punch bowl, S58, is 24cm diameter with two Animal prints on the exterior and the Flower sprays decorating the inside. The bold gilding of pattern 1222 can clearly be seen on both pieces.

S59

S60

S61

S62

S59 and S60 Two examples of covered bucket chocolate in bone china 12cm high although two sizes are recorded in the 1820 Shape Book. S59 is in pattern 500 with P100 Flower sprays in charcoal grey and is the most restrained of the Bat printed patterns. S60 shows pattern 558 the most exuberantly gilded of all Bat printed patterns and printed with P200 Landscapes prints. This example is reputed to have been in the ownership of Sir Walter Scott.

S61 French Cabinet cup and stand in bone china in pattern 613 with Landscapes in blue with band and line gilding. This shape first appeared in the Pattern Books on a painted pattern in the year 1805 and continued in the 1820 Shape Book and no doubt continued even longer.

S62 French shape garden pot and separate stand in bone china pattern 557 printed in charcoal grey with P200 series Landscapes. These pots are illustrated in the 1820 Shape Book in three sizes.

S65–1

S63   **S64**

S63 Match pot in bone china, 12cm high, pattern 557 printed with P409 in charcoal grey. The 1820 Shape Book illustrates this shape made in three sizes.

S64 Beaker on a foot in bone china, 15.5cm high, pattern 557. Transferred with P226 in charcoal grey.

S65 Flat-rimmed chamber-pot in bone china in pattern 557. Transferred with Landscape views both inside and out. The 1820 Shape Book lists this chamber-pot as being available in 9 sizes.

S65–2

S67

S66 Two handled antique jar in drabware pattern 1191, the first pattern in the Pattern Books naming Animals in the illustration. Transfer printed in charcoal grey with P412. The 1820 Shape Book show that eight sizes of this jar were available in bone china as well as drabware.

S67 A small porter mug also in drabware coated with white slip inside, 7.5cm high. Bat printed in charcoal grey with P411 and with gilt banded edge. The same shape and size of mug was used in illustration S69 but with Revived Jackfield ware.

S66

S68–1

S68–2

P68 An earthenware Dutch jug with brown slip banded neck. Bat printed with greyhounds P414–2 and P415 on the body and initialled 'T' in black.

P69 A small porter mug, 7.5cm high, in Revived Jackfield ware with a redware body covered with black and white slip. The external white slip panel printed with P410 in charcoal grey.

S69–1

S69–2

S70

S71

S70 Dutch jug in drabware 18cm high, transferred with P414–1 in charcoal grey pattern 1191. The jug is of early manufacture with the greyhounds chasing the fox and not the later hare.

S71 Large covered Dutch jug in drabware 20.5cm high, pattern 1191. The covered jugs were fitted with a strainer behind the spout. Decorated with Animals prints in charcoal grey.

Chapter 6

On-glaze Pluck and Dust printing

Pluck and Dust is the Cinderella of Spode's ceramic printing. It is a Cinderella with a difference, however. Forever overshadowed by its 'handsome sisters', Bat and underglaze, no fairy prince in the form of Mr. Battam even acknowledge its existence in the *1851 Exhibition Catalogue*. Being, as it is, an in-between type of printing apparently stemming from both Bat and underglaze, it has some of the advantages and disadvantages of both. This hot-press method using tissue paper, transferred a stiff oil which allowed a heavier print of far greater size than could be achieved with Bat printing. Nevertheless, the delicacy of Bat printing was missing and it had none of the hard wearing quality of underglaze. The enamel colour dusted on the oil was of the same constitution as that for Bat printing. Again, the enamel firing temperature was critical, but with a greater deposit of colour the differences in results of even slight misfiring were more apparent. When underfired, the prints remained matt, easily damaged and in obvious contrast to the glassy glaze. With overfiring the print sank into the glaze and pits and bubbles could easily form and mar the printed surface.

Its recorded use at Spode Works commenced with pattern 981 in 1806, although it is one of the possibilities that the earlier 'black printing' was either this or a very similar method. The period of the initial introduction of entirely new designs was brief lasting until about 1810, although a few variations of colour and finish of prints from existing copperplates were issued after this date. It is probable that the continued development of the printing method was limited by the improved and widened range of underglaze high-temperature colours coupled with the decline of creamware dinner services decorated on their borders only. However, the Spode – Copeland Red Shop for Pluck and Dust printing of iron red was only closed in 1943 on health grounds as the dusting colours contained lead.

Red was an essential colour for ceramic decoration, particularly for the brilliant designs fashionable in the early nineteenth century. It was, and continues to be, a most awkward ceramic pigment. Iron-red, the most practical, could not withstand the high temperature of glost firing ($1100^{0}C$) and was thus unsuitable for use in underglaze printing. It was, and is, satisfactory at the lower enamel kiln temperatures, but even then over- or underfiring, conditions not easy to control in the early nineteenth century, produced very noticeable changes in colour. Nevertheless, it was the basis of red enamel and a range of allied colours both for painting and printing on the glaze. As already discussed in Chapter 5, the handcraft of Bat printing could not be used for large, all-over patterns or continuous borders and was confined to separate impressions of limited size. To fill this dual gap of colour and size in the range of less expensive printed wares Spode introduced Pluck and Dust printing.

Within the limited range of the wares available at the time of our first edition published in 1983, the Pluck and Dust designs appeared to fall into two very distinctive groups of all-over decoration and secondly of designs for borders alone. The print numbering system for Pluck and Dust printing, therefore, was devised to take notice of these two groups with a substantial gap left between the chosen numbers for each section so that any additions could be placed in the correct group. With additional information obtained in the last twenty years, it now appears that the borders and centres were not always used in the manner that had been expected, and that the division into two groups was not maintained in the production of the wares. In consequence, the additional prints found on Spode ware since 1983 have been allocated print numbers that follow on from the last example (P527) illustrated in the first edition. These additional prints commence with P528 Dragons third.

The first design used for Pluck and Dust printing appears in the Pattern Book under the number 981 and is not shown decorated on a piece of ware as are the majority of the pattern number entries. It is described in the Pattern Book as 'Red willow gold traced and gold edge'. To search for such a version of the ever popular 'Willow' pattern would be a fruitless task. Pattern 981 is not of that design. In 1806 'Willow' was obviously a more general descriptive term and did not solely imply the 'Willow pattern' as we now know it. Pattern 981, a handsome union of red and gold, was based on the bamboo rather than the willow and it is under the title of 'Bamboo' that it is known today. Its use was universal for tea, dinner and dessert wares.

Two new variations of Bamboo P501 were produced about fifteen months later. One, pattern 1185, was again in iron red and gold but with a more elaborate border, but the other, pattern 1178, was printed in blue also with some gilded leaves. Close examination of the ware does not resolve the question whether the cobalt blue was dusted on-glaze in Pluck and Dust printing or whether the underglaze method of the colour in the oil was adopted. The gilding is, of course, on-glaze but the blue is now in-glaze and, on firing, it could have dropped into the glaze from the front or equally could have risen through the glaze from below. An example of the action of the volatile cobalt blue when firing in contact with lead glaze is illustrated and described in Chapter 7. Pluck and Dust copperplates of Bamboo were certainly used for underglaze printing after 1822 with three variations shown in the B series of pattern numbers which were reserved for simple underglaze printing and painting. The most commonly found is B76 which is printed in cobalt blue but with the gilding substituted by yellow or poor man's gold.

In 1811, six on-glaze variations of Bamboo were printed in black and washed over in green and four further colour modifications were subsequently issued. The last two patterns, 4873 and 4874 did not appear until 1831/32 and were handsome prints in brown and orange with neat continuous borders.

Appearing in the Pattern Books just two places later than 981 of Bamboo was a second Pluck and Dust pattern being numbered 983. Again it has only a written description without illustration and reads 'Full red flowers – gold band edge'. Now known as Rose border, P521 it appears both as a border pattern without further printed embellishments and used as a border enclosing other red Pluck and Dust printed designs placed centrally. The pattern number that should have followed is no. 984, but this is entirely omitted from the Pattern Books. Fortunately the number does occur written in red in the usual way on the back or underneath a number of pieces. It is a second and a richer looking

A Pluck and Dust printing team at work. The printer has added just sufficient lampblack to the printing oil so that the print shape will still be visible on the tissue and can be seen by the cutter, on the right, and the transferrer, in the centre, thus aiding the placing of the print on the glazed ware. After dusting the oil transferred on the ware from the tissue, the woman on the left is cleaning off the surplus colour, in this case a crimson a derivative of gold.

version of Rose border with the red roses set into a wide gilded band making quite an expensive form of printed decoration. The Rose border was revived in 1826 as pattern 4031, without the expensive gilding, shown on a London shape teacup on the Pattern Books. This number is within half a dozen of the revival, as pattern 4025, of its earlier companion Bamboo. This joint re-appearance, after twenty years, of the first two Pluck and Dust designs must be further evidence of the decline of management in the late 1820s through the acceptance of repetition rather than insistence on originality which had brought earlier success to the Company.

However, evidence of some attempts at originality have been found by collectors in the last twenty years. Print pattern P528 Dragons third, print pattern P529 Bolton's Birds with Rose border and print pattern P530 Curtis flowers combined with prints from P506 were all taken from fresh sources although the rarity of the surviving printed ware does not suggest great initial or continued sales. Of the other designs, Vine border P522 and Oak border P523 are the best known both being printed in red with later variations in colour. They both were used extensively on dinner ware as an inexpensive border pattern and are also found on tea and coffee services. In many cases they are extremely well transferred with the joins in the patterns well made and very difficult to find. Vine border is the only Pluck and Dust pattern mentioned by name in the No.1 Colour Recipe Book. On page 23 is given Recipe no. 60 – French Brown for Printing Vine Border by Richd.Bell:

9 Calcined Ferra Sienna
8 Shining black   } All three ground together for use
30 Flux No. 7

Judged by the colour in the Pattern Book this would probably be pattern 1048, one of a group of various brown Vine border prints introduced in 1806, as can be seen in the table of Pluck and Dust printed designs. Richard Bell, the elder of the two Bells, is named as the printer of this Pluck and Dust pattern. He is similarly occasionally named for recipes for Bat printing colours. From this evidence it would appear that the two on-glaze printing methods were undertaken, at least at times, by the same printers despite the very different method of hand and machine printing. At least powdered colour was used in both on-glaze methods in contrast to the oil and colour mixture used for underglaze printing.

One other type of on-glaze print is found in red, magenta and allied colours. These were prints taken from the copperplates used for underglaze blue printing but in colours that would not withstand glost oven temperatures and therefore had to be printed on the glaze. It is impossible to tell whether these were printed entirely by the Pluck and Dust method without the colour in the oil or by a combination of some colour added to the oil to be further strengthened by dusting after transfer. As the copperplates were not engraved for on-glaze printing, very variable results were obtained and in consequence specimens are rare. The underglaze designs known to have been used for on-glaze prints are noted at the end of the Pluck and Dust prints catalogue. They are listed by their underglaze reference numbers to which group the copperplates belong. Illustrations will be found at the appropriate reference in the underglaze prints catalogue. It is likely that more of these designs will be discovered in on-glaze printing colours.

Catalogue of Pluck and Dust Prints

Pluck and Dust print P501, the most successful, was based on Chinese art. The remaining designs are in the European tradition but do not have the grace and simplicity of the first. The range of printed border pattern designs was produced to reduce the cost of handed painted creamware plates in an endeavour to undersell the market leader, Josiah Wedgwood, in this type of ware. After 1806, the date of origination of the printed borders, the further introduction of Spode's painted designs for creamware was much curtailed and new production soon ceased to be recorded in the Pattern Books. This can, no doubt, be attributed to the lower cost of printed borders and to the decline in popularity of the plainer creamware services decorated on the borders alone.

P501 Bamboo This design, derived from a Chinese original, was widely used in red and also black washed over in green and mostly with gilding. It is also found in blue with yellow replacing the gilding. In addition to the main pattern illustrated, matching sprigs were produced, used to decorate cups and other small pieces.

P501

P502–1

P502–2

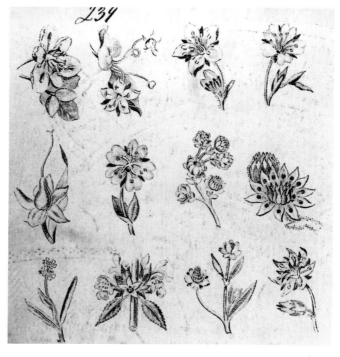

P502–3

P502 Red Plants and Insects This is the description for pattern no.1019 in the Pattern Books, which is unillustrated. The second pattern 1025 is shown as P502–1 with prints on a Bute teacup which include a plant from illustration P502–3 and insects and shells as does the coffee can of P502–2. The original coppers no longer exist and the plants shown at P502–3 are taken from a Sprig Proof Book.

P503

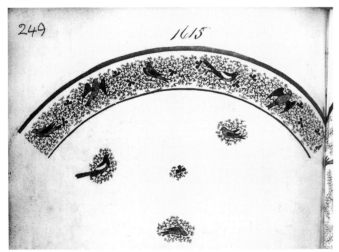

P504

P503 Red Flowers This all-over flower print was first produced in iron-red and shortly after in overpainted enamel colours. A piece of ware has not yet been found and the illustration is taken from the Pattern Books.

P504 and P505 These two rather similar patterns of Birds, according to the Pattern Books which supplied the illustrations, were only printed in red. P504 is named as Red Birds first. A piece of Red Birds second, P505, has not yet come to light.

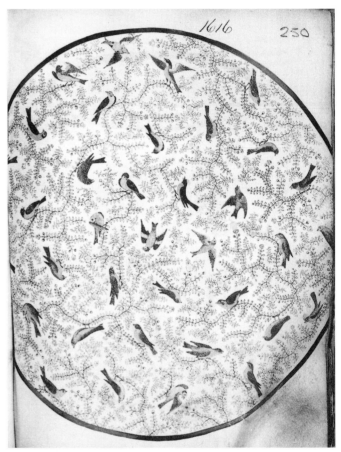

P505

P506 Butterflies and Moths with Sea Shells This odd mixture is illustrated from a print taken from a copperplate still held at Spode Works. Sets of six of the larger pieces form the border for red printed designs with centres of Curtis flowers P530.

P506

P521

P521 *Rose border* This border is most often found on tea wares printed in red but occasionally has been found printed in black and overwashed in green enamel on earthenwares. It was used as a border for P529 Bolton's Birds.

P522

P522 and P523 *Vine and Oak borders* These were the most popular of the printed borders for dinnerware. They are often seen in red or brown on creamware services and appear on tea wares.

P523

P524–1

P524–2

P524 Love Chase border This small border design was produced in red on tea and coffee wares. It is the border from the underglaze blue print Love Chase P717. P524–1 is an illustration of a copperplate and P524–2 shows a Bute coffee can in the Pattern Book being used to illustrate pattern no. 1119.

P525 Convolvulus border This print is found transferred in brown and chocolate to both dinner and tea wares. It was produced both with and without coloured ground panels behind the main print.

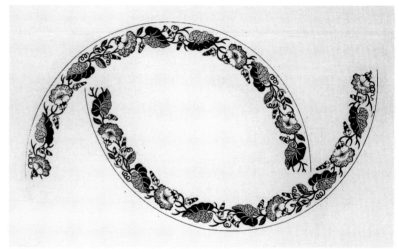

P525

P526

P526 and P527 Geometric border first and Geometric border second
These two borders were designed for creamware dinner services and were printed in brown and red.

P528

P528 Dragons third A breakfast set of felspar porcelain impressed with mark 16 and printed in red with this pattern has some pieces marked with the Spode name and some marked with that of Copeland & Garrett late Spode.

P527

178

P529 Bolton's Birds Through the researches of Bill and Marguerite Coles the centre prints of a Pluck and Dust red printed dessert service have been traced. The border on each piece is the fully gilded version of Rose Border surrounding a centre of a bird taken from the first edition of James Bolton's *Harmonia Ruralis or An Essay towards A Natural History of British Song Birds*. This was published in two volumes in 1794 and 1796 with later impressions dated 1824, 1830 and 1845. A search at Spode Works added two further bird copperplates to the four found of those used in the dessert service which are numbered as follows: P529–1 depicts the Bullfinch taken from plate 11 in Bolton's book. P529–2 shown on a pull from the copperplate depicts a Goldfinch on a Thistle taken from plate 21. P529–3 depicts a Goldfinch in its Nest taken from Bolton's plate 22. P529–4 taken from plate 31 shows a Red pole (Redpoll). Plate 35 shown as P529–5, despite its colour, is The Canary Bird and P529–6 is the Wood Warbler. Recently found at Spode Works is another copperplate showing a bird chasing a fly. From the black and white pull from the copperplate it would appear to be a Spotted Flycatcher and has been numbered P529–7. A Dutch jug enamel overpainted with P529–1 and P529–3 has been found regrettably with the birds and the border spruced up in fanciful colours.

P529–1

P529–2

P529–3

P529–4

P529–5

P529–6

P529–7

P530–1

P530–2

P530 Red Plant centre with Insect and Shell border A Pluck and Dust red printed dessert service combines two different forms of decoration. In the centre of each piece is placed a differing red plant, very similar to those shown at P502–3 but not exactly similar. The border of each is made up with six of the larger items taken from the copperplate shown as illustration P506. The pieces are finished with a gilt edge. P530–1 and P530–2 show the plain oval shape dessert comports and P530–3 and P530–4 two of the dessert plates. The plain oval shape of the comports suggests an earlier production than P529 where the later shaped comports were used.

P530–3

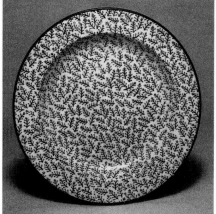

P530–4

P531

P532

P531 Botanical Flowers This use of botanical flowers was introduced by the Wedgwood Company using the same border design. This red printed plate is a copy of the Wedgwood design whose pieces were usually produced in underglaze blue. Spode's design is named on its copperplate as *Spring Crocus*.

P532 Fibre A simple sheet pattern printed in red and designed to make life easier for both printers and transferrers. It never became popular as might be guessed.

List of prints found transferred on-glaze in low-temperature colours in designs engraved for underglaze printing.

Underglaze print Catalogue reference	Name	On-glaze colour
P701	Girl at Well	Purple
P815	English Sprays	Brown
P821	Geranium	Magenta
P822	Blue Rose	Red
P828	Vandyke	Red
P903	Botanical	Purple
P906	Greek	Red

It is unlikely that this list is complete. Not all on-glaze prints were entered in the Pattern Books. Both additional colours for listed designs and the use of other engraving may well be found.

Table 6.1 Pluck and Dust printed designs showing variations of colour and finish by their pattern numbers P500 series

Print no. and name	Pattern number	Probable year of introduction	Description
P501	981	1806	Red with gilding – gold edge.
Bamboo	1178	1807–08	Blue with gilding – plain edge.
	1185	1807–08	Red with gilding – elaborate border.
	1652	1811	Black washed green with gilding – gold edge.
	1653	1811	Black washed green with gilding – plain edge.
	1664	1811	Black washed green only – green edge.
	1665	1811	Black washed green with gilding – Coloured edge.
	1666	1811	Black washed green with colour – Coloured edge.
	1719	1811	Black washed green only – Gold edge.
	3686	1824	Enamelled in blue and puce – Flower border.
	4025	1826	Black washed green with gilding – Gadroon gilded edge.
	4873	1831-32	Dark brown with orange – Wavy border.
	4874	1831-32	Dark brown with orange – Wavy border.

Bamboo copperplates were also used for underglaze printing on the later B series patterns. B76–Blue and yellow. B254–Brown, yellow and puce. B256–Chestnut brown.

Print no. and name	Pattern number	Probable year of introduction	Description
B502 Red plants & Insects.	1019	1806	Red – gold edge.
	1025	1806	Overpainted in enamels – gold edge.
	3164	1821	Red – gold edge as 1019.
P503 Red Flowers.	1024	1806	Red – gold edge.
	1113	1807	Overpainted in enamels – gold edge.
	1910	1812	Black washed in green.
P504 Red Birds first.	1610	1810	Red – pale brown edging colour.
	1615	1810	Red – red edge.
P505 Red Birds second.	1616	1810	Red – brown edge.
P506 Butterflies, Moths and Shells.	Not illustrated in Pattern Book but see P530.		
P521 Rose border.	983	1806	Red – gold edge.
	984	1806	Red on gold band.
	2120	1814	Black with green wash on pink band.
	2605	1817	Black with green wash and yellow set between brown trellis.
	4031	1826	Red – plain edge.
P522 Vine border.	1030	1806	Red – red edge.
	1031	1806	Black – black edge.
	1032	1806	Chestnut – chestnut edge.
	1033	1806	Chocolate – chocolate edge.
	1045	1806	Red – gold edge.
	1047	1806	Chocolate – gold edge.
	1048	1806	French brown – gold edge.
	2931	1819	Blue – blue edge.
	2940	1819	Blue – gold edge.
P523 Oak border.	1050	1807	Red – gold edge.
	1475	1809	Red – red edge.
	1476	1809	Brown – brown edge.
	1501	1810	Enamelled in colours – brown edge.
	1611	1810	Enamelled in colours – dark brown edge.
	2121	1814	Queen's brown – Queen's brown edge.
P524 Love chase border.	1119	1807	Red – gold edge.
P525 Convolvulus border.	1160		On all three used as border pattern on coloured backgrounds with centre prints of Greek outline over-enamelled.
	1161		
	1171	1807–08	

Print no. and name	Pattern number	Probable year of introduction	Description
	1740	1811	Brown border – plain edge.
	2112	1814	Enamelled border in full colour.
	2436	1816	Brown border on gold panel.
P526 Geometric border first.	1518	1810	Brown – brown edge.
	1519	1810	Red – red edge.
P527 Geometric border second.	1564	1810	Brown – dark-brown edge.
P528 Dragon's third.	4198		Cup in red Bell shape.
P529 Bolton's Birds.	Not in Pattern Book.		
P530 Red Flowers, Insects and Shells.	Not in Pattern Book.		
P531 Red Flowers.	Not in Pattern Book.		
P532 Fibre Sprigs. All Red Printed.	1447		Gold edge.
	1504		Gold edge plus lozenge bead and brown edge.
	1507		Brown edge.

Shapes of wares decorated with Pluck and Dust prints

No special shapes were designed to receive these prints. Indeed, the method was developed to fill a gap in the printing range rather than break new ground. Most of the pieces illustrated here are from Spode's straightforward production of table wares, the decoration of which was the major use to which the process was put.

S72

S73

S72, S73 and S74 Each bone china piece is printed with Bamboo P501 in iron red with gilding. The teapot, size 25.5cm over the spout and handle, is in New Oval shape. Compare the four pieces illustrated which show pleasing variations in the print so that the design fitted each shape of ware and yet retained the same feel. The print on the saucer of the New shape cup and saucer, S74, is perhaps the basic Bamboo design.

S74

S75

S75 A dessert plate in bone china with wicker embossed rim, Pluck and Dust printed in red and gilding with Bamboo with additional elaborate border, pattern 1185. It is marked with the rare Prince of Wales mark no.39.

S76

S77

S76 Felspar porcelain egg cup, 5.7cm high, printed in red with P528 Dragons third, part of a breakfast service.

S77 Coffee can. Bone china marked '984' in red, the can is printed in red on a wide gold band with Rose border P521. The pattern, 984, is one of the few numbers omitted from Spode's Pattern Books.

S78

S78 A 20cm saucer-shaped bread and butter plate matching the can S77.

S79 Small moulded basket with twist handles, 11cm long overall. Drabware with white slip band printed in red with Vine Border P522, pattern 1030.

S80 Creamware dinner plate of plain circular shape 25cm diameter. Printed with Vine Border P522 in chocolate with chocolate edge, pattern 1033.

S79

S80

Chapter 7

Underglaze printing

A blue derived from cobalt for the decoration of pottery and porcelain was in use long before its appearance in England transferred on to earthenware from about 1780. Found painted on early Persian pottery it was taken up by the Chinese during the Yuan dynasty about AD 1300, and was used extensively both on-glaze and underglaze to decorate Ming porcelain as well as all later Chinese wares.

Cobalt is a silvery-white metal element, which is found in two natural forms of which one, smaltite, a greyish mineral of cobalt arsenide, occurs in veins associated with silver. The English name cobalt is taken from middle high German 'Kobalt', meaning a goblin, named from the German silver miners' belief that malicious goblins placed it in the silver ore. It was used in Europe as a blue painted decoration on tin glazed pottery and earthenware and from about 1725 on European porcelain where it continued to be used as a painted and enamel decoration both on and under glaze. In the United Kingdom the earlier supplies were imported from Saxony in the form of 'Zaffre', an impure cobalt oxide, or further refined as 'Smalt', a fused body of 'Zaffre', potassium carbonate and silica. In 1815–1816 cobalt was found in Cornwall and British cobalt oxide, known as 'Calx', became available for use by the potters.

Simeon Shaw, in his *History of the Staffordshire Potteries* published in 1829, attributes the first blue printing to Thomas Turner at Caughley near Broseley in Shropshire, although the possibility remains that Worcester was the first to use underglaze blue transfers. However, the introduction of blue printing into Staffordshire is credited to a number of Turner's workers leaving Caughley and joining Staffordshire potters, with an engraver and a printer being engaged by Spode about 1784 to commence underglaze blue printing on earthenware. Simeon Shaw named Spode's first engraver as Lucas with the first printer as Richards although the names of Lucock and Rickett have been suggested as being more likely to be correct.

The process, when adopted by Spode in 1784, was still in its infancy, particularly on earthenware, Spode's first production. The gradual development in Spode's blue printed ware were brought about by increased understanding of the nature of cobalt blue and by improving techniques of engraving and transferring. No sudden mature appearance this, but rather the same slow growth of experience that we ourselves undergo, which culminated in mastery about 1810.

The nature of cobalt has already been discussed particularly with reference to blue Bat printing in Chapter 5. For underglaze printing one further aspect must be considered. Unfired cobalt oxide when mixed with printing oil is a pallid dull purple not easily seen through the tissue paper of the transfer. Since it is essential when placing tissue transfers on the biscuit body to see the position of the print, this natural pale shade was strengthened by a vegetable dye added to the cobalt and oil printing mixture, thus ensuring that the design

Forest Landscape dish, P607–1.

was visible through the transfer tissue with the present stain giving a dark-grey printing colour. Before the transfer printed biscuit ware could be glazed the print was 'hardened on' by firing in a kiln at about 700°C. At this temperature of about red heat, the printing oil and vegetable colouring was driven off and burnt away and the cobalt, reverting to its natural, dull purple colour, became firmly fixed to the biscuit body which on cooling was ready for glazing. After dipping in the liquid lead glaze, incidentally the chief cause of lead poisoning or 'potter's rot', the ware was then fired in a glost oven with the temperature increased to about 1100°C to develop and give brilliance to the glaze.

Having previously been subjected to a temperature seven times as hot as boiling water in the hardening kiln it could well be supposed that the cobalt colour, well burnt on to the biscuit body, would now be inert and immovable. On emergence from the glost oven, the print could be expected to reappear unchanged but now covered by a brilliant transparent glaze, an underglaze print in fact. This would be true of many of the later underglaze colours but not of cobalt blue. When in contact with lead glaze at temperatures between

Back of Forest Landscape dish, P607–1.

1000°C and 1100°C cobalt blue changed colour from dull purple to the fine lustrous translucent blue so well know to antique collectors. Furthermore, as discussed in Chapter 5, its volatile nature was activated by the additional heat and it permeated and passed through the glaze.

An example of this can be seen in the Forest Landscape dish, P607–1, illustrated. This early Spode production was printed in the dark cobalt blue of the period, probably before 1800, and in the flat Chinese landscape style with a lakeland scene with small islands, tongues of land and a waterman in his boat. The dish's face is marred by pits and dirty specks and missing sections of the glaze. The back is similarly marked but in addition has portions of the neighbouring dish stuck to it at one end. It was a victim of a collapse in the glost oven during firing. The supporting stilts or spurs at one end had slipped and the dishes dropped one upon the another. The one above marked the face of this dish which, in its turn, stuck to the face of the one below. When breaking them apart the lower dish must have been destroyed leaving its broken fragments fused to this survivor. Normally such an article as this, damaged in manufacture, would have been destined for that pottery scrap-heap known as the shraff tip. Perhaps this dish was surreptitiously taken home by a workman and, with the broken fragments smoothed down, continued in use indefinitely.

Close examination reveals ghostly traces of a blue pattern in the plain undecorated glaze on the back of this illustrated surviving dish. Signs of the pattern of the left-hand side of the Forest Landscape print can be detected. The large island at the top with two of the buildings on the left, the tongue of land above the boatman and a vague suggestion of his boat, as well as a clearer impression of the diaper cell of the inner border can all be seen. How have they appeared? The activated cobalt print from the lower dish, passing through its glaze, has jumped the accidentally close gap between the two dishes and is imprinted in the clear glaze on the back of the dish above. This 200-year-old accident demonstrates the volatile nature of cobalt blue which, although first printed underglaze, after firing passed into and through the glaze and thus might be better termed 'in-glaze'.

The Recipe Books and Mr Grocott's notebook give numerous differing formulas for blue for underglaze printing and further involuntary variations would, no doubt, occur in mixing and in the materials themselves. However, a gradual change in colour can be detected. The early wares, before about 1800, were printed in hard strong blues of slightly dull appearance. This basic tone gradually changed to the brighter, more lustrous, vivid blues of the middle period. Comparison of the pieces still shows a wide variation in shade, and some patterns, the best known being Castle P711 with its paler shade, were always printed to give a different look. Nevertheless, overall a more lively appearance was achieved. Towards the end of the Spode period in the late 1820s and the 1830s a softer more lavender blue was introduced and can be found with such designs as Floral P901 and Portland Vase P720.

The body of the ware upon which the prints were placed also affected the appearance. Prints on earthenware, which partially absorbed the colour, have a softer look than those printed on the more impervious bodies of bone china, feldspar and stone china into which the cobalt was not imbibed. On the porcelain bodies, the prints stand in sharp contrast to the white background giving a harder appearance. The blue-stained body of Spode's stone china coupled with its close texture resulted in both a sharper and harder look than was found on earthenware. Changes in the colour mix and in the glaze probably purposely accentuate the quite noticeable differences in appearance of underglaze printing on the various bodies.

Generally the alterations in the colour show firstly a greater understanding of the use of cobalt, culminating in Spode's best printed wares of the middle period. Later changes show no improvement in technique but rather an endeavour to offer something new to meet perhaps the dictates of fashion.

Having discussed the variations of cobalt blue it seems appropriate to turn now to the designs printed in these diverse shades. Spode's choice of designs can be placed into three continuing groups based, for the most part, on the body of the ware. The first group included all earthenware with pearlware glaze, excepting tea wares. The second was bone china and felspar to which must be added tea services in earthenware. The last group was stone china.

The first group, which was by far the largest both in number of printed designs and in variety of shapes, covered wares for dinner and dessert, for the bedroom and the kitchen and every other household use. Designs of every sort are found in the wares included in this group. The second group, bone china and felspar porcelain, is not found underglaze transferred with European and Mediterranean subjects, except the very rare Shepherdess P705. Neither Indian Sporting P904 nor Caramanian P905 are found on tea wares, although two designs adapted from the Caramanian prints but with flower borders, The Turk P715 and Turkish Castle P716 are uncommon earthenware examples. Otherwise the sharp division between European art used for Bat printing and Chinese for blue underglaze on the first bone chinas was most marked. A new range of underglaze Chinese-type patterns was designed especially for this new ware of which the most usually found are Temple P613 and Broseley P614. Some of the earlier floral patterns such as Lily P801 and Lyre P802 and the floral sheet patterns Daisy P805 and Leaf P806 were also used. These were followed by the later flower designs, one of which Union Wreath first P823 was used only on Gadroon-Edge wares. Tea services in earthenware generally follow those of bone china, although the European designs Girl at Well P701, Milkmaid P702 and Italian Church P709 can all occasionally be found. Earthenware services are not common in any case, although it must be presumed that they started life in their millions. The death-rate of everyday earthenware teapots with damage-prone handles, spouts and covers and continuously poured full of boiling water must have been enormous and very few are found today.

Spode's stone china body, the basis of the third and last group, was introduced, it is thought, in 1813. It was a conscious and deliberate copy of the Chinese hard-paste porcelain export dinner ware of the late eighteenth century. The body was lightly stained with cobalt to a similar colour to that of the Chinese ware and Spode's printed mark was a copy of a Chinese seal with pseudo-Chinese characters. Not surprisingly the designs printed or painted on this ware were all after the Chinese. Spode produced a number of new underglaze patterns for this body used exclusively for its decoration as well as some that did duty for both stone china and the later earthenwares. Stone china was followed and superseded in 1822 by a very similar but rather whiter body known as Spode's New Stone. It had a wider decorative application in that, although many of the stone china designs were continued, it was also used for the later floral patterns.

The designs with approximate date of their origin and a note of the ware upon which they are usually found are shown in the catalogue of underglaze blue prints immediately following this chapter. The popularity of some designs was short-lived; others defied every change of fashion and remained long in production; Italian P710 and Tower P714 are still manufactured to this day. A new series of engravings was not necessarily the death-knell of those previously issued, but it is likely that the general popularity of earlier prints markedly declined on the appearance of new designs.

One design is worthy of particular note. Two early copperplates and a portion of a third are extant. In each the central design and inner border are engraved and the outer or main border is omitted. The copperplates have been reused with a later design engraved upon the back. In the case of the truncated portion, the original copper was later cut up for smaller engravings with the surviving piece used for the Animals Bat print P410. This design, which gives the impression of Spode's eighteenth-century Chinese engravings, is a most curious mixture of Chinese and European art. The main design is European, yet two Chinese islands hang unsupported in the sky and an overlarge moth flits above the buildings. It could be that an empty sky on blue-printed ware was too much for the engraver schooled on Chinese scenic designs entirely covering the ware which were the accepted Spode eighteenth-century productions.

How can it be certain that this design was engraved in the eighteenth century? Indeed, on one copperplate with the engraving exactly fitting an Early Indented shape dinner plate is a small cartouche worded 'SPODE FORE ST' set in a curled ribbon to be used to mark the ware. Fore Street was the address of the Spode's London sales business managed by Josiah Spode II until his father's death. In

The Rotunda at Ranelagh Gardens. *Above is Spode's copperplate for print P707 taken from the original engraving shown below it. Beyond the changes needed to squeeze the shape into a circular format, Spode's engraving is very similar to the original with added Oriental touches. Why the trees were changed to hollyhocks is not clear nor is the appearance of a Chinese fisherman in the sky endangered by a giant moth.*

1796 the London business left Fore Street, City, and moved to Portugal Street in the West End just off the Strand. This dates the engraving between 1784, the commencement of Spode blue printing, and 1796 at the latest.

A further surprise awaited Paul Holdway who first came across these copperplates. With research he found that the main building depicted was that of the Rotunda at Ranelagh Gardens with Spode's engraving taken from an exterior view reproduced in Volume V of *London and its Environs Described* — published in 1766. One of London's pleasure gardens, Ranelagh in Chelsea, was opened in 1742 and was described as 'one of those public places of pleasure which is not equalled in Europe and is the resort of people of the first quality. Though its gardens are beautiful, it is more admired for the amphitheatre'. This, named the Rotunda, was a circular building with an external diameter of 56 metres (185 feet). In it was served tea and coffee and twice-weekly entertainments of music with which supper was provided. Rather than a design

View of Ranelagh.

for general use, perhaps these copperplates were engraved especially for the proprietors of Ranelagh Gardens to print supper ware to be used in the gardens. The quantity of dinner and soup plates used by such a place would surely warrant the engraving of special copperplates and this would account for the use of a mark including Spode's London address. No plate so decorated has yet been found and, if it was a special order, perhaps never will. However, a hope can remain for every Spode collector that he or she may become perhaps the only possessor of Rotunda, P707.

Examination of early Spode blue-printed dinner plates decorated with designs derived from the Chinese reveal that three separate components made up the complete decoration. In the centre was the main design and placed around it an inner border, termed a nankin in Staffordshire, thus revealing the origination of this feature, with the whole encircled by the main border design. In later Spode blue-printed productions the first and last were always present but the nankin was often reduced to insignificance used only to divide the central design from the border or was finally often omitted. For the decoration of holloware two additional sections of pattern were normally provided. A quite separate and usually entirely different design was engraved for each pattern to provide prints to cover the handles. In some cases shaped sections were engraved to fit curved handles, but included amongst the engravings for a set of dinnerware pieces was a copperplate engraved all over in sheet form with this special design known as the 'handle sheet copper'. From a tissue printed from this copper, transfers could be shaped for most handles, tabs and similar extensions. The second items for transferring on to the footrim of soup and sauce tureens and similar vessels was straight or curved strips of pattern. The design of these was often based on or derived from the nankin or border design.

The provision of this full set of engravings of main pattern, nankin if used, border, handles and footrim was the mark of Spode and other large well-organised manufacturers. The handles, in particular, on the blue-printed hollowares of many of the smaller potters will be found washed over with plain cobalt blue, not that hand finishing was never used by Spode on underglaze blue printed wares as will be seen.

With on-glaze printing, a misplaced transferred pattern or a gap left by error in a join could be rectified by immediately wiping the print from the glaze and reprinting. With underglaze printing, wiping could not remove the colour from the biscuit ware and such an error thus entailed a significant cost to the potter in the loss of the nearly completed ware. To avoid this, small gaps in joins and in difficult positions under or around handles were touched in by hand painting or filled in by a specially cut piece of matching transfer. The process known as 'piecing and mending' is still practised in the Potteries and is not always the result of slips in transferring. With Spode's Geranium, P821, a handled cover had the geranium spray divided with the parts transferred on the cover above and below the handle. The flower stalks were often 'mended' by hand painting beneath the handle to rejoin the spray, no doubt at the same time as the addition of a painted blue line around the handles' terminals, a feature of the normal finish of this particular pattern. Again 'piecing' was needed for 'Well and Tree' dishes with printed designs joined at border and centre. A single copperplate was engraved to cover both a flat dish and one of the same overall size but moulded with a gravy well and runnels. The transfer pressed into the additional contours of the Well and Tree necessitated insertion of an additional strip of transfer at one end if a gap was not to be left between the border and centre pattern.

By 1822 a number of additional colours able to withstand high-temperature glost firing had been developed and were used underglaze. The B series of patterns, a numbering system especially for underglaze wares, was started in that year and some of the underglaze blue designs in new colours were included in the series. These new colours were not so translucent as cobalt blue nor was the same lustrous 'inglaze' look obtainable. Consequently, the prints in the new colours transferred from copperplates designed for cobalt blue gave a flatter look with less contrast of tone and not exhibiting the liveliness so often found with the best underglaze blue printed ware. Examples are not common, green and brown being the most frequently found, and an odd shade known as Payne's grey is sometimes seen.

The introduction of these new underglaze colours heralded what was probably the world's first two-colour underglaze printing commencing not later than 1824. It thus pre-dated by many years the method of multi-colour printing, the first manufacture of which is usually attributed to Felix Pratt. It must be admitted that Spode's method of two-colour printing was laborious and was based on skilled hand painting with a difference.

The method depended on a substance described by the Spode workers as 'ackey' with its use as 'ackeying'. These glorious English words are potters' descriptions for dirty or sticky. The substance of 'ackey' needed two essential qualities. It had to be impervious to oil and colour and secondly it had to dissolve in water. Regrettably no exact composition of Spode's 'ackey' has come down to us but it is variously described as a composition of sugar or treacle and possibly a stain or of potash, sugar and rose-pink colouring. Either meets the necessary qualifications.

Its first use may have been as a coating painted on the biscuit body over the new Gadrooned Edges of plates and dishes which were introduced in the 1820s. With plain rimmed ware any blue mistakenly transferred over the edge could be and was removed before glazing by a rub with a pumice-stone. With gadrooned edges this was no longer possible as the pumice could not reach into the indentations. The 'ackey' received any mistransfers, guarding the gadroon edge from the print, and then dissolved when the tissue was stripped and floated off in water. Any lingering vestige was burnt off in the 700⁰C of the hardening kiln. A commercial resist is used today to overcome similar difficulties and is termed 'ackey' at Spode Works, although the name is not in common use throughout the Potteries.

This simple operation was adapted to produce two-colour prints first using the popular 'Tumbledown Dick' design. This originated in 1819 and by 1827 fifteen variations of colour and background had been produced. The basic print of a bird standing on or tumbling off a branch of flowering prunus was designed, and nearly always used, for overpainting in various enamel colours with the background left uncoloured or 'washed' in a single tone. In 1824 the new underglaze colours and the use of 'ackey' opened the door to two-colour underglaze printing. First a cobalt blue print of the basic design of bird and prunus was transferred to the plain biscuit ware and hardened on. This transferred print was then carefully hand painted all over with 'ackey' leaving only the background uncovered. A second print in a contrasting colour of an all-over sheet pattern known as Marble or Cracked Ice was then transferred over the surface of the background and the 'ackey', with no reference to fit other than entire coverage of the ware. After rubbing down, the tissue was floated off in water leaving the marbled pattern transferred to the background but not upon the bird and prunus which has been protected by the 'ackey'. This second print was then hardened on and the ware given its glazed finish and final firing.

The first two-colour prints in the Pattern Book are 3715 and 1716 showing the bird and prunus flowers further coloured by enamelling and with the written words 'on a buff printed marbled ground'. A very usual colour for the marbled background was a shade of khaki green. Although perhaps especially mixed, this could also be the end result of mixing the unused dregs of all the other underglaze printing colours in a single pot. No doubt 'invented' by the same master of the English language who had introduced the term 'ackey', the Works name for this delightful colour is pigmuck green.

This method, although quicker than hand painting a marbled background, could not compete with the later Prattware close register Multicolour printing and has long since vanished into the past.

A comparison of blue printed dinner plates.
The single article in greatest production of Spode blue printed ware was the dinner plate. It was the basis around which new printed designs were composed, and is still the most easily found source of Spode blue prints. Wherever possible, a dinner plate is illustrated for this very reason as it shows the print to best advantage. A study of this most simple shape, the so-called 10 inch plate, surprisingly perhaps, also demonstrates the changes that fashion and taste made to shape and size. The large majority of Spode blue printed dinner plates fall into five main categories of shape.

1. Early Indented

This, the smallest plate in size 23cm diameter and light in weight, is found only printed with earlier patterns. P601, P603 and P628 have all been found, as have the earlier engraving of Forest Landscape P607–1 and Willow P609–1. It was certainly in production before 1800 since the engraving of Rotunda P707 fits the centre of the plate exactly. It could well have been the earliest shape of Spode blue printed dinner plate in use in 1784 when underglaze printed ware was first produced at Spode Works. Notice the rather octagonal outline and compare with the next shape New Indented which superseded it. Although difficult to see in photographs, edges and indentations of the Early Indented plates were usually left sharp and rectangular in section. With the New Indented, Double Indented and Circular plates the edges were softened and rounded by sponging after trimming.

2. New Indented

This plate is both larger, 25cm diameter, and more heavily potted than those previously made. The shape is similar to Early Indented but is more circular and less angular than its predecessor. The earliest pattern found printed on this shape is Greek P906 introduced in 1805 or 1806. The two indented plates do not seem to have been used concurrently for long, the second entirely superseding the first. The additional size and altered outline most probably were the cause of re-engraving Forest Landscape P607–3 and Willow P609–2 so that the transfers would fit the new size and the printed design could continue in production. This was the most common Spode dinner plate for many years.

3. Double Indented

This variation was manufactured for the Caramanian pattern P905 in about 1809. It was a little larger, 25.5cm diameter. The Caramanian designs were introduced both with this new plate shape and matching new oval shape dishes. The dishes were evidently not popular and a return was made to the more practical rectangular shape dish. Double Indented plates continued in use for all plate sizes. However, the rectangular dishes can be found with prints taken from new or re-engraved coppers or from the original oval coppers with the transfers clumsily pieced to cover the rectangular shape. As far as can be found, no other prints made their debut on this shape of plate until the late 1820s to early 1830s with Botanical P903, Aesop's Fables P907 and Portland Vase P720. This last printed design is sometimes found on plates of similar outline but with small moulded ridges running in from the indentations on the face and a double semi-footrim on the back.

4. Circular

Who can say when the plain round plate was first 'introduced' since it has been with us since the invention of the potter's wheel. It is equally difficult to be sure with Spode's blue printed dinner plates but it was certainly used for Rome P713, thought to have been originated in 1811, and for Convolvulus P819 in 1812. Spode Circular plates are rather smaller, 24.7cm diameter, than New Indented, much as though the latter shape has been rounded off from inside its indentations.

5. *Gadroon Edge*

This plate with a moulded edge and a raised footrim was first manufactured about 1825. It was both larger, 26cm diameter, and heavier than any previously made. It is often found in Spode's 'Imperial' body, a so-called improved earthenware, and printed with patterns including Jasmine P820, Blue Rose P822 and Union Wreath second P824. Its appearance added to Spode's range and the earlier nineteenth century shapes were not abandoned. Indeed, Double Indented was revived after the 1824 or 1825 origination of this shape. Nevertheless, Gadroon Edge probably captured more of the feeling of the age than did the continuation of the earlier shapes.

Comparing the first dinner plate, Early Indented, of the eighteenth century with the last, Gadroon Edge of 1825, the overall size was increased from 23cm to 26cm diameter and the weight from an average of 300g to 500g. The later proud owners of Spode blue printed dinner services, spurning earlier economy and simplicity required visible prosperity in size, weight and ornamentation for their dining tables.

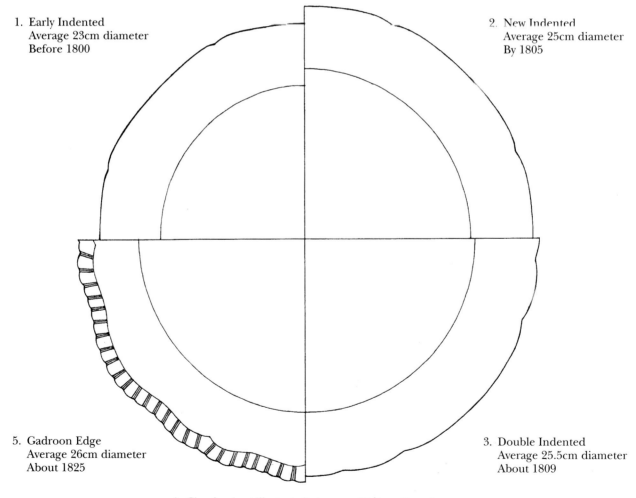

1. Early Indented
   Average 23cm diameter
   Before 1800

2. New Indented
   Average 25cm diameter
   By 1805

5. Gadroon Edge
   Average 26cm diameter
   About 1825

3. Double Indented
   Average 25.5cm diameter
   About 1809

4. Circular (not illustrated) Average 24.7cm diameter
   Used for printed ware from about 1811

Comparison of Spode's earthenware dinner plates showing their probable dates of introduction.

Catalogue of underglaze blue prints

Divided by subjects

The illustrations are of printed examples of Spode manufacture and marked with the name Spode unless otherwise stated. A plate has been chosen for the illustrations wherever possible to give the best representation of the printed design. The names used in this catalogue are generally based on those adopted by the late Leonard Whiter in his book on Spode. With further knowledge some of Whiter's names have been changed or modified. Designs not included in his book owe their titles to Works tradition, to the collectors that first identified the design and, if all else failed, to your authors. In a number of instances noticeable variations occur within a design, some of which Leonard Whiter treated as a separate pattern, notably Forest Landscape shown as two patterns and Willow shown as three. In this catalogue a print number has been allocated to each major design with variations treated as subdivisions and placed under a numeral suffixed to the main print number. The same treatment is given to multi-scene patterns such as Indian Sporting. Each engraving within the main design is similarly numbered with the separate scenes distinguished by a different suffixed numeral or numerals.

A very few of the prints illustrated in the catalogue have not yet been found on ware marked with the name Spode and in each case the reason for inclusion in the catalogue is given in the description of the pattern shown with the photograph of the piece. Two patterns included by Leonard Whiter as possibly being Spode are omitted and one, P619 Long Bridge, has been retained although some doubt still remains about its place of manufacture. Since Leonard Whiter's book was published in 1970, no piece of Camilla or Warwick Vase has been found marked Spode and it must be concluded that both patterns were engraved after the withdrawal of Spode and that they belong to Messrs. Copeland & Garrett whose name is found on ware printed with either pattern.

P600 Series   Orientally inspired designs

Designs from this series were printed on ware manufactured from all the bodies used for Spode's underglaze printing except perhaps Spode's Imperial. Having made this exception, it would be no surprise to stand corrected. The hold that the original Chinese dinner services had gained upon the tastes of the British public was shown by their continued demand for pottery and porcelain so decorated. No manufacturer could afford to be without such patterns however much he preferred the later styles. Thus Spode's orientally inspired designs include the very earliest prints, their subsequent re-engravings, designs for the new bone china and for the later stone china, itself a copy of the Chinese porcelains. Furthermore, all possible shapes for every use seem to have been demanded and received their quota of prints.

P601   Temple Landscape first   (Buddleia)
Early Indented earthenware plate printed with a hard blue of flat tone. Likely to have been manufactured before 1800. The more easily remembered name of Buddleia is the suggestion of Robert Copeland.

P602   Two figures
Early Indented earthenware dinner plate with the same flat look as P601.

P603   Dagger landscape first
Early Indented earthenware soup plate again of early manufacture and light in weight. It has a hazy blue glaze.

P604 (Right)   Dagger landscape second
18.2cm Circular plate impressed Spodes New Stone and with Copeland & Garrett printed mark. A copper plate still at Spode

Works has the same centre as this illustration but the border and nankin are similar to that shown on P603. Whiter's name of Dagger Landscape second would be appropriate for a print from the copperplate although not for this print where a plain border has been used in place of a dagger border and with the nankin now with additional embellishments.

P605   Mandarin   (Dagger Landscape third)
Either name seems equally unsuitable as a description of the design but purely on the grounds
of ease of memory the first seems preferable.

P605–1   13cm deep saucer with gilded scalloped edge part of an earthenware tea service with the copperplates still held in Spode Works.   The service marked only by a variety of workman's marks.

P605–2   16cm breakfast cup saucer in Bute shape and in bone china.   The design re-engraved to fit the new bone china ware.

P606   Parasol figure
Base of 23cm square earthenware cover dish.   This is an uncommon later production and evidently did not meet with great success.   Compare the centre design of this print with that of Temple Landscape second P611.   Both prints must surely stem from the same Chinese design.

P607 Forest Landscape This design was first produced to fit the Early Indented dinner wares and later re-engraved for the larger New Indented dinner service.

P607–1 Early indented soup plate likely to be made before 1800.

P607–2 Coffee can of much the same early appearance also in earthenware but with a different border similar to that used on Bungalow P617.

P607–3 New Indented earthenware dinner plate. This re-engraved version of P607–1 now fits the larger plate. Differences in the designs can be seen.

P608–1 Rock This pattern uses Forest Landscape border on its first earthenware version but not on the second which is printed on bone china. A 20cm plate in the first earthenware version.

P608–2 22cm bone china plate almost differing sufficiently in the main pattern and the borders to be numbered and named as a different design.

P609–1 Willow A pattern of early origination and continued production A large number of copperplates were engraved in this design for transfers for an extensive range of shapes. Early Indented earthenware plate. Various shades of blue are found from similar early copperplates. It seems likely that the differences occurring in the engravings on the first series of copperplates were not intentional alterations in design but rather were differing interpretations by individual engravers.

P609–2 New Indented earthenware plate. These copperplates were re-engravings to fit the new shapes of plates with an advance in technique of engraving and printing. From this point a greater control appears to have been exercised on the engravers and the individualities of P609–1 disappear.

P610–1   Flying Pennant
From the appearance of the two variations of this pattern it would seem to be a nineteenth century introduction designed to fit the New Indented size of dinner ware. The name is taken from the pennant on the vessel at the bottom of the print. New indented earthenware dinner plate. Note the bridge joining the two main blocks of land and the small nankin encircling the centre design.

P610–2   41cm oval scalloped edge dish in earthenware with gilded rims. The bridge has been removed making a more open lake or sea in the centre. The main border remains the same but the nankin has been enlarged to become a very noticeable feature.

P611–1   Temple Landscape second
Designed for and found on stone china body. The prints are usually very clear and a vivid blue. The central design closely resembles that used on Parasol Figure P606 with a temple type border.

P611–2   A variation with a dagger border.

P612–1 Queen Charlotte
Two variations of border occur in this design for use on bone china and earthenware. The name is an old factory tradition. Here shown on a bone china dinner plate. The design is that most regularly found on blue printed bone china dinner services. Note the butterfly in the border and the cell border nankin.

P612–2 24.6cm earthenware plate. The butterfly is omitted from the border as is the nankin. The prints are found on a wide range of articles including jugs and general utility wares.

P613–1 Temple
A design following the Oriental form of Art used chiefly on bone china tewares. A saucer in bone china from a New Oval service with Bute cups and saucers with simple gilding.

P613–2 A small tea plate without gilding.

P614–1

P614–3

P614 Broseley

This pattern, almost a variation of P613, was used on bone china teawares in a plain ungilded form. Sometimes known as Pale Broseley through the deliberate use of a paler blue. Occasionally found on earthenware and felspar porcelain.

P614–1 Shown here on 23cm felspar plate.

P614–2 The design is reversed when decorating holloware as can be seen on this teapot.

P614–3 Earthenware plate printed in a darker shade of blue with a nankin separating a different border from the centre which remained basically the same design.

P614–2

P615 Tall Door
Circular earthenware dinner plate. Although never popular, the design seems to have been used for many years. It has been noted transferred to an earthenware Old Oval cream jug, but pieces of much later appearance have been seen.

P616 Buffalo
20cm earthenware plate. Another pattern which continued long in production. Its first appearance is likely to have been before 1800 yet it is found on New Indented plates as the illustration here. Many factories made it yet marked Spode's pieces are hard to find.

P617 Bungalow
An extremely rare pattern of rather crude design with all known pieces being in bone china. The Old Oval teapot illustrated is unmarked but a matching cream jug is impressed SPODE. It appears to have been manufactured between 1800 and 1805.

P618 Trench Mortar
13cm earthenware saucer. This pattern, copied from the Chinese, is found very rarely with a Spode mark. It can be dated to the 1790s and is most often found on earthenware tea services. It is named after the curious trench-mortar-like bamboo stumps in front of the house.

P619   Long Bridge
Earthenware dinner plate. Similar patterns were manufactured by a number of potters. A fully marked Spode piece has yet to be found and possible attribution rests on two factors. Geoffrey Godden illustrates a most complicated unmarked supper set with this pattern in his book *British Pottery*. Sections of the same complicated design but in Willow P609–1 have been found impressed SPODE. Secondly, plain semi-circular supper set sections printed with this pattern which coincide with Spode's sizes and shapes are found with

workman's marks used by the Spode factory. However, no extant copperplate engraved with this pattern can be found at Spode Works and the attribution as Spode manufacture must remain in doubt.

P620   Net
New Indented earthenware dinner plate (shown above). This pattern was in production for a number of years both by Spode and by competing manufacturers. It is often unmarked.

P621–1   Grasshopper
A pattern found only on Stone China and probably designed for its introduction in 1813. Original design shown on a New Indented stone china plate.

P621–2   A later variation with Grasshopper centre and the border taken from Group P814.

P622   Lange Lijsen (Long Elisa) (Jumping Boy)
New Indented earthenware dinner plate. As the name suggests, this copy of a Chinese design may have reached Spode by way of Dutch delftware. It is a middle-period production.

P623   India
New Indented earthenware dinner plate. Despite its name this is a copy of the Chinese. It is one of the patterns that sometimes carries the inscription regarding cobalt from the Sparnon Mine with the date August 1816, which is the probable year of introduction of the India pattern.

P624   Old Peacock
This earthenware soup plate illustrates a very uncommon pattern. The name used by Leonard Whiter has been retained although it must be admitted that the birds hardly look to be peacocks. It is a late production.

P625   Japan
The illustration, a 22.5cm earthenware muffin dish base, is of another uncommon pattern. Again the birds are unrelated to any known living example.

P626   Dragons first
An 18cm bone china plate. The design usually decorates bone china services for breakfast and tea. In 1996, Anthony Bunce pointed out in an *NCS Newsletter* that the original design by the Chinese featured the complete dragon divided in half with the head and front claws painted in the centre of the inside or upper surface with the rear claws and tail painted on the outside and appropriately united with the front half at the rim. Spode's copy design attempted this on cups and bowls but unfortunately not on plates or saucers where the two

halves, still divided, writhe separately on the front of the flat ware and the rear surface is left plain. 'Going over the top' is easier with hand painted designs than with transfer printing it would seem.

P627   Dragons second (shown above)
16cm bone china saucer. A most unusual pattern for Spode; it is more thought of as Davenport, Masons or Coalport who produced very similar ware in quantity. Without the underglaze blue SPODE mark, a collector might well pass it over.

P628   Trophies – Nankin
Early Indented earthenware dinner plate. This, the first of the Trophies or Hundred Antiques pattern, has the typical hazy blue tinted glaze of a pre-1800 production.

P629   Trophies – Etruscan
26cm circular earthenware dessert or cake stand, footed and with raised rim. A late introduction of about 1825 which shows a very different technique and treatment of a similar subject as P628.

P630–1 Trophies Dagger (Fitzhugh)
A close look at the first three marked Spode versions of this pattern will reveal considerable differences in the border, the centre and in the motifs, yet the three are basically the same design. The fourth example is also marked but lacking trophies can hardly warrant the first word of the name. The circular 22cm earthenware plate of P630–1 has a small raised footrim not usual with Spode ware.

P630–2 23cm octagonal earthenware plate. A Chinese shape as well as pattern.

P630–3 21.5cm octagonal bone china plate, perhaps for dessert. This version was revived for modern production until recently.

P630–4 24.5cm Bone china New Indented plate with centre and main border as P630–2 but the trophies replaced by a dagger nankin.

P631   Chinese Garden
21cm earthenware muffin dish base. The print has every appearance of being designed for additional enamel colouring. However, a number of plain blue pieces such as this are known. The first coloured version, pattern 3424 of 1822, has a Chinaman standing by the urn of 'trifid'-like flowers.

P632   Chinese of Rank.
21cm earthenware bread and butter plate of saucer shape. Felicity Mallet traced the source of this design to an aquatint entitled 'A Chinese of Rank' by Thomas and William Daniell in *Picturesque Voyages to India by the way of China*, published in London in 1810. It is a very rare pattern with the only piece marked yet recorded being an egg-cup stand.

P633   Oriental Birds
13cm earthenware saucer. This print has yet to be seen on ware marked SPODE. It can be found on Bute earthenware teacups and cans with the Spode typical kinked loop handle and shards printed with the little birds on the border have been discovered in excavations during alterations at Spode Works. It probably dates from 1800–1805.

P634   Peony and Willow
Stone china dinner plate printed in clear blue. The pattern is not often found but it is likely to have been introduced especially for Spode's Stone China between 1813 and 1820 in imitation of Chinese porcelain. The rarity of the surviving pieces gives some guide to its initial popularity.

P635   Pagoda
Bute earthenware coffee can printed with six storey Pagoda set within a hutted village. The handle large and well defined in Spode's kinked loop form. Unmarked. The original copperplate is still at Spode Works and is illustrated by Robert Copeland in his book *SPODE'S WILLOW & other designs after the Chinese,* page 88, No.25.

P636   Bud and Flower
A single handed shell shaped earthenware dish transferred in plain underglaze blue named by George Worlock from the list of printed pattern names published by Llewellyn Jewitt in 1878 and hitherto unidentified. The pattern is usually over-enamelled and numbered 3088 in the Pattern Book giving an approximate date of 1821 for its introduction if taken from the 'Whiter' scale of dating. It seems likely that the pattern was adapted from a Chinese original.

P637   Chinoiserie
An early 18.1cm tea plate with pierced and moulded border and impressed SPODE with mark 2a. The border pattern can be more clearly seen in an unmarked porcelain saucer illustrated by Robert Copeland in his book page 157 no. 30. No original design has been found but the Spode version is likely to have been introduced before 1800.

P700   Series   European and Mediterranean subjects
This series, which includes many of Spode's most popular designs, is based on the perspective of modern western art with the exception of Love Chase P717 and, in some degree, Rotunda P707. The majority of the designs are not found printed on bone china or felspar porcelain and none decorated stone china. A study of the illustrations of blue printed shapes following this prints catalogue will show these designs used for decoration of every type and shape of earthenware.

P701 Girl at Well (Font)
New Indented earthenware dinner plate. This pattern, probably dating from the early 1820s, uses the same border as Union Wreath third P825. As well as on dinner and toilet wares, it can be found both on tea and on doll's tea services.

P702 Milkmaid
New Indented earthenware dinner plate. The probable date of introduction was 1814 or 1815. The border is the same as that used for Tower P714. Another pattern found on tea services in earthenware.

P703 Woodman
Earthenware dish. Surprisingly this attractive pattern is uncommon. It seems to have more about it than either of the two preceding patterns, which are far more often found. The original print illustrated here shows the centre design was followed closely by Spode's engravers but the border was far too

plain and has been substituted with one of Spode's own designs. The publisher is not named on the original print but it is inscribed 'Published October 25th 1807' and the engraver is known to have been Francis Eginton.

Original print of Woodsman used in P703.

P704 Country Scene

Earthenware breakfast saucer. This pattern is a rarity. The original copperplates still exist and shards have been found at excavations at the Works yet very few actual pieces are known.

P705 Shepherdess

An 18.5cm Circular bone china dessert plate. Another extreme rarity. A pair of basket and stands and six dessert plates all marked Spode are all that is known of this pattern. The illustrated print has been fitted to a circular plate and yet has been engraved to fit the indented shape as can be seen, so perhaps more pieces can be expected to be found. This print or a very similar design has been noted on ware marked 'Stephenson'.

P706 Musicians

32.5cm earthenware basin. Whiter named this design 'Village Scene' having seen only a small pot decorated with the May Tree Dance. Further discoveries have revealed the complete design, based on musicians, shown here. A number of other plain blue pieces have been found, not all from the toilet ware range, and two pattern numbers, 4207 and 4215, are illustrated in the Pattern Books showing small blue prints washed over in puce.

P707 Rotunda

Print taken from one of the two complete copperplates. Cut up sections of the pattern have been found on the back of the copperplate engraved with bat print P411 of about 1808–9. The design of Rotunda is discussed within the main chapter and is a curious mixture of Chinese and European art. Originating before 1796, by 1808 it was no longer expected to be reused with some of the copperplates salvaged and re-engraved on their reverse.

P708

P709

P708   Gothic Castle

New Indented earthenware soup plate. Another mixed design with both Chinese and European features but later in design perhaps 1811/12. Even the vignettes in the border are a mixture of European and Chinese scenes and African animals.

P709   Waterloo (Italian Church)

19.6cm Circular earthenware plate. The church depicted is that of the Belgian village of Waterloo very close to Wellington's Headquarters before the famous 1815 battle. The design appears to have been used chiefly for earthenware breakfast and tea sets. The first enamel version appeared in 1820.

P710   Italian

An unsigned grey pen and wash sketch seems to be the source for the central design of the famous Spode Italian pattern. The central male figure on the nearer bank in the sketch is waving to the couple standing on the far bank who are returning his salutations. They can clearly be seen in the enlargement of the sketch illustrated here but have been omitted in Spode's engraving. The sketch is now held by the Spode Museum Trust and is said to have been copied from a Claude Lorraine pastoral landscape of 1638 which can be seen at Parham House in Sussex. The border design is a straight copy of a Chinese original.

P710

Detail of sketch from which the Italian pattern was taken.

P711

P712

P711 Castle

New Indented earthenware dinner plate. This and the two prints, P713 and P714, are both adapted from aquatints contained in *Views of Rome and its Vicinity* published by J.Merigot, 28 Haymarket and R. Edwards, 142 New Bond Street, London in 1796–98. The Castle pattern is from the aquatint entitled *The Gate of Sebastian at Capena*. Other potters used the same design which is thought to have been introduced by Spode in 1806 and was always printed in a special paler blue.

P712 Lucano

The scene represented here is 'The Bridge of Lucano near

Tivoli to the East of Rome'. The tower is the tomb of Plautius Lucanus. Again the use of the pattern was not confined to the Spode factory. The source print for Spode's Locano was probably an engraving by George Hackert.

P712–1 New Indented earthenware dinner plate printed with the full pattern.

P712–2 Small vignette used occasionally as a supplementary decoration.

P712–1

P712–2

P713

P714

P713 Rome (Tiber)

Circular earthenware dinner plate. The engravings of this design are some of Spode's finest, producing clear sharp prints of clean appearance. The design is a combination of two of Merigot's engravings. The main composition *The Castle and Bridge of St. Angelo* has interposed an out-of-place *Trajan's Column*. With the addition of the trees, the whole makes a handsome if not strictly factual picture. The border differs from most in that it does not encroach upon the main design.

P714 Tower

New Indented earthenware dinner plate. This, the third reproduction of Merigot's aquatints, is taken from the engraving *The Bridge of Salaro near Porta Salaro*. Again it is a free adaptation with the trees and other detail added to fill up a circular space. The border is shared with Milkmaid P702. Thought to be introduced in 1815, the design was engraved in a wide range of sizes and will be found decorating many of the more unusual utility shapes as well as dinner ware. It continues in production to this day.

P715

P715 The Turk

21cm earthenware plate. The main design is taken from the print *Ancient Granary at Cacamo* and appears here exactly as it does on a slightly smaller plate in the Caramanian service as P905–18 differing only in the completely changed flower border shown here. Several copperplates engraved for prints of this design are still held in the Works. Both the centre pattern and the flower border are the same on all the copperplates and on all known prints in this pattern leading to the conclusion that this design is not a multi-scene pattern as is Caramanian P905.

P716

P717

P716 Turkish Castle
9cm earthenware jug. Again the main motif is a design from the Caramanian P905 series, but the flower border differs from that of The Turk P715. The very limited range of known earthenware pieces in this and the previous pattern would suggest that manufacture was limited to earthenware breakfast and tea ware.

P717 Love Chase
18cm earthenware plate. Some pieces printed with this pattern are of early nineteenth century manufacture well within the Spode period of manufacture. Despite being available for many years, the last piece noted was a Copeland dinner plate date

marked for 1910, it is uncommon and tells the story of Atalanta, Milanion and the golden apples.

P718 French Birds
22.5cm single-handed shaped earthenware dessert dish. An uncommon late engraved design. This shape of dish dates from the later 1820s or early 1830s. French Birds was one of the first prints used with the new underglaze pink.

P719 Dresden Border
23cm New Indented earthenware plate. A rare design that obviously could not have proved popular.

P718

P719

P720

P721

P720   Portland Vase
Double Indented and ribbed earthenware soup plate. The vase depicted bears little resemblance to the original Roman glass vase of this name. Another uncommon Spode design of 1831.

P721   Blossom
A print named as 'Blossom' appears in a factory proof book and two copperplates are still held in the Works store. The name 'Blossom' must refer to the border design rather than the

central scene and was listed by Llewllyn Jewett as a Spode pattern introduced in 1817. Some eighty pieces of 'Blossom' fragments were found in the foundations of former Spode workmen's houses used to form a damp-proof membrane for the houses. These were found in London Road, Stoke by Paul Holdway amongst a mass of fragments of twenty-six patterns of Spode blue printed ware. None of the 'Blossom' fragments were marked with Spode's name although the plate shown here is impress marked Spode.

P801   Lily
32.5cm earthenware supper set dish. The design is of early origin used both on earthenware and a little later on bone china. The pattern was also used at Worcester and by other potters.

P800 series   Floral patterns
Decoration by painted flowers or floral designs was first practised as soon as a ceramic surface was made able to accept such a decoration. Spode's underglaze printed wares are no exception and floral or flower-based designs were in production throughout the Spode period. Early designs were formal or restrained and in some cases could easily be classified as orientally inspired. In the middle Spode period a number of sheet patterns based on flowers or foliage were designed but only with limited success. Finally in the 1820s, the main flow of successful floral designs was produced to meet the popular fashions of the times.

P801

P802

P803

P802 *Lyre*
13.5cm earthenware saucer. This is a rare design. The saucer illustrated is part of a Bute shape set of tea ware with gilded edges. A matching cup but with a cheaper brown edge has been noted.

P803 *Lattice Scroll*
New Indented earthenware dinner plate. The gadroon edge on this design is printed and not moulded. First produced in 1810, it can be found on a wide range of wares.

P804 *Flower Cross*

Circular earthenware dinner plate. Pieces are often unmarked but it appears to be a design solely used by Spode.

P805 *Daisy*
Earthenware coffee can. This is one of the few examples of this sheet pattern found on marked ware. The object in designing such a sheet pattern was to avoid the necessity for a 'fit' for each shaped piece and thus the need for the multiplicity of engravings. One copperplate engraved all over with the design produced a transfer that, once trimmed, fitted any shape. This boon to the manufacturer did not meet public approval and examples are extremely rare.

P804

P805

P806

P807

P806   Leaf

Bute shape earthenware tea saucer. This is the most easily found of the sheet patterns, with Bute tewares in earthenware perhaps the most common. The design gives a very dark all-over blue appearance to the ware.

P807   Marble (Mosaic) (Cracked Ice and Prunus)

21.5cm   New Indented earthenware dessert plate. The engravings for this pattern were produced partly as 'fitted' designs and partly in sheet form used for large vessels and awkward shapes. A nine-pint Dutch jug is illustrated in the shapes section (S172) and shows how well the design transfers to large pieces. The print was introduced about 1821 and is sometimes found on stone china as well as earthenware.

P808

P808   Peony

32cm earthenware bowl. This pattern is rarely found in plain blue and is shown as an enamelled version as pattern 2217 of 1814 in the Pattern Book. It has been carefully laid out and transferred on the bowl with the flower placed centrally.

P809–1

P809–2

P809 Fence

Probably produced in the first decade of the nineteenth century, the pattern is not common in its original form and is likely to be rarer still in the later variation.

P809–1 Circular earthenware plate. Shows the original simple diaper border used without an inner nankin border.

P809–2 New Indented earthenware plate. Re-engraved centre pattern with a nankin interposed between a new border being four of the six parts used on examples of Group P814.

P810 Chantilly Sprig

New Indented earthenware soup plate. As its name suggests, this pattern derives from a design on French porcelain. Spode's version is not common although it decorates both earthenware and bone china.

P811 Gloucester

Early Indented earthenware soup plate. The shape of the plate and its early appearance all suggest manufacture before 1800. The pattern was revived for a long period in the twentieth century.

P810

P811

P812–1

P812–2

P812 *Peplow*

Two versions of this rare pattern have now come to light. That already illustrated in our first edition would appear to have been the later of the two and now has been listed as the second version.

P812–1 Early Indented earthenware dinner plate with nankin surround to centre pattern and flower type border and star rim. Probably early nineteenth century.

P812–2 19.5cm earthenware plate with a re-engraved centre and a wide star rim supported by floral designs. Probably issued about 1819–1820 in both earthenware and bone china with London shape cups. A copperplate at the Works is marked with the plate maker's backstamp J HARLOW STOKE.

P813 *Bowpot*

Circular earthenware dinner plate. The design is rarely found printed in plain blue as is this piece and is usually over-enamelled in colour. The first enamelled version was introduced in 1812.

P814 *Group*

Circular earthenware dinner plate. Introduced about 1809, the design is usually found on dinner ware. Towards the end of the Spode period the six floral groups in the border appeared on other patterns although only four were used other than on Group.

P813

P814

P815

P816

P815 English Sprays
Earthenware tea cup saucer. This a very late and rare design introduced about 1829. A cup, together with part of the press mould to make the handle, is shown in the tea ware section of the shape illustrations.

P816 Chinese Flowers
15cm earthenware tea saucer. The design was also transferred to New Indented dinner ware as well as tea services. It was one of the few outline prints that were regularly issued in plain blue without added enamel colours. Manufacture commenced about 1815.

P817 Fruit and Flowers
19cm Circular earthenware plate. A late design, about 1826, printed on both earthenware and bone china.

P818 Filigree
Circular earthenware soup plate. One of the most successful of Spode's floral patterns. On the smaller pieces the baskets from the border are used as centres with a reduced width border. Thought to have been originated about 1823.

P817

P818

P819

P820

P819 Sunflower (Convolvulus)

Circular earthenware dinner plate. Dating from 1812, this all-over sheet-type pattern is rare from the early Spode period although it has been recently revived and now appears in the shops again. It will be seen that the design features two flowers, Sunflower and Convolvulus. It is likely that the original name was Sunflower and that the special 'Sunflower blue' noted in Mr. Grocott's pocket book was used to print this pattern.

P820 Jasmine

Gadroon Edge earthenware dinner plate. Introduced in 1825, this design is usually found with the new gadroon moulded edge dinnerware, for which it was an early designed decoration. The jasmine itself is in the border.

P821 Geranium

This extremely handsome border is made doubly attractive to David Drakard by the little worried faces that peep out of each section. The pattern was designed in 1818.

P821–1 Circular earthenware dinner plate which shows the central Geranium sprig used on round pieces.

P821–2 Base of rectangular earthenware cover dish. This shows the alternative central sprig designed for rectangular shapes.

P821–1

P821–2

P822

P823

P822   Blue Rose
Gadroon Edge earthenware dinner plate. Another introduction of 1825 designed for the Gadroon Edge dinner ware. It is usually found on dinner services using the round soup and sauce tureens.

P823   Union Wreath first
20cm Gadroon Edge bone china plate. This design, again from 1825, is found in Gadroon Edge bone china or felspar tea wares, examples of which will be found in the tea ware section of the Shapes catalogue.

P824   Union Wreath Second
Gadroon Edge dinner plate in Spode's Imperial body, being a

slightly improved earthenware body. The design consisted of a Blue Rose P822 centre surrounded by the border of Union Wreath first P823 and was engraved to fit the new Gadroon edge wares.

P825   Union Wreath third
New Indented New Stone dinner plate. Although numbered third by Leonard Whiter this was probably the first production of an underglaze blue printed Union Wreath design with a likely introduction date of 1822. It is chiefly found on earthenware and New Stone examples are not so frequent. The border is shared with Girl at Well P701.

P824

P825

P826

P827

P826 Nettle
21.5cm octagonal New Stone plate. This design was named by
Kathleen Holdway. After negotiations for a pair of these plates was
completed she remarked: 'We were properly stung — I would call
them Nettle'. It is a printed design. Careful inspection discloses
joins in the border and in the nankin and a comparison of the pair
show them to be printed from the same copperplate.

P828 Vandyke
20.5 cm earthenware plate. This design is named after the
beard-like shapes in the border. Although a dozen Bute shape
cups and saucers have been examined, all of typical Spode shape
with the usual Spode kick handle, none included printed marks
and only an occasional impressed Spode mark has been found.

P827 Daisy and Bead
10cm earthenware dolls' dinner service dish. This little dish is both
impressed and printed with SPODE marks. It is an unusual pattern,
a combination of a separate printed border with a sheet copper
print for the central design roughly trimmed and transferred on
top. Shards from a very large bowl or chamber pot with unrecorded
extra panels were found during building excavations at the Works
so production was evidently not limited to toy pieces.

P829 Honeysuckle and Parsley
27cm earthenware comport. As can be seen, the border is
honeysuckle and the background is termed parsley. The first
illustration appearing in the Pattern Books is 3244 of 1820
which states 'Printed in blue' and shows the design fully
enamelled over the print. This 'blue only' print has the
appearance of a later production.

P828

P829

P830

P830 Star Flower
Gadroon Edge earthenware bowl transferred in a similar manner to P827 with a narrow border fitted around the main sheet pattern which has been trimmed to fit the space available. The neatness and balance of the pattern speaks well of the skill of the transferrer. Pattern 2383, of about 1815, shows the design enhanced with gilding and enamelled versions are known as well as other printed colours. The Gadroon Edge shape did not make an appearance until about 1822 so that the all blue version shown here was issued some years after the first use of the design.

P831

P832

P831 Radiating Leaves (Patience)

25cm New Indented Spodes New Stone dinner plate. Being on an impress marked plate the all blue print transfer must have been made after 1822. A version printed in brown and coloured is illustrated in the Pattern Books as pattern 3909 giving a Whiter scale date of 1824–25. The name 'Radiating Leaves' is that of Robert Copeland and 'Patience' is that of Joan Hoyes who found a pair of the plates.

P832 Worcester Wheel

33cm Stone China drainer. Many versions of this design were produced including several in the B series. The plain blue version is a rarity on a pattern obviously designed for the use of colour. The name is that favoured in the factory.

P833 Chrysanthemum and Bamboo

Gadroon Edge. Hot water plate impressed Spodes New Stone. Another design more often found with added colour particularly on the flower heads. As well as the impressed mark the base in printed 'H.M 44th Regt.' so this hot water plate must have had a quantity of similar dinner plates in the cheaper plain blue.

P834 Grapes (Uva)

Earthenware Tooth brush box and cover printed in an all blue version of the well-known pattern known at the Factory as Grapes. This is usually found over enamelled in colours and very rarely seen in plain blue. The name 'Uva' is the choice of Michael Attar its present owner.

P833

P834

P835

P836

P835 Flower Sprays
Gadroon Edge ewer and basin in Spode's Imperial body. Seven differing sprays of flowers have been used to decorate these late pieces which have not been seen on other ware.

P836 Rose and Flowers
20cm Circular earthenware dessert plate with border and centre made up of a selection of various flowers predominated by roses. As can be seen, some parts of the pattern appear to have been left plain as though there could be a coloured version although this single plain blue plate, the property of Martin Pulver, is the only example yet noted.

P837 Union Wreath fourth
25cm Gadroon Edge soup plate which must be the final mixture of Union Wreath plates. The centre decoration is that used on Union Wreath third P825 but with the added initials I U S C placed on both sides of the ribbon holding the bunch of flowers. The border is that used on Union Wreath first P823.

P838 Starship
20cm New Indented plate impressed Spodes New Stone. This plain blue printed plate is a combination of the centre pattern in Star surrounded by the border pattern in Ship. Both these patterns are illustrated by Leonard Whiter in his book showing the fully coloured versions which are illustrated in the Pattern Books as 3072 and 3067

P837

P838

P900 Series   Multi-scene patterns

Spode produced seven multi-scene patterns where a series of different centres of similar theme were placed within a common border. Initially the sets of designs were based on dinner service pieces with each size of plate, dish and major piece printed with a differing scene. With the earlier patterns in particular, the popularity of the prints soon ensured their appearance on a wide range of other articles although not upon tea wares. The earlier designs, Greek P906, Caramanian P905 and Indian Sporting P904 were all probably in production by 1812, although no exact date can be found for Indian Sporting. Surprisingly, considering the success of these, it was 1828 before the next multi-scene designs were offered, of which Botanical P903 was perhaps the most successful.

P901–1

P901 This pattern is the rarest of the three flower-based multi-scene designs. It was printed on earthenware using the Double Indented shape. The colour used, a lavender shade of blue, was introduced with this pattern in 1830 and is also found on the wares of the Copeland & Garrett period. Notice the reversed presentation of the centre and the border. The flowers in the border are in white, shaded blue, standing on a blue ground. The centre design has blue flowers on a white background. The design, shares with Aesop's Fables P907, the distinction of being provided with a printed cartouche naming the pattern as Floral.

P901–1   25cm Double Indented dinner plate.

P901–2   25cm Double Indented soup plate.

P901–3   21cm stand for sauce tureen.

P901–4   33cm drainer.

P901–5   47cm dish.

P901–6   10.5cm scalloped pan.

P901–7   Sauce tureen, cover and stand, a very attractive design.

P901–8   23cm plate.

P901–9   52.5cm dish.

P901–2

P901–3

P901–4

P901–5

P901–6

P901–7

P901–8

P901–9

P902–1

P902–2

P902 British Flowers

This pattern and the next, Botanical Flowers P903, were both issued in 1828 based on similar designs of flowers. Comparing P902–2, the soup plate from this pattern, with P903–1, the dinner plate of Botanical, it is clear that the two derive from the same source. The British Flowers dinner plate is Double Indented in shape and is in earthenware. The five pieces shown represent all the differing centres.

P902–1 25cm Double Indented dinner plate.

P902–2 25cm soup plate.

P902–3 16cm circular plate.

P902–4 Jug 14cm high.

P902–5 52cm Well and Tree dish.

P902–3

P902–4

P902–5

P903–1

P903 Botanical

This pattern reverses the colours of British Flowers with basically white flowers on a blue ground, giving a softer look. The earthenware dinner service is printed on the Double Indented shape. A variety of nine centres are shown.

P903–1 25cm dinner plate.

P903–2 25cm soup plate.

P903–3 Interior of scalloped edged bowl, 28cm diameter.

P903–4 Exterior of same bowl.

P903–5 52cm dish.

P903-6 47cm dish.

P903-7 26cm dish.

P903-8 24.5cm dish.

P903-9 23.5cm plate.

P903–2

P903–3

P903–4

P903–5

P903–6

P903–7

P903–8

P903–9

P904–1

Original aquatint – *Shooting a Leopard in a tree*

P904   Indian Sporting

The source of this multi-scene service is a publication of monthly issues by Edward Orme of Bond Street, London entitled *Oriental Field Sports, Wild Sports of the East* written by Captain Thomas Williamson and illustrated by Samuel Howitt. Twenty monthly issues of large size were made, each consisting of two aquatints and descriptions published at one guinea per issue commencing 4th June 1805. These were followed by publication of the same forty incidents in smaller book form in two volumes in 1807. Both sizes were reprinted in 1819. Spode used adaptations from seventeen of the original prints plus sections of others to produce the border pattern and the two composite pictures used for the sauce tureen cover and stand.

The name of the scene, in many cases, is printed on the back of the ware. The Spode title does not always exactly follow that of Captain Williamson and the titles shown here are those used by Spode in marking the ware. Indian Sporting prints were most commonly transferred to earthenware dinner services of the New Indented shape but different handles and knops were also supplied and pieces for other uses can be found.

P904–1   'Shooting a leopard in a tree'. 52cm Well and Tree dish. Shown with original large hand coloured aquatint.

P904–2   'Dooreahs leading out dogs'. 47cm dish.

P904–2

P904–3   'Driving a bear out of sugar canes'. 42cm dish shown with original book aquatint.

P904–3a   Interior of 24cm square salad bowl.

P904–4   'The Hog at bay'. Exterior of square salad bowl shown with the original book aquatint.

P904–4a   Soup tureen base.

P904–5   'Hunting a buffalo'. 32cm dish shown with original book aquatint named as 'The Buffalo at Bay'.

P904–6   'Shooting at the edge of a jungle'. 37.5cm dish shown with original book aquatint.

P904-7   'Hunting a civet'. 27cm dish shown with original book aquatint 'Hunting a Kuttauss or Civet'.

P904–3

Original aquatint – *Driving a Bear out of Sugar Canes*

P904–3a

P904–4

P904–4a

Original aquatint – *The Hog at Bay*

P904–5

Original aquatint – *The Buffalo at Bay*

P904–6

Original aquatint – *Shooting at the Edge of a Jungle*

P904–7

Original aquatint – *Hunting a Kuttaus or Civet*

P904–8

Original engraving – *Battle between a Buffalo and a Tiger*

P904–9

Original engraving – *The Dead Hog*

P904-8 'Battle between a buffalo and a tiger'. 23.5cm dish shown with original book aquatint. Notice the difference between the dish and the original engraving.

P904–9 'The dead hog'. Base of sauce tureen shown with original book aquatint.

P904–10 Composite picture for cover of sauce tureen.

P904–11 Composite picture for stand of sauce tureen.

P904–12 'Hog hunters meeting by surprise a tigress and her cubs'. Square cover dish base. The cover has the same print and a drainer was also made to fit this dish decorated with the same pattern.

P904–13 'Death of the bear' 21 cm deep plate and P904–13a 25cm dinner plate. The same copperplate was used for both sizes with the centre trimmed in size to fit the smaller piece.

P904–14 'Chase after a wolf' shown on a soup plate together with the original book aquatint.

P904–10

P904–11

P904–12

P904–13

P904–15 'The hog deer at bay' 18.5cm plate.

P904–16 'Syces or grooms leading out horses' — shortened by Spode on this very small 16cm plate to 'Groom leading out'.

P904–17 'Common wolf trap' 21.5cm plate shown with the original book aquatint. The building has been given greater prominence by Spode.

P904–18 and 18a Adapted from Spode's 'Common wolf trap' shown on 14cm oval serving tray 3cm deep and on the cover of 11cm covered dish fitted with a separate pierced drainer.

P904–14

Original aquatint – *Chase after a Wolf when carrying off a Lamb*

P904–15

P904–16

P904–17

Original aquatint – *Common wolf trap.*

P904–18

P904–18a

P904–19

P904–19a

P904–20

Original aquatint – *Koomkies leaving the Male fastened to a Tree*

P904–21

P904–19 and 19a   Border pattern used a main decoration shown on the base of the three part covered dish and as P904–18a on 6.5cm pail shape custard.

P904–20   'Koomkies leaving the male'. This very rare transfer seems only to have been used on the base of the three-piece vegetable dish. Perhaps being a long narrow engraving it was found unsuitable for any other piece. Reading Captain Williamson's description of the scene, it would appear that the wild male elephant, having been attracted by the females or koomkies and captured, was left tethered to a tree until subdued by thirst and hunger when taming could commence. The original aquatint is shown with the 'Spode' print.

P904–21   'Hunting a hog deer' shown transferred to a 27cm comport. It would appear that the unfortunate animal met its end at P904–15.

P905 Caramanian

The original views from which Spode's engravings were taken were published in 1803 as Volume Two of a large size three part work entitled *Egypt, Palestine and the Ottoman Empire*. Part One, covering Egypt, and Part Three, Palestine were not copied by Spode. Volume Two is headed *Views in the Ottoman Empire chiefly in Caramania, a part of Asia Minor hitherto unexplored, with some curious selections from the Islands of Rhodes and Cyprus and the celebrated cities of Corinth, Carthage and Tripoli, from the original drawings in the possession of Sir R. Ainslie, taken during his embassy to Constantinople by Luigi Mayer.* A longer title would have needed an even larger book.

This volume contained twenty-four large aquatints titled in English and in French, despite the Napoleonic wars. Some were copied by Spode in their entirety; features from others were combined into composite pictures and nine were ignored completely. This last is surprising since Spode's engravers produced two fanciful engravings in the Caramanian style for the series, designed the border using *Oriental Field Sports* prints rather than the Caramanian originals and incorporated into various scenes trees and animals from the same Indian series of prints.

The Caramanian service was introduced on a new Double Indented dinner ware shape with dishes, oval in form, with double indentations matching the plates. The rectangular shape of the New Indented dish superseded these oval dishes although the Double Indented plates continued in service. The reason for the change in shape from the oval to the squarer shape of dish may have been that both shapes used the same weight of pottery and thus would be sold at the same price yet the squarer shape held more food. Some of the dish copperplates were extended or adapted for the squarer shape of dish and some of the other sizes would seem to have had entirely new engravings which was a more satisfactory although more expensive solution. With others no such work seemed to have been undertaken immediately and dishes can be found with sections of prints 'pieced' to fill up the additional space as can be seen particularly on P905–3. The names used by Luigi Mayer have been retained although in the last 200 years much has changed on the southern Mediterranean coast of Asia Minor now named 'The Turquoise Coast' by the Turkish Ministry of Culture. The name of Cacamo is now Kekova although the coastline was considerably altered in a nineteenth century earthquake. An article by David Lewis in Volume One of the *Spode Society Recorder* updates many of Luigi Mayer's names.

P905–1

P905–2

P905–3

P905–3a

P905–1 'A Triumphal Arch of Tripoli in Barbary'. 61.5cm dish in original Double Indented oval shape. The centre was designed for the largest normal size of dish, 52cm. Two larger sizes could be obtained by special order. That illustrated, which had an extended area of 'blue grass' added between the border and the centre, as can be seen, and an even larger dish which was decorated with two borders to cover the additional space. This particular print was used with a double impression of the centre which cleverly covers a massive 80.5cm dish shown in the Shapes section following this catalogue of prints. This arch still stands in the ruins of the Roman city of Leptis Magna although the last 200 years have rather reduced it in bulk with many fallen stone blocks now surrounding the building. At least the weedy top knot has been cleaned which gives it a better sense of order.

P905–2 'The Castle of Boudron in the Gulf of Stancio', 46.5cm oval, Double Indented earthenware Well and Tree dish

P905–3 'Antique fragments at Limisso', 42cm New Indented earthenware dish. The inserted or 'mended' piece along the bottom of the centre design intrudes and spoils the pattern.

P905–3a 42.5cm Circular dish using a different treatment of the same scene. P905–3 is nearer the original print.

P905–4 'Principal entrance to the harbour of Cacamo', 37cm Double Indented earthenware dish. The original aquatint was followed more closely on the dish than on the cover dish.

P905–4a Variation of the same scene on base of 23cm square cover dish. The hills in particular have been changed.

P905–5 'Ruins of an ancient temple near Corinth', 26.5cm base of a round cover dish. This view is a combination of two prints with the background of a third added. The name refers to the capped and joined columns to the right of the picture. The figures in the centre are of 'A Caramanian family changing its abode' and the background depicts 'The City of Corinth'. A slightly different engraving of basically the same scene appears on dishes.

P905–4

P905–4a

P905–5

P905–6

243

Catalogue of underglaze blue prints

P905-6 'Citadel near Corinth', 27cm comport. This is a Spode fanciful production without an obvious original. Why anybody would cross a river by boat within a few feet of a stone bridge is beyond imagination. Putting on one side these ludicrous boating exercises, *The Dictionary of BLUE and WHITE PRINTED POTTERY 1780–1880,* Volume II, illustrated on page 58 a 30cm oval dish under the same title, but with minor variations in the engraving, and with the centre view entirely reversed with the distant Corinth shown on the right and the river, bridge and boatmen on the left. A search by Paul Holdway in the Spode copperplate store, revealed the upper half of the original copperplate which had been divided to be re-engraved on its underside with a later design. No trace could be found of the copperplate engraved with the lower section of the reversed view of the 'Citadel near Corinth'.

P905–7 'Part of the harbour of Macri' 22.5cm baker or baking dish. The original aquatint, from which the transfer was copied, was followed closely by Spode.

P905–8 'Colossal sarcophagus near Castle Rosso'. The soup tureen illustrated in this print is not the first and most usually found tureen shape of the Caramanian service but was introduced for use with the later New Indented dishes although retaining the knop and handle shape used for the Caramanian service. The original tureen shape can be seen in the illustration of the sauce tureen P905–15. Spode, when reproducing the 'Colossal sarcophagus', did it no service in reducing it to a single storey whereas it still stands in the town of Kas three storeys high.

P905–9 This is the normal print found on the covers of the soup tureen and the oval vegetable dish. It is a combination of two original prints 'A colossal sarcophagus at Cacamo in Caramania' and 'A colossal vase near Limisso in Cyprus' together with various items from the border design.

P905–10 'Caramanian vase'. Base of a circular footed comport or supper set centre piece. A made-up view with no exact original.

P905–7

P905–8

P905–9

P905–10

P905–11

P905–11 'Caramanian Castle'. Circular plate or stand. Another Spode production with no original source print. It is the basis of a separate pattern with a flower border, P716 Turkish Castle. Prints on oval Double Indented dishes can also be found.

P905–12 'Sarcophagi and Sepulchres at the head of the harbour of Cacamo', 25cm Double Indented earthenware dinner plate. Although the Double Indented oval dish fell out of favour, the plates continued in use.

P905–12a A less common version of the dinner plate with the flying birds replaced by clouds.

P905–13 'City of Corinth' 25cm Double Indented soup plate. This design generally follows the original print except the additions of the boat in the foreground and the temple ruins on the right.

P905–14 'Ancient bath at Cacamo in Caramania' 19cm Double Indented plate. The term bath is more likely to have meant a covered water reservoir than a swimming pool or bathing place.

P905–12

P905–12a

P905–13

P905–14

P905–15 'Entrance to ancient granary'. Sauce tureen of the first shape used for this and the soup tureen of the Caramanian series. See P905–8 for the later alternative shape. Spode's printed design is much changed from the original source print and shows only the entrance arch. P905–18 gives a better impression of the whole.

P905–16 'Necropolis or cemetery of Cacamo'. Sauce tureen stand. Compare with P905–16a.

P905–16a 21.5cm plate with the same view as P905–16 but differently engraved.

P905–17 'Sarcophagi at Cacamo'. 20cm square dish. Another design put together from pieces of several.

P905–18 'Ancient granary at Cacamo'. 16cm Double Indented earthenware plate. This shows rather more of the original print than does P905–15 on the sauce tureen. This design, a little modified and set in a flower border, is the centre of a separate pattern, P715 The Turk.

P905–15

P905–16

P905–16a

P905–17

P905–18

P905–19

P905–19a

P905–19 13cm Diamond pickle tray. A similar print with the three figures taken from the dinner plate was made up to fit various small pieces.

P905–19a 10cm Toy dinner plate basically of the same design but altered to suit the space available. This variation was used also to decorate Bell custards.

P905–20 15.5cm New shape ewer. Not a single piece of this design is taken from Luigi Mayer's aquatints. They all derive from Samuel Howitt's *Oriental Sports*. However, the composition of the border and the decoration on the handle must classify it as a Caramanian print. A very similar engraving was used to decorate the side of the base of the three-part vegetable dish.

P905–21 Border pattern used as main decoration. The sauce ladle and toothbrush box show the small pieces that can be expected to be seen so decorated. The ladle clearly shows the Caramanian design of handle print.

P905–22 17cm Old Shape Broth bowl with cover. The transfers decorating the cover of this set have already been listed as part of the Caramanian service. However, that on the bowl, at least in part, is a new design. The single seated and the two standing figures appear in both P905–15 and P905–18. However, the house, or perhaps sarcophagus, and its outbuilding have not made a previous appearance but would seem to be of Spode imagination.

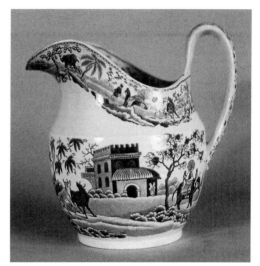

P905–20

P905–21

P905–22

Catalogue of underglaze blue prints

P906 Greek

This series of designs was taken from a publication in 1804 giving details of the collection of Sir William Hamilton. It was a large work entitled *Outlines from the Figures and Compositions upon the Greek, Roman and Etruscan Vases of the late Sir William Hamilton, with engraved borders. Drawn and engraved by the late Mr. Kirk.* Spode lost no time in putting this publication to use to catch the fashion of the day. The Greek pattern was ready by 1806 using New Indented earthenware dinner shapes. This was no mean feat considering the crowded nature of the designs and that every size of engraving had no less than five different multi-scene features. The four urns or vases standing in the border remain constant throughout the design. The centre pattern and four cartouches placed in the border between the urns vary in content from piece to piece. A close study of the pattern is rewarding and the quality and speed of the initial production puts many a modern potter to shame. A selection from the prints is shown and where known the name of the centre scene is added below the illustration. Many of these central scenes have been identified or named by Margaret Buxton and this information is shown on ten of the fourteen examples of differing wares shown here.

P906–1

P906–1   25cm New Indented earthenware dinner plate. 'Zeus (or Jupiter) in his Chariot'.

P906–2   A similar plate 21cm diameter. 'A Wreath for the Victor'.

P906–3   18cm plate. 'Heracles fighting Hippolyta'.

P906–4   Interior of 21cm square salad bowl. 'Artemis drawn by a Griffin'.

P906–5   47cm dish. 'Artemis drawn by a Griffin and a Lynx'. Compare with P906–4.

P906–6   26cm dish.   'Iphigenia told of the death of Agamemnon'.

P906–7   36.5cm drainer. Notice the extensions to the original print transferred to each end. Name of centre scene unknown.

P906–8   52cm dish, the largest standard size. The centre scene is adapted from an original print.

P906–9   23.5cm dish, the smallest size. 'Four figures in battle'.

P906–10   24cm soup plate.   'Refreshments for Phliasian Horseman'.

P906–11   42.5cm dish. 'Centaurs battling Theseus'.

P906–12   37.5cm dish. 'Artemis with two lynxes'.

P906–13   33cm drainer. Name of centre scene unknown.

P906–2

P906–3

P906–4

P906–5

P906–6

P906–7

P906–8

P906–9

P906–10

P906–11

P906–12

P906–13

P907   Aesop's Fables

This series was produced right at the end of the Spode period. Special cartouches were engraved to mark the pieces giving the name of the fable above the wording AESOP'S FABLES and SPODE (Mark 64). After change of ownership of the factory, the name SPODE was obliterated from these marks which continued to be used with a separate Copeland and Garrett mark. The designs were adapted from the illustrations used in the 1793 edition of the Rev. Samual Croxall's *Fables of Aesop*. Croxall was published many times in different formats and illustrated by many artists. Spode's designs are most frequently found printed in green, with other colours, including blue, being rare, particularly those marked SPODE. The dinnerware shape was Double Indented plates with New Indented dishes and the moulded foot 'BS' shape tureens. The peculiar head growing from a long neck in the border might almost be an object seen from the shores of Loch Ness. The following fables are illustrated in the series:

The Ass, the Lion and the Cock; The Crow and the Pitcher; The Dog in the Manger; The Dog and the Shadow; The Dog and the Sheep; The Dog and the Wolf; The Fox and the Goat; The Fox and the Grapes; The Fox and the Lion; The Fox and the Sick Lion; The Fox and the Tiger; The Hare and the Tortoise; The Horse and the Loaded Ass; The Leopard and the Fox; The Lion, the Bear and the Fox; The Lion in Love; The Lioness and the Fox; The Mountains in Labour; The Oak and the Reed; The Peacock and the Crane; The Sow and the Wolf; The Stag looking into the Water; The Wolf and the Crane; The Wolf and the Lamb, The Wolf, the Lamb and the Goat.

A total of fifty-two copperplates still exist covering the above centres with borders. All the pieces in the selection illustrated are marked SPODE and are printed in blue unless otherwise shown. They are in earthenware.

P907–1

P907–2

P907–3

P907–4

P907–5

P907–1 25cm Double Indented soup plate — 'The Lion in Love'.

P907–2 22cm Double Indented plate — 'The Dog and the Sheep'.

P907–3 18.5cm Double Indented plate — 'The Fox and the Tiger'.

P907–4 24cm baker — 'The Dog and the Shadow'.

P907–5 29cm comport — 'The Ass, the Lion and the Cock'.

P907–6   48cm dish — 'The Dog in the Manger'.

P907–7   Interior of scollop edged bowl — 'The Fox and the Sick Lion' [printed in black].

P907–8   Exterior of same bowl — 'The Leopard and the Fox [printed in black].

P907–9   Double handled dish — 'The Crow and the Pitcher'.

P907–10   New Indented dish — 'The Horse and the Loaded Ass'.

P907–6

P907–7

P907–8

P907–9

P907–10

P950 series   Special and Armorial productions
This section illustrates underglaze blue printed ware with designs printed for a special use or to special order. All the pieces illustrated are marked SPODE, either impressed or printed. As discussed in Chapter 4, many of Spode's private customers who ordered dinner or tea wares printed with their armorial bearings in underglaze blue additionally ordered a more splendid service enamelled in full colour. History does not tell us whether the servants treated the splendid service more tenderly than the cheaper underglaze wares which were perhaps used every day. Judging by the remains of each that can be found, there could have been little in it.

P951   23.5cm dish perhaps for serving smoked or potted fish. It would not have been worth engraving the dish for less than 200–300 transfer prints so perhaps they were for commercial use, a forerunner of potted meat jars.

P952   14cm bone china tea saucer with Geranium border P821. The Arms are those of Captain Grace. The Arms Book lists a fully enamelled version of the Grace achievement.

P953   25cm New Indented earthenware dinner plate. Printed with a Greek P906 border surrounding the Arms of the City of Newcastle upon Tyne.

P954   34cm Gadroon Edge circular soup tureen stand. Jasmine P820 border with the Arms of Alderman Thompson MP — alderman of the City of London. Perhaps a colleague of Alderman W.T.Copeland.

P951

P952

P953

P954

Catalogue of underglaze blue prints

P955 46cm Gadroon Edge well and tree dish with the decoration a Union Wreath mixture. The border is that used by Union Wreath first and second P823 and P824. The central group is from Union Wreath third P825 shortened to allow the inclusion of the laurel wreath and number, the insignia of the 59th Regiment of Foot. Sir Frederick Robinson was promoted Colonel of the Regiment in 1827, about the date of the manufacture of the dish. A dinner service, of which this formed part, was likely to have been used in the Mess on informal occasions.

P956 23cm base of a square cover dish in stone china. This was obviously not best ware for Earl Ferrers whose Arms decorate the piece.

P957 Hot-water plate in Double Indented shape. Dresden border P719 surround the Arms of General Fagan KCB. A fully enamelled armorial service was also supplied.

P955

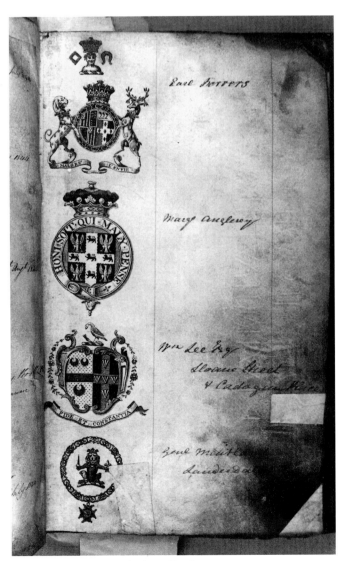

Entry for Earl Ferrers in Arms Book

P956

P957

Page of Arms Book

P958 29cm circular dish with Geranium P821 border with the impaled Arms of the Copeland and Yates families. William Taylor Copeland is named against the entry in the Arms Book.

P959 Gadroon Edge dinner plate with Jasmine P820 border and the lozenge of Miss Hackett.

P960 Modern dinner plate using Geranium P821 border surrounding a print taken from a copperplate engraved at Spode Works in the 1820s of Simon Bolivar, the Liberator who helped six Latin American countries break free from the rule of the Spanish Monarchy. Spode's copperplates, engraved in two sizes, were taken from a Paris engraving by Mariaga published in 1820. A series of Spode pieces was made and exported to South America between the late 1820s and Bolivar's death in 1830 and probably a little after. The illustrated plate was a trial for a quantity made to the order of the Republic of Venezuela for the Bicentenary celebrations of Bolivar's birth in 1783.

P958

P959

P960

P961, P962 and P963 A small creamware mug with a double laced strap handle and a printed Spode mark appears to be the sole Spode survivor commemorating an event which took place in Brazil on September 7th, 1822. In 1807, to escape the grasping hand of Napoleon, the Portuguese King John VI and his family, with the help of the British fleet, fled to his huge colony of Brazil. In 1816 despite the final defeat of Napoleon, he still remained in that salubrious colony and was declared 'King of the United Kingdom of Portugal, Brazil and the Algarve'. It was not until 1821 that he was finally persuaded to return to Lisbon leaving his son Crown Prince Pedro, as Regent in Brazil. On 7th September 1822 the Regent received despatches ordering him to obey the directions of the Cortes in Lisbon and return Brazil to the status of a colony. On reading the despatches he drew his sword and declared 'The Hour has come! Independence or Death! We have separated from Portugal'. It was a nearly bloodless revolution since the South American continent was ripe for independence.

P961 Dom Pedro first King of Brazil 1822–1831.

P962 Leopoldina his wife and Queen Consort of Brazil.

P963 The standard of Independent Brazil.

P964 A set of Spode ointment pots and syrup jars marked with the small printed capitals SPODE was supplied to the London firm of Corbyn, Stacey & Co. These were decorated with two bands in blue of Union Wreath border P823 and P824 and named in black with the drug contained. Twenty electuary and ointment pots and twenty-seven syrup jars continued in daily use until closure of the retail shop in 1896.

P964–1 18.4cm earthenware ointment pot to hold the drug BALS:LOCATEL a balsam for the treatment of ulcers on the skin.

P964–2 19cm high Syrup Jar inscribed SYR:RHAMNI a purgative and laxative derived from the bark or fruit of the Buckthorn plant.

P961   P963

P962

P964–1

P964–2

P965

P966

P965 24cm base of square cover dish printed with Geranium P821 border encircling the Arms of the Skinners Company. The reverse of the dish enlivened with two further impressions of the Arms, two impressions of print P821–2, and a Roundel reading Master 1821, 22 and the initials TG, placed centrally, being the initials of Thomas Gainsford.

P966 26cm oval Comport printed with Geranium P821 border and a paddle steamer with a very tall funnel and two masts supporting furled sails with the boat heading straight into the wind under the wording NETHERLANDSCHE STOOM BOOT MAATSCHAPPY.

P967 New Indented shape vegetable tureen and cover printed with Lattice Scroll P803 and an armorial device with an oval supported by two husky naked men each holding a large club.

P967

Shapes of wares decorated with underglaze blue prints

The study of Spode underglaze blue printing will not confine the student only to fine and interesting prints but can add a window to the world of the late eighteenth century and the early nineteenth century. *The Penny Magazine* in a supplement dated May 1843 entitled 'A day at the Staffordshire Potteries' and written after a visit to the Stoke Works described the blue-printed ware as:

> A kind of ware, the introduction of which, to use the words of Mr. Porter ('Treatise on Porcelain') has added materially to the decent comforts of the middle classes in England and has more than any other circumstance contributed to the great extension of our trade in earthenware with the continent of Europe.

In making this true, Spode's designers appear to have summoned up their ingenuity not only to produce a huge and varied range of traditional wares but also to create ceramic shapes which encroached on the spheres of both metal and wood. Most were decorated by blue printing, the study of which, therefore, gives an insight into the way of life of their first users. As intimated by Mr. Porter, blue printed ware was aimed at the fast-increasing middle classes. With printed ware costing, on the average, two and half times as much as plain undecorated ware it was obviously not bought by those with restricted means. Judging by the number of crested armorial blue-printed services supplied, it also entered the homes of the rich even if only for everyday use. The shapes found can therefore be expected to reflect the way of life of the middle classes and perhaps in some degree the more well-to-do.

In an endeavour to assist this look into the past, the blue printed wares illustrated have been divided into four groups by use:

> Dinner and dessert
> Breakfast and tea
> Toilet and personal hygiene
> Useful, ornamental and toys

Dinner and dessert wares

Nearly all Spode's underglaze blue-printed dinner services are earthenware with the plates in one of the shapes described earlier in the chapter. Some bone china dinner ware was decorated in this manner with the design Queen Charlotte P612-1 being especially engraved for this use with the plate shape combining features of both the New and Double Indented earthenware shapes. However, underglaze blue printed bone china is uncommon in dinner ware although not so rare in dessert ware. From 1813 Spode's stoneware was introduced with a new range of patterns based on Oriental art and made in imitation of the no longer imported Chinese dinner services.

Of the earthenwares the majority of the blue-printed pieces found to-day

S81 A table laid for dinner with Spode underglaze blue printed earthenware made in the first quarter of the eighteenth century.

will be from this dinner and dessert category of wares. For those able to afford to buy Spode's underglaze printed wares, dinner was the main meal of the day and lasted through many courses followed by dessert. Vast services were made and even now six dozen dinner plates is not an uncommon number to find in services offered in the larger auction rooms.

Before the introduction in about 1822 of the Gadroon Edge plate, Spode's dinner and soup plates and the smaller suppers, twiflers and muffins were made with flat bases without footrims, as were many of the plain dishes. On the other hand, stands for tureens were fitted with an applied raised footrim even though their shape was sometimes that of a dish. Dessert plates have a recessed footrim unlike that on stands.

Spode's eighteenth-century print-decorated holloware is rare and most of the surviving tureens, cover dishes, salad bowls and similar pieces date from the second and third decades of the nineteenth century, although some may be a little earlier. The Works' records of sizes and shapes of moulded wares have not survived, and this lack cannot be made good by workmen's notebooks as it is in part for thrown and turned wares. By the very nature of the work, holloware pressers and casters were not individually responsible for the dimensions of their productions, as were throwers and turners, and thus had no particular need to note the size and

S82

S82 The four standard sizes of plate in the Double Indented shape used for the introduction of the Caramanian P905 series of views and subsequently used in other series of multi-scene patterns. The sizes of the plates, from left to right, are 25cm, 21cm, 19cm and 16cm.

S83 Three shapes of dishes. Left — plain oval Oriental Birds P633, Centre — New Indented shape Filigree P818, the most used shape introduced about 1805, and Right — Double Indented oval shape, used for the introduction of the Caramanian P905 series. This dish shape did not prove popular and was withdrawn in favour of the New Indented shape. The double indented plates remained in use.

shapes. A record of Spode's moulded wares can only be built up from surviving examples.

Illustrated in this shapes section, amongst other items, are a selection of the different shapes made for the soup and sauce tureens and stands. These are by no means all that were supplied but give a good representation of the more usual shapes made. On the introduction of a new printed pattern, the shapes of the holloware were either also newly designed or chosen from the existing shapes, and the engravings were 'fitted' to them as described in Chapter 3. Thus, of necessity, the shape of the holloware and the printed pattern were married and will nearly always be found together. The later designs of tureen are sometimes found with early patterns as an alternative with the aid of 'piecing and mending' but not always with great success.

Dishes were made in sizes from 7inch to 20inch in multiples of 1inch as standard productions, with larger sizes available to order and in the same variety of shapes as were available in plates.

S83

S84

S85

S86

S84 47cm New Indented shape earthenware dish in Castle P711 shown fitted with a removable drainer for serving wet food such as fish.

S85 Three oval shaped comports. Left — printed with Indian Sporting patterns P904–21 *Hunting a hog deer.* The extended ends form handles and are decorated with the handle pattern of the Indian Sporting design. Centre rear — Footed comport of early flat design Willow P609–1, Right — The later version of the Willow pattern P609–2 and printed in a lighter shade. of blue.

S86 Two three-part vegetable dishes each fitted with a liner in which the food would be placed and held in a warming oven and then served in a cooler base and cover. Rear left — Rome P713 with the liner in a single compartment. Front and right — Caramanian P905, an exploded view showing a divided liner.

S87

S87 Vegetable dish in three parts. Trophies Dagger P630–3 with liner divided into four sections.

S88 Four covered dishes without liners. Rear left — Circular footed dish in Filigree P818. Rear right —

Square dish Indian Sporting P904–12 — *Hog hunters meeting by surprise a tigress and her cubs.* Front left — Earthenware muffin dish in Japan pattern P625. Front right — Stone china oblong dish in Grasshopper P621–1.

S88

S89 Group P814 circular sauce tureen and cover. It originally may have been supplied with a stand.

S90 Two sauce tureens covers and stands. Left — Rome P713. Right — Tower P714.

S91 Two further sauce tureens, covers and stands. Left — India P623. Right — Lattice Scroll P803. The stand and the tureen are supplied as a single piece. In most services the sauce and soup tureens are of the same shape but of differing sizes. This tall shape does not seem suitable for the larger soup tureen and an example has not been noted. The sauce tureen may have been made for dessert rather than for dinner ware.

S89

S90

S91

S92

S92 A final pair of sauce tureens, covers and stands. Left — Lange Lijsen P622. Right — Rome P713.

S93 30cm circular Soup tureen, cover and stand in Greek pattern P906. The circular tureen shape was used for the

introduction of the Greek pattern in 1806 although later examples are found on the shapes used for Tower P714.

S94 Another example of the circular form of tureen used with Grasshopper P621–1 on a stone china body.

S93

S94

S95 Soup tureen, cover and stand in earthenware in a rarer shaped and handled form used with Indian Sporting P904 prints.

S95

S96 Two sauce or gravy boats in earthenware. Left — 19cm overall in Greek P906. Right — 16cm Lange Lijsen P622. The original name for these was sauce boats. Gravy boats seem to be a modern description. Most manufacturers seem to have supplied them with or without stands. Spode's examples are surprisingly uncommon and no stand has been identified as being especially made for Spode boats.

S96

S97 Argyll, being a gravy warmer with a similar external appearance to a coffee pot. The vessel is formed with two separate compartments. The lower, to contain hot water, is fed through a tube set behind the handle and covered by an extension from the removable cover of the vessel. The upper chamber, which holds the gravy, discharges through the spout and is not connected to the lower chamber. The vessel is said to have been invented by the third Duke of Argyll about 1750, and was designed to obviate a skin forming on the gravy during its slow and devious underground passage from kitchen to dining room at Inveraray Castle. This example is decorated in Tower P714 pattern.

S97

S98 Three round scalloped pans with twist handles. Earthenware, the largest 23.5cm diameter, Italian P710. The smaller pair 10.5cm diameter, Filigree P818. On the smaller pieces decorated with Filigree, the main decoration consists of a basket of flowers taken from the border of the larger transfers surrounded by a smaller modified border.

S99 Three earthenware bowls. Left — Two-handled, low antique salad bowl, 26cm diameter, Geranium P821. Made in two sizes of which this is the smaller. Right — Scalloped edge footed bowl 26cm diameter, Trophies Etruscan P629. A later shape produced after 1825. Front — Punch bowl again 26cm diameter Queen Charlotte P612-2. Ten sizes of this plain bowl were produced, the largest holding 2 gallons, an appreciable quantity of punch.

S98

S99

S100

S101

S100 24cm basket on stand in earthenware, Lange Lijsen P622. The basket has but a single row of piercings and could have been used for fruit or salad.

S101 23cm pierced basket and stand Castle P711 with a border used from a section of the complete border print and used to cover the whole of the pierced interior surface which is placed at the top of the basket.

S102 Pierced basket and stand, Willow P609–2. Piercing in diamond pattern placed at the foot of the basket side and on the edge of the 25cm stand.

S102

S103

S103 Slightly smaller basket and stand, India P623. The piercings placed low down on the sides of the basket and based on a plain oval shape.

S104 Plain oval dish in earthenware, 24cm Rome P713. The plain shape and narrow border is typical of this pattern which is based on a simple round dinner plate.

S105 34cm oval handled deep straight sided container Union Wreath third P825. Sides circled with four ribs at top and three at the bottom. Later sold as oyster tub.

S104

S105

S106

S107

S108

S106 34cm footed salad bowl Union Wreath third P825. Compare with the salad bowl appearing in S99 on the left.

S107 Root dish. Earthenware, 30cm long, Tower P714. A somewhat similar shape in the *Leeds Catalogue of Creamware* is described as a radish dish. This may have been the original name for Spode's shape.

S108 32cm circular dish consisting of four joined quadrant sections surrounding a centre core of four smaller sections and a fitted large loop carrying handle, all decorated in Castle P711.

S109

S109 Dessert centre piece. Earthenware, 40cm overall. This is one of a number of shapes used for this purpose.

S110 65cm extra large New Indented dish transferred with Italian P710 with the largest copperplate available covering a 52cm dish and a second border added to cover the additional size.

S110

S111

S112

S111 52.7cm circular Well and Tree dish printed with a double impression of Castle P711 with the second truncated impression fitted below the first.

S112 15cm Caramanian P905 vinaigrette or oil bottle with cover. The print shows part of the view 'Entrance to an ancient granary'.

S113 A lidded mustard pot with rams head handles, cone shaped and decorated with Rome P713. A particularly fine example.

S114 Drum shape mustard pot, earthenware 7.5cm diameter, Rome P713. The complete item may have included a round stand.

S113

S114

S115 Three pepper pots in earthenware. Left — In Queen Charlotte P612–2 and on the right, in the same shape, Italian P710. In the centre, a taller and slimmer version, Tower P714.

S116 Page 21 of Shaw's pocket book. The first five items are all different shapes of individual cups for custard, demonstrating its popularity at the beginning of the nineteenth century.

S117 On right — Pail shape custard in the normal single person size 7cm high in Tower P714. On left — Giant pail shape custard, Greek P906, 24cm high. Obviously custard was made in quantity, probably in a large plain basin, from which the individual servings were taken. The giant size pot is extremely rare, perhaps made especially to order and used for refilling the individual portions within view of the users.

S115

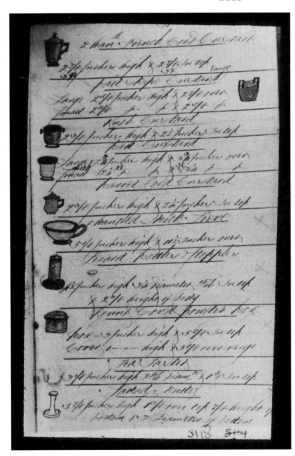

S116

S117

S118

S119

S120

S121

S118 Open custard cups in Flower Cross P804. On the left — Knob custard, 5cm high. On the right — Pail custard 8cm high. This shape was also made with a pierced cover with the internal shape of the main body slightly varied so that the cover, dropping inside the lip of the body, rested on a flange moulded into the body. A covered pail shape custard has not been recorded with printed decoration, they are usually very elaborately painted and gilded.

S119 French covered custard 9cm high overall in earthenware Greek P906. Examples when found without the cover appear to be rather plain teacups.

S120 Bell custards in earthenware, average height 5.5cm. On the left — Union Wreath third P825. Centre — Caramanian P905–19. Right — Trophies Etruscan P629. The most common shape of custard, sometimes called syllabub cups.

S121 Barrel covered custards in earthenware decorated in Lattice Scroll P803 and complete with stand. The handle shape is similar to that used on the French Covered custard.

S122

S123

S122 Knife rests. Earthenware, 10cm long made in all the main patterns used for dinner ware. Designed to hold the knife blade from the cloth between courses.

S123 Set of ten asparagus rests in earthenware, each 9.5cm at widest, Willow P609–1. The prints are taken from two engravings showing the usual minor differences found on early coppers. The shapes are variously described by different manufacturers as asparagus rests, shells or small plates. The exact method of use is not known, but it is probable that the asparagus was placed in them in the kitchen and was thus preserved from damage when being transferred to the diner's plate.

S124 Four diamond trays in earthenware the largest piece 25.5cm long in Rome P713. Left centre — Caramanian P905–19. Right centre — Tower P714, and in front an earlier production, Willow P609–1.

S124

S125

S126

S125 30cm butter dish in Parasol figure P606 formed with a central butter container with cover fixed centrally into an extended upright sided stand with tapered cut off ends. It has been suggested that the stand may have been shaped to hold ice during hot weather or perhaps a butter knife.

S126 Divided pickle tray. Earthenware 9cm long, Willow P609–1. An early production with a very blue glaze.

S127 Three earthenware leaf dishes shaped and moulded with veins and stalks on the underside. The average size varies but is usually about 11cm wide and printed with the usual dinner ware patterns.

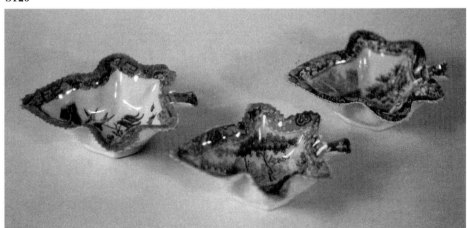

S127

S128

S128 Earthenware pickle tray in Castle P711, 28.5cm wide fitted with two pairs of separate quadrant-shaped trays and a central narrow compartment possibly to hold a serving spoon.

S129 Soup and sauce ladles in earthenware. Soup ladle 31cm long and sauce ladle 17cm both transferred with Jasmine P820. The 1820 Shape Book shows these with an additional cream bowl ladle. From the detail shown this appears to be much the same as the sauce ladle, except that the handle is set at a steeper angle to the bowl.

S129

276

S130

S130 and S131   Little dessert ware appears to have been decorated with underglaze blue prints. A canoe-shaped sauce tureen and stand, still with its ladle, is transferred with the same prints of Indian Sporting as are found on the dinner ware tureen P904–9 and cover P904–10. However, the stand is decorated with a version of P904–18, a rather longer print to suit the canoe-shaped stand. Shown separately as S131 the well in the stand to hold the tureen can clearly be seen.

S131

Wares for breakfast and tea

It is difficult to be certain of the exact form and shape of Spode's early tea-wares since the first productions were unmarked. It is likely that all early ware was manufactured in earthenware and that the first bone china was not available much before 1800. The forty-five piece tea set in bone china printed with chinoiserie underglaze blue transfers with the major pieces in Old and New Oval shape are likely to have Bute shape teacups and saucers with coffee cans although tea bowls continued in production with the most common shape being Royal Flute.

S132

S132 An earthenware fluted teapot closely following a Chinese form transferred with an early version of Willow P609–1 with the nankin widened and used as the border which, in itself, was omitted. The teapot and cover are covered with a heavy pearlware glaze in imitation of Chinese porcelain and well gilded, overall 24cm wide. Base inscribed with large numerals 157 with matching inscription under the cover of 156.

S133 Although this sugar box in earthenware was described as French shape in our first edition, it is decorated in the same early printed design as the teapot just illustrated in S132, Mandarin P605–1. The fluted shape of both pieces makes it most likely it is of the same service.

S133

S134

S135

S134 A chocolate/coffee cup, a tea bowl and a saucer of fluted and gilded form from the service of which the teapot forms part. Shown in front of these pieces is a print on paper taken from a copperplate, one of a number still held in the Spode Museum. It would seem probable that this service was made before the introduction of bone china perhaps in the late 1780s or in the 1790s.

S135 An earthenware Old Oval teapot decorated with Trench Mortar P618 and impress marked SPODE. The handle is of the usual Old Oval form but at the upper junction with the pot has been brought down the side and secured with an imitation of the cross strap used on metal ware. This probably indicates manufacture before 1800.

S136

S136 A fluted and gilded saucer decorated with Trench Mortar P618 of exactly the same form as the teapot shown in S135.

S137 An earthenware Old Oval teapot decorated with Gloucester P811. The upper junction of the handle is that usually found on Old Oval teapots and is similar to that in S135 except that the unusual imitation cross strap has been omitted. Although neither of the two Old Oval teapots, S135 and S137, are illustrated with a teapot stand this probably would have been supplied originally.

S137

S138

S138 and S139 The most easily found of the underglaze blue printed tewares is transferred in Temple P613 on bone china with the major pieces in New Oval shape and supplied in forty-five piece sets using Bute shape cups and coffee cans. The two illustrations show the teapot, with cover and stand, and the sucrier and cream jug.

S139

281

S140

S140 and S141   Although gilded plain Bute shape teacups and coffee cans were supplied in many cases, an odd selection of other shapes could be ordered.   S140 shows a Bute handle fixed to a Royal Flue tea bowl and the coffee can fluted to match together with a fluted saucer.   S141 shows the same pattern transferred to a Porringer shape teacup and saucer, the shape introduced about 1810.

S141

S142

S143

S142 Earthenware teapot 17cm wide overall decorated in Queen Charlotte P612–2.

S143 Bute shape teacup and saucer in earthenware transferred with Queen Charlotte P612–2.

S144 Large teapot 37 cm wide including spout and handle decorated in Broseley P614 This pattern, sometimes called Pale Broseley due to the shade in which it was usually produced, was long in production, most frequently in a bone china body.

S144

S145

S145 Bute shape teacup and saucer in bone china shown on left in Broseley P614. This shape was the most frequently used Spode teacup until ousted about 1815–16 by the London shape shown here on a coffee cup on the right.

S146 Etruscan shape bone china teacup and saucer transferred in Broseley P614. The cup is fitted with a serpent handle and the saucer with a well to steady the cup during use. Probably not made until after 1825.

S147 23.5cm low Egyptian teapot in earthenware transferred in Geranium P821, the pattern designed in 1818.

S146

S147

S148

S151

S148 Cottage shape 23.5cm earthenware teapot printed with Girl at Well P701. This shape was much used by Staffordshire potters but infrequently by Spode.

S149 Coffee pot 24cm wide in earthenware also transferred with Girl at Well P701 and fitted with a similar shaped spout as the teapot S147.

S150 Gadroon Edge Antique shape teapot, cover and stand in felspar porcelain decorated in Union Wreath first P823. Notice the handle shape and the lack of gilding.

S150

S151 Gadroon Antique shape cup and saucer in felspar porcelain similarly decorated with Union Wreath first P823 but with expensive added gilding. Notice the cup handle matches the design of that used on the teapot.

S152 Low cup and saucer of a shape similar to plain Pembroke in earthenware decorated with English Sprays P815. Shown with the cup and saucer is a press mould together with a handle moulded from it found nearby during excavations at the Works in 1981. The mould, made in two parts in low-fired earthenware, was filled with clay. The sections were pressed together on the bench and produced the handle which was then fitted to a thrown or moulded cup. In 1843, the charge for making and fitting a handle to a cup was 1d. per cup. The user's name, Simpson, is inscribed on the side of the mould and part of a date, placing the mould in the 1830s, is inscribed on the back of this remaining portion.

S153 Named by Whiter as 4643 shape from its first appearance in the Pattern Books under that number, it is unfortunate that pieces of the shape have been found since with earlier pattern numbers inscribed upon their bases. Research by Robert Copeland in the Works' records found that in 1881, the shape was known at the Works as Persian which is the name adopted here. Comparing the cup in S151 with the taller cup on the left in this illustration the only obvious difference with the two shapes appears to be the shape of the handle and that the decorative print is now Fruit and Flowers P817.

S151

S152

S153

S154

S155

S154 Low Oval Shape teapot, cover and stand and sucrier and cover in bone china decorated in Love Chase P717. A very similar shape was made by the Davenport factory and used in their canewares. Love Chase is an unusual pattern telling the Greek story of Atalanta, Milanion and the golden apples.

S155 Two Bute shape cups and saucers. Left — Breakfast cup in bone china with bowl of cup measuring 10cm diameter Mandarin P606–2. Right — Teacup in earthenware with bowl of cup measuring 8cm diameter Love Chase P717. The breakfast cup has twice the capacity of the teacup.

S156 Two coffee pots in earthenware. Left — Italian P710. Right — Tall Door P615, of Vase shape with an early shaped handle.

S156

S157 Vase-shaped coffee pot in earthenware, Fruit and Flowers P817. Compare the later shape of handle on this pot made about 1826 with the earlier handle on the Tall Door P615 in S155.

S158 and S159 Three creamers in earthenware. S158 low round Egyptian shape decorated in Chinese Garden P631. See illustration S147 for a teapot of the same shape although decorated with Geranium P821. S159 — on Left, Cottage shape in Broseley P614 which is a common Staffordshire shape little used by Spode. On Right — Old Oval shape with Tall Door P615. See S156 for a coffee pot in this pattern.

S157

S158

S159

S160

S160 Two round butter tubs or perhaps sugar boxes in earthenware. On the left Waterloo P709 and on the right Tall Door P615.

S161 Large wavy edge tea bowl and saucer in earthenware decorated with Waterloo P709. Tea bowl 9.5cm diameter and the saucer 14cm.

S162 Two Bute shape coffee cans in earthenware. One in Tall Door P615 and the second in the clumsy Bungalow P617 to which expensive gilding has been added not only to the rim and handle but with an elaborate circlet of complicated gilding added inside the can.

S161

S162

S163

S163 Teabowl and saucer in earthenware decorated with Fence P809–1. This simple uncommon pattern is transferred to a tea bowl and saucer based on the Bute shape of cup and saucer.

S164 Covered muffin dish in earthenware, 23cm diameter Japan P265. The cover fits into a circular groove in the dish.

S165 The centre section of the two forms of Spode toast racks are exactly identical each holding four pieces of toast in earthenware dividers. However, the canoe shape decorated with India P623 is 25cm long and the straight ended version is only 16.5cm long in Broseley P614 The second shape would be much handier for serving breakfast in bed.

S164

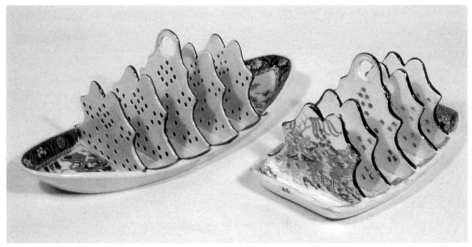

S165

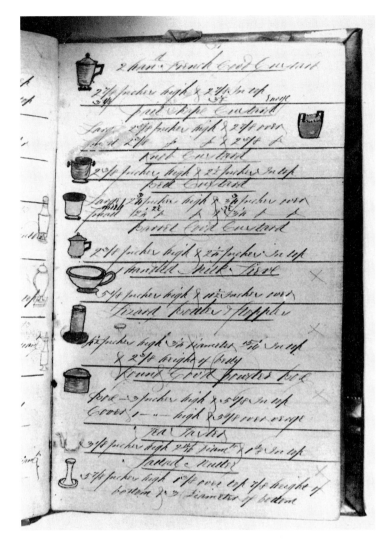

S166

S167 Four egg hoops and a Bell egg cup in Tower P714. As can be seen, the egg hoops can be used either way up with the smaller end used for duck or bantam eggs.

S166 Page 18 Shaw's pocket book, showing small thrown pieces.

S167

S168

S168 Two egg cup stands with Frame egg cups in earthenware. Frame egg cups are moulded with a ridge around the centre so that the cup remains suspended in the stand until lifted out for use. That decorated in Rome P713 holds five egg cups with one placed in the centre. The Italian P710 stand with the carrying handle is arranged with the holes for five egg cups arranged in the outer circle.

S169 Three egg drainers in earthenware, a pair in Willow P609–1 and the third slightly larger with a diameter of 8.5cm in Castle P711.

S170 Beehive in bone china 11.5cm high in Temple P613. Illustrated in three sizes in the 1820 Shape Book. The stand is fixed to the base.

S169

S170

Toilet and personal hygiene

Modern plumbing and the National Health Service have decimated the demand for these most interesting items. Gone are separate chamber-pots except in baby sizes, which are now produced in plastic. No more is there a call for bidets in stands, coach slipper pots, spitting pots, wash hand sets, ewers and basins, toothbrush boxes and other items of unplumbed bedroom toilet. Hardly a single item now graces the present potter's list and those surviving from the past are keenly sort as reminders of a less comfortable age.

S171

S171 Waiting for the fire to be lit for ladies' ablutions at *The Sow and Pigs Hostelry* in Cow Street, Winslow early in the nineteenth century. The individual Spode earthenware pieces are shown separately.

S172 Two earthenware Dutch jugs 29cm high. On the left — Marble P807. On the right — Tower P714. Both are fitted with lifting tabs and each has a capacity of 9 pints. The shape was made in nine sizes with these the largest.

S172

S173 Bidet in mahogany stand with cover. Bidet 47.5cm long in earthenware decorated with Tower P714, with rare Crown impressed mark 5a. Stand overall 52.5cm x 32cm and, without the cover, 46cm high – a comfortable height. The stands were tailored to fit the pans as can be seen. The bidet is decorated on the inside only with the outside left in plain undecorated white earthenware.

S174 Two further items were for ladies' comfort. The bidet shown here is rather larger than the last shown in a stand. Again in earthenware and decorated both inside and outside in Tower P714. It is 53cm long and in itself must have been a more expensive item than a pan decorated on the inside only. The object standing in front of the bidet is a *Bourdalou* or ladies' coach or slipper pot in earthenware, 20cm long and decorated in Italian P710. Ladies' undergarments at that time still had separate legs and were not joined at the centre. The vessel could be used with great convenience during a coach journey although the French name is taken from that of a Jesuit priest at the court of Louis XIV whose discourses detained the ladies of the court so long as to make the use of such a vessel a necessity.

S173

S174

S175

S176

S177

S175 Footbath in earthenware 44.5cm overall in Caramanian P905–8. This is one of the largest of several sizes of footbath. In Shepherd's watercolour of Spode's London warehouse, painted in 1811 and illustrated in Chapter 1, a porter can be seen carrying such a vessel into the building.

S176 Sponge box in earthenware 24cm diameter and 10cm deep decorated in Tower P714. Fitted with a concave dished removable cover pierced for quick drainage. Shown holding a natural sponge.

S177 Open soap box with pierced draining tray in earthenware, 17cm long in Tower P714. The base is of flat slab construction luted together with slip. The moulded draining tray is pierced and is shown holding a piece of bar soap.

S178

S179

S180

S178 Three part soap box in earthenware 12cm long in Tower P714. The base is of flat slab construction with a moulded pierced liner and fitted with a drop in moulded cover.

S179 Ball soap cup in earthenware of circular form decorated in Tower P714. The cup raised on a plain white base.

S180 Earthenware eye bath raised on a moulded stand and printed with a part design overall 7cm high.

S181 Toothbrush box with cover. Earthenware, 20cm overall Union Wreath third P825. The base is fitted with two rests to support two toothbrushes.

S181

S182

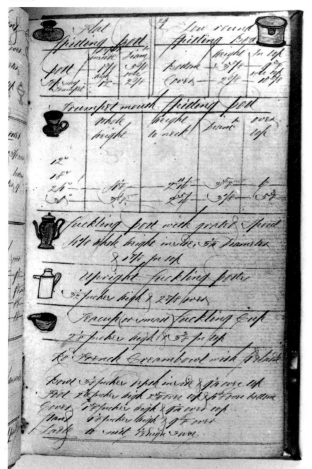

S183

S182   New Shape covered slop bowl in earthenware 25cm diameter, Italian P710. This piece is named in the 1820 Shape Book as the New Shape, although a previous design in not shown. Slop bowls are now rare, as they must have been awkward vessels to handle.

S183   Page 29 of Shaw's pocket book of 1817 illustrating spitting and suckling 'Potts' together with throwing sizes.

S184   Suckling pot with grated spout. Bone china, Temple P613. As can be seen from the illustrated page of Shaw's book, a small cover was originally provided.

S184

S185

S186

S187

S188

S185 Tea cup (or small) suckling cup in earthenware, 5.5cm high, decorated in Tower P714. In our first edition this description was mistakenly given to the Pap boat shown in the next illustration S186.

S186 Pap boat in earthenware 10cm overall, Castle P711. A simple design easy to use.

S187 Churn bottom suckling pot in earthenware 7cm high decorated in Tower P714. The name is taken, once again, from Shaw's book. A neat vessel to hold in the hand.

S188 Upright suckling pot in earthenware 10cm high, Tower P714. The larger size and design of this vessel suggests that it may have been designed for the elderly.

S189 Low, round spitting box with cleaning spout in earthenware, Caramanian P905-21. Cleaning this must have been delegated to the most junior member of the household staff.

S189

S190

S191

S190 Low round spitting pot with cleaning spout and separate removable funnel. In earthenware, 17.5cm diameter Tower P714. It is unusual with a utilitarian vessel such as this to find separate pieces still together.

S191 Trumpet-mouthed spitting pot in earthenware, the trumpet 12cm diameter, Tower P714. The size corresponds closely to the '36' shown by Shaw.

S192 Round divided dressing table box with screw top. In earthenware 12cm diameter, Milkmaid P709. Screw-top toilet boxes were made to prevent the contents being spilled during the hazards of travel. Ceramics were not often used for this purpose.

S193 Covered dressing table or ointment pot in earthenware, 5cm diameter, Tower P714. This little pot is somewhat stained from the contents of previous use. It is described as a 'Covered Pot' in a list of dressing table items in the 1820 Shape Book.

S193

S192

S194

S195

S194 The earthenware flat rimmed chamber pot shown at the rear is 13.5cm in diameter being probably the smallest of the nine sizes made in this shape. Front left is a miniature doll's chamber pot 5.5cm diameter in Filigree P818. On the right is a broken shard of a full size flat rim chamber, dug up during alterations at the Works, decorated in Indian Sporting print P904.

S195 Hand bowl or basin in earthenware 43cm diameter Girl at Well P701. Eight sizes are listed in the 1820 Shape Book; this is one of the largest with a capacity of 2 gallons.

S196 Gadroon Edge ewer and hand basin in earthenware, ewer 27cm high and basin 33.5cm diameter, Jasmine P820. The shape and the print are of the late 1820s.

S197 Second Gadroon Edge ewer and basin decorated in Star Flower P830. Notice the variation in handle shape on the ewer and the differences in the body shape although the ewer shows the seam lines of having been cast in a two part mould. The handle may be of a slightly different shape or perhaps a variation made by the handler when applying the handle.

S196

S197

Useful, ornamental and toys

Additional items from Spode's extraordinary range of ceramic articles which were decorated with underglaze blue prints are included in this section. Of particular interest are the toy pieces. These were made to two markedly different scales of sizes. Dinner ware was made in a much smaller size than were the tea wares. With the latter, teapots and teacups were small but were of a size that could actually be used by the young ladies playing with their dolls. On the other hand, dinner services were smaller still. Soup tureens held insufficient soup to give their proud owners even the smallest taste, but the size was perhaps more in keeping with the dolls themselves. These two sizes remain with us unchanged 200 years later. Such is the hold of tradition. However, to follow the order of the title for this section, first must come useful wares followed by ornamental thus leaving the toys until last.

S198

S198 Supper sets, in their mahogany trays, were made in two shapes, circular and oval. The set illustrated here fits in a 48.5cm tray with four covered sections and centre piece, decorated in Rome P713. The cover of the nearest quadrant section has been removed so that the inside pattern can be seen. Similar sections can be found sub-divided to hold three portions.

S199 A similar supper set in its circular tray fitted with quadrant sections and centre piece uncovered and decorated with Forest Landscape P607, an earlier production.

S199

S200

S200 Complete oval supper set in mahogany tray, 58cm overall. In earthenware and decorated in Flower Cross P804. The four dishes are in two shapes and include covers.

S201 The centre piece of the oval shape supper sets are fitted out as shown with the Rome P713 piece. A raised centre piece with cover and base was fitted internally with a removable bowl, shown separately and a pierced tray to take four frame eggcups and a divided container for salt and pepper. With this tray in use, with the boiled eggs in place, the cover was not used. With the tray and eggcups removed, the contents of the bowl could be kept fly- and dirt-free by the cover.

S202 Cheese cradle in earthenware 31cm overall, Forest Landscape P607–3. Designed to take a large circular cheese on its side. Similar cradles are found in wood with silver fittings.

S201

S202

S203

S204

S205

S206

S203 Stilton pan and cover in earthenware, 32cm overall, Caramanian P905–8. An early and not very practical shape.

S204 New shape Stilton pan and cover in earthenware 25cm Italian P710. The change of shape allowed the cheese to be more easily cut.

S205 Storage jar and cover, earthenware 34.7cm high, Gothic Castle P708. This very large jar can be seen at Spode Works Museum and was a part of the Alexander collection.

S206 Oyster tub in earthenware, Italian P710. This vessel is moulded on the sides to simulate the woven osier of earlier tubs.

S207

S207 Deeper pan than S206 in earthenware and of similar shape, 33cm long overall ribbed at the top with four parallel bands circling the piece but otherwise plain. Decorated with Lucano P712. Exact use uncertain.

S208 Earthenware covered circular pot decorated with Blossom P721. A search through the 1820 Spode Shape Book has not revealed this exact shape amongst the mass of thrown circular lidded boxes so its exact purpose remains unknown. However, the rare decorative pattern makes the piece.

S209 Ornate pierced basket and stand in earthenware with Italian P710. Basket 27cm overall and stand 24cm.

S208

S209

S210

S211

S212

S213

S210 Porter mug in earthenware, 14cm high decorated in Caramanian P905–8. 'Colossal sarcophagus near Castle Rosso'. With a capacity of 3 pints. this must have been a mug for the farmer in the harvest field.

S211 Two smaller mugs in earthenware both decorated with Tower P714. The mug on the left is 10.5cm high and the smaller one is 6.5cm high. Notice the shape of the example on the right is similar to the larger example in S210.

S212 Round foot, New Shape candlestick in earthenware 26cm high, Italian P710. An uncommon survivor of what must have been a large production.

S213 Double extinguisher tray, 13cm in earthenware, Musicians P706, is shown on the left. These were available as single or double trays and were supplied with the extinguishers. A double tray was used, perhaps, for 'his and hers' candlesticks and for reading in bed. On the right is a French Flat candlestick in earthenware, Lange Lijsen P622. Spode listed twenty-three different shapes of candlestick in the 1820 Shape Book.

S214

S214 Four new shape Ewers in earthenware. From left to right — Italian P710, Tower P714, Caramanian P905–20, Union Wreath third P825. The largest holds four pints and the smallest one pint. Shaw, in his pocket book lists twelve sizes of this good-looking and well-designed jug.

S215 Low Dutch jug in earthenware 14cm high Castle P711. A useful size and shape for everyday use.

S216 A covered low Dutch jug in earthenware 13cm high, Milkmaid P702. These covered jugs were made with a strainer behind the spout to hold back the skin forming on boiled milk or other hot liquids. The choice of Milkmaid P702 for decoration would appear very suitable.

S215

S216

S217

S218

S217 A large Dutch jug in earthenware, 29cm high and decorated with one and a half sections of Indian Sporting P904–4. Although this print was used on the soup tureen base, it was the wrong shape for a Dutch jug and a cut down section of the same print was used to fill the white space appearing below the full print on the jug.

S218 Plain barrel jug in earthenware, 17.5cm high, Queen Charlotte P612–2. Another well-designed jug made in nine sizes. Jugs of the same basic shape but wih added moulded hoops were also made.

S219 Dog trough or feeding bowl in earthenware, 18cm overall and decorated in Tower P714. These were made in several sizes; this would suit a small dog. A trough in creamware of similar design, but by Wedgwood, has been noted decorated with a ducal coronet. No doubt the thoroughbred animal using such a superior bowl would not give the user of this blue printed bowl even a friendly sniff.

S220 Wall tile in earthenware 13.3cm square, Italian P710. Spode is not noted for tile manufacture as was his neighbour Minton. This, one of the few marked PODE (without the S), shows no evidence of having been wall mounted. Indeed, wear on the face suggests it might have been used as a teapot stand.

S219

S220

S221

S222

S221 Garden seat in earthenware, 48cm high, Peony P808. The careful arrangement of this bold pattern to give a neat symmetrical appearance, pleasing to the eye, speaks well of the skill of the transferrer and all members of the decorative team. The shape follows a Chinese original.

S222 Earthenware leech jar of ball shape, 25cm high including stand, decorated in Tower P714. It would have had a cover, now missing, to stop the living contents from escaping. Originally a useful article that has outlived its day.

S223 Footed comport in Flower Cross P804, length 30cm overall and complete with set of four trays in two shapes arranged around a raised central dish. Used perhaps for spices or comfits.

S223

S224

S224 Spode's largest dish, 80.5cm long and weighing some 7.25 kilos. The pattern is a double impression of P905–1 'Triumphal Arch', in itself a monument to the skill of the transferrer and a surprise to the local Tripolitanians.

S225 Covered circular container, 25.5cm high and 39cm diameter. Used possibly as a bread bin and decorated in P712 Lucano.

S226 Old shape broth bowl and stand in earthenware, 17cm overall in Italian P710. The New shape broth bowl was very similar, except the cover was ogee shape rather than convex. Both were made in a number of sizes.

S225

S226

S227

S228

S227 Soup tureen and stand in earthenware. Stand 40cm long, of wide oval shape and with redesigned close fitting handles. Less deeply boat-shaped than the previous stand made for this oval-shaped tureen. The tureen shape much used for Filigree P818 was based on a circle, no doubt to match the plain circular dinner plates.

S228 New Shape jar in Stone China, Temple Landscape second P611–1 with additional gilding. This handsome piece is listed in the 1820 Shape Book as having been made in nine sizes. Very

few were decorated with prints as is this example.

S229 Beaker match pot in earthenware, 12cm high, Queen Charlotte P612–2. Another shape not often found with underglaze transfer decoration.

S230 Barrel covered bowpot in earthenware 12cm high, Queen Charlotte P612–2. It appears in the 1820 Shape Book in seven sizes — either plain, as with this example, or for dipping and figures.

S229

S230

S231 Barrel-shaped scent jar with perforated cover. Earthenware and decorated in Tower P714. Two examples are illustrated by Whiter; a plain shape 25cm high and an example moulded with cherubs 18.5cm high. The size of the jars suggests that they would be filled with potpourri to perfume the room rather than the person.

S232 Three miniature items of toilet ware in Filigree P818 backed by a pierced and footed cress dish, 18cm in diameter, to provide a contrast of scale. The toy pieces are a chamber pot, a tooth brush box and a soap box with a pierced drainer.

S233 Toy teaware pieces in Geranium P821, consisting of a plate, a London cup and saucer and a cream jug. The low round Egyptian teapot placed behind is full size 23.5cm overall yet does not look too out of place with the toy pieces which were made to a larger scale to allow their owners to take tea with their dolls.

S231

S232

S233

S234 Toy teaware pieces in earthenware in Milkmaid P702. Although to the same scale as the previous dolls tea service the use of tea bowls rather than cups and saucers is unusual.

S235 A toy earthenware dinner service in Tower P714. A full size 25cm dinner plate is the larger piece shown behind which gives a clear idea of the reduction in scale for toy dinner services when compared with toy teawares. No hope for meat and two vegetables on those tiny plates.

S236 Unmarked earthenware toy sized jug 7cm high with P637 Chinoiserie print showing the border pattern more clearly than does the Spode impressed marked tea plate. The jug is placed before a print taken from a copperplate, still held in Spode Works, engraved with two versions of this pattern. A comparison between the upper and lower versions, both engraved on the same copperplate, shows the latitude allowed to the early less regimented engravers.

S234

S235

S236

Chapter 8

Marks and marking, dates and dating

Before examining the matters foreshadowed in the heading, it might be of interest to discuss three questions that are not always so simple to solve as would be expected. They are:

1. Is it printed or painted?
2. What was it for?
3. Is it all there?

Dealing with the first question, Bat printed designs really should not be a problem. When examined closely, particularly through a magnifying glass, the separate stipple dots, even when mixed with line engraving, will clearly be seen and cannot be mistaken for a hand painted design. Pluck and Dust engravings were nearly always partly stipple punched and therefore on close inspection are not likely to be confused with painted decoration. Underglaze blue, particularly if of simple line engraving without punch work, is not so easy. Sometimes, most often on shaped ware, obvious joins or 'mended' insertions occur. Animals appear in most unhappy half-states missing their hindquarters, or a headless human mounts a shortened stairway. No painter, however slapdash, would perpetrate such butchery and, it must be added, nor would the best of the transferrers that took pride in their skills. However, particularly on plates, such obvious indications of transfer printing will not occur. The design on the centre of the plate will be a single entity without joins and, if line engraved alone, the slight spread of the cobalt into the glaze makes an answer hard to give even with a close inspection. It is in the nankin and outer border that the solution lies. If these are painted rather than printed, the artist will have divided the circular distance in his mind and regulated the pattern so that when working round to the starting point no obvious join appears. Depending on the painter's skill, the pattern may have been squeezed or stretched a little to achieve this aim but its regularity will hardly be impaired. Although both the print designer and the engraver did their best to shape the transfer to fit the piece exactly, a sticky intractable transfer that once in contact could not be adjusted was far more awkward to control than a painter's brush and perfect transfer joins are hard to achieve. This difficulty can be seen in the illustration of the octagonal plate of Nettle P826. The design was line engraved without punch work. The fineness of the shaded lines on the central flowers may suggest engraving and confirmation can be found in the nankin and border. In the nankin a section on the right has been 'mended' with an added inserted piece. In the border on the left two beads fall nearly together and slightly out of line, and close by a section of transfer is entirely missing. Careful inspection of the border will usually give a clear answer to the question: 'Is it printed or is it painted?'

Marks and marking, dates and dating

Is it printed or painted?

1. Enlargement of Bat print P411 showing central portion.
2. Further enlargement to show central punched dots of stipple engraving.
3. Enlargement of Pluck and Dust printed Vine Border P522.
4. Further enlargement showing the use of punch and graver.
5. Section of underglaze blue printed dish in Two Figures P602 showing the simple line engraving used for early underglaze prints.
6. Similar section of underglaze blue printed dish in Floral P901 demonstrating underglaze printing using the fully developed techniques of engraving. Spode engraving at its best.
7. Section of octagonal plate underglaze decorated with Nettle P826 showing faults in transferring the borders.

1

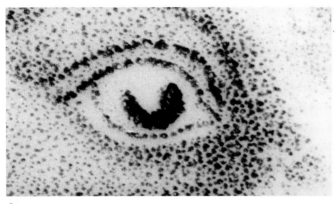

2

3

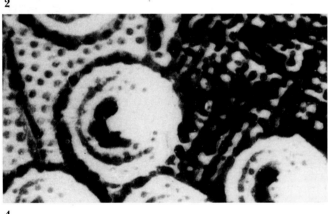

4

5

6

7

The answers to the second question: 'What was it for?' are in many cases most obvious, but it is not these that add to the particular pleasure of collecting 'shapes' in printed ware. The illustrations of Spode's wares at the end of Chapters 5, 6 and 7 will provide some of the answers but not of all the moulded pieces. By some odd mischance no shapes book for moulded wares has survived at Spode Works and now the exact use and proper description of some of the pieces shaped in a mould is still open to speculation. However, the understanding of the use of a piece of Spode's ware will help with the last question: 'Is it all there?'.

Certain items, to perform their function, were made in more than one piece. The teapot springs to mind as the most obvious example. The pot is not complete without its lid or cover; indeed, some teapot shapes were supplied with an additional separate stand. Generally, if a vessel was to

Is it all there?   **8**

8. Low Dutch jugs. On the left with cover and strainer. On the right, an open jug not made with a cover or strainer, showing transferred border inside jug and open spout.
9. French covered custards. Notice that the border is transferred inside the custard although a cover was provided
10. Ends of two soap boxes with draining trays in Tower P714. The tray on the left is rounded on its uppermost edge and cannot be fitted with a cover. The one on the right is indented to take the cover supplied as part of the set.
11. Baker or baking dish in Indian Sporting P904. Note that the pattern is also transferred on the outside and the plain turned out rim would not support a cover.
12. Liner in Castle P711, a sectional part of a covered tureen. The indentation in the rim is to hold a cover or tray. The outside of the liner was not decorated since it would not be seen, fitting as it did into the base.

9

10

11

12

serve a hot liquid or solid, it was made with a cover and was sometimes also provided with a stand. The most commonly found shapes that were first supplied with covers and stands included soup and sauce tureens which also included ladles. However, with the less expensive dinner services these last may have been that item so beloved by the modern motor trade, an optional extra. They were certainly priced separately but perhaps only to cover the cost of the inevitable replacements. Other items that were supplied with both cover and stand were broth bowls and chocolate cups. Items that were not covered but always had a stand were cups, whether the stand was so named or was called a saucer, and round or oval pierced baskets. It is with the articles that could be supplied with or without covers or stands that difficulty arises. The low Dutch jug was made both with and without a cover. With a cover, a strainer was placed behind the pouring lip to hold back the skin on hot milk or other heated liquids, and the inside rim of the jug was not decorated. The open jug was not provided with a strainer and a decorative border was transferred on to the inside rim of the jug, which of course was always visible. Also shown (No.9) are two French covered custards. Although supplied with a cover, the inside rim of these small pieces was transferred with a border pattern of the design used for the external decoration.

A further design supplied both with and without covers was for soapboxes fitted with draining trays. The tray of the box supplied without the cover was rounded on its uppermost edge and was quite unsuitable to take a cover. The top edge of the other tray was indented to take the square cover as can be seen in the illustration. The larger box is complete with two pieces but the smaller requires a cover to complete its original design. An article of dinnerware that can cause difficulty is the three piece oval vegetable tureen. The three parts making the whole are a cover, a liner and a base. Occasionally four-part tureens are found with a handled flat tray added between the cover and the liner. There is a close similarity between the liners of these tureens and a plain oval dish known as a baker. This last, as the name implies, was a dish used for heating or cooking in the oven and yet could be used on the table, a forerunner of ovenproof tableware. Such a useful article must have been made in enormous quantities but they are now uncommon, no doubt due to a distressingly high mortality rate associated with handling over-hot dishes. Illustrated in Fig.11 is a baker from the Indian Sporting service. Note the plain out-turned rim upon which no cover could balance and particularly notice that the exterior is also decorated with transfer prints. Compare this baker with the liner illustrated in No.12. This is a sectional part of a four-part covered tureen. Provision for the tray to fit above is clearly shown. Secondly note that the exterior of the liner is not decorated, indeed, in this example the printed mark of SPODE appears on the side, which would not have been countenanced if it had not been hidden by the base. The Indian Sporting baker is complete in itself but the Castle liner is not, although it looks much the same on cursory inspection. Only with care can a definite answer be given to the question: 'Is it all there?'

Having discussed shapes and designs and the decoration of Spode's printed wares, a look can now be taken at the back and under the base where makers place their marks. Spode's mark falls into two distinct categories. The first group of marks are those put on by the manufacturer to keep his name before his customers in the hope of future business. With these can be coupled the pattern numbers used to ensure continuity of design when repeat orders were obtained. The significance of the second group of marks, generally termed workman's marks, ceased soon after the successful production of the piece and did not extend to the retailer or to the final customer. Spode's workers, in common with the rest of the industry, were paid basically by the piece rather than by the hour. Team production, such as underglaze transfer printing, was paid by the total successful production of the team with each member receiving an agreed proportion. It was the manufacturers' insistence that the count for all piecework included only pieces that were satisfactory after the last oven firing, known as 'good from the oven', that caused the difficulty. As soon as more than one team of printers and transferrers or clayworkers were employed each needed a distinctive mark that would withstand firing so that their pieces could be properly counted. Although not originally designed for such a purpose, workman's marks can now be an aid in the attribution and dating of pieces, but naturally the first group, put on with the very purpose of naming the ware, are of the greater help.

Spode's maker's marks were applied in three forms, by impressing a stamp into the body of the ware before firing, termed an 'impressed mark', secondly by painting or writing the name on or under the glaze and lastly by transferring a printed mark on or under the glaze. All Spode's maker's marks incorporate the word SPODE and most are just this single name alone. Any mark including the words LATE SPODE is what it suggests, a mark used on wares manufactured at the Works after the withdrawal of the Spode family. Pattern numbers were always hand written or painted, usually on the glaze but occasionally under glaze when used in conjunction with the later high-temperature colours.

Like most factories of the period, the use of makers' marks increased as the years went by. The earliest wares were never marked and the variations of the large impressed mark 1 are very rarely seen. The very small mark 2a is the first that appears in any regularity and its use on underglaze blue printed ware is an almost certain indication of early manufacture. The first bone china printed tea services were marked, if at all, only on the major pieces and then frequently with just the pattern number. Initially cups and saucers were unmarked, then later perhaps only by the pattern number before full marking became more frequent. The felspar marks 40, 41 and 42, expensive items applied by Bat printing, were normally confined to the larger pieces and again are unlikely to be found on cups and saucers which had to make do with a pattern number, a cheaper painted mark or sometimes with no mark at all. Generally, by about 1815, unmarked printed ware became the exception although some patterns continued to be sparsely marked, particularly blue and gold Bat prints and a few underglaze blue patterns where an occasional pressed mark is all that can be found. As marking was a definite expense, some patterns may have been left unmarked to sell at a lower price.

In listing and numbering the makers' marks used on Spode printed wares, use has been made of the applicable section of the full schedule of Work's marks devised and annotated by Robert Copeland. Marks not found on printed ware have been omitted and added are a number of impressed marks, the purpose of which cannot definitely be explained, yet are helpful in the attribution of the ware. The description of the use of the various marks has been limited to their application on printed wares alone.

Spode's maker's marks used on printed wares

Impressed marks

These marks are made by impressing a stamp into the unfired clay. The stamps themselves were of clay formed in a sprig mould and then hard fired. With continuous use they wore down and were replaced perhaps by a later design, thus marks 2, 3 and 4 would have had an overlap period between changes of design.

Reference Number	Mark	Probable years of use	Description and usage
1		1785–90	Several variations of this mark occur, all of large size approximately 16mm long. This is an early mark which has been found on pieces of Two Figures P602.
2a		1790–1805 and perhaps 1810	Small, varying in size from 8 to 10mm. long. Probably the first regular mark found on early underglaze printed ware.
3		1800–20	Found on earthenware and very rarely on bone china. The mark is usually straight but is sometimes very slightly curved perhaps through variations in the moulding of the stamps.
4		1812–33	An impressed mark found on earthenware and very variable in size. Distinguishable from mark 2a by the serifs on the letter S. The numerals 22 are not part of the marker's mark but are a workman's mark.
5a		1815	A rare mark found on large moulded earthenware pieces. The bidet in the stand S173 (page 294) is so marked. The probable year of use should only be treated as a guide. It has been suggested that the mark may have been especially brought out for the coronation of George IV in 1820.
7		1822–33	Impressed, with several minor variations, into the body so named.

Additional impressed marks of uncertain original use

Reference Number	Mark	Probable years of use	Description and usage
15		1803–1812	These letters, either singly or together as shown, are found impressed into the footrim of bone china teapots, sugar boxes and cream jugs usually of the New Oval shape. The letter O in particular varies in form. Sometimes the pattern number is added but with a single exception they have not been noted used in conjunction with a full Spode maker's mark.

Impressed body marks on the later felspar porcelain wares

A number of these are listed in the various Recipe and notebooks and will be found impressed into the ware. Their use continued after March 1833 and the mark alone cannot give an exact date of manufacture. Each different body had its correct and most compatible glaze and a probable explanation for the use of these impressed marks was to ensure the use of the correct glaze on what are visually identical bodies.

Reference Number	Mark	Probable years of use	Description and usage
16	✛	From February 1828	As shown in the larger Recipe Book, this impressed mark indicates felspar porcelain no. 10, the body chosen for the introduction of the felspar porcelain in November 1821 although this mark was not used until February 1828.
17	✝	From December 1829	Shown as an impressed mark in Thos. Grocott's book, this indicates body no.13 coming into use in December 1829.
18	F	From September 1832	An impressed mark denoting felspar body no.17, the last introduction before the change of ownership.

Painted marks individually written by painters and guilders

Reference Number	Mark	Probable years of use	Description and usage
22		On printed ware 1803–33	These marks were painted on the glaze in the Enamelling Department. The marks shown are a selection of the various handwriting of the many gilders and decorators. The principal colour was red but also used were purple, black, brown and gold. Pattern numbers were often written close to these marks in the same handwriting and at the same time. In printed wares, painted marks are normally found on bone china decorated with Bat prints.
23			
24			

Transfer printed marks

With underglaze printing the earlier transfer marks were engraved on the copperplates with the pattern design, thus a mark was available with each print from that copper. Not every copper was so engraved hence the erratic application of the earlier printed marks in particular. Somewhat later this method was supplemented with special engraved marks coppers from which a sheet of marks was printed to be cut up and used as required. Mark 33 was used in this way and occasionally a green printed mark can be found transferred on blue printed ware and vice versa. The elaborate felspar marks were individually Bat printed with the application of a mark being the same cost as a decorative Bat print. It is not surprising that full felspar marks do not often appear on the simpler felspar shapes of Bat printed felspar porcelain such as cups and saucers.

Reference Number	Mark	Probable years of use	Description and usage
31 32		1800–20	This and its slightly curved variant Mark 32 are found on both underglaze blue printed earthenware and bone china.
33		1810–33	The most common underglaze printed mark found on earthenware, bone china and felspar porcelain.
33a		1817–33	A smaller version of Mark 33 found with Bromley P614, a pattern introduced about 1817.

Reference Number	Mark	Probable years of use	Description and usage
34	SPODE	Perhaps before 1800	Seen on copperplates of Temple Landscape first P601 and Trophies–Nankin P628.
35		1814–1833	This variation seems to have been confined to Milkmaid P702.
36		1810–25	The most usual mark found with patterns Lattice Scroll P803 and Rome P713 introduced in 1810 and 1811 respectively. Has also been found on a few pieces of other patterns of a similar developed engraving. It could be the mark used by a particular engraver.
37 and 37a		Perhaps 1810–15	Both marks 37 and 37a, two sizes of the same design, are rare. Being rather indistinct with the blue running into the wording may account for this rarity.
38a		Before 1796	This scroll mark is engraved on a single copperplate of Rotunda P707. Spode's London showroom left Fore Street in 1796. A piece with this mark has not yet been found.
39 and 39a		1806–18	Probably introduced after the visit of the Prince Prince of Wales in 1806. It was rarely used, but copperplate still exists engraved with six of these marks arranged for transfer press printing. Mark 39a is a similar mark, but this time Bat printed from a different copperplate. Oddly enough the dish with flower sprigs of pattern 500, illustration S41, has a press printed mark no.39 in Iron Red.
40 and 40a		1821	The first felspar mark used in 1821 only. Not so far found on Bat printed pieces. This and Marks 40a and 40b are always Bat printed on the glaze in puce.
40a		1822–33	This is mark 40 with the date removed. Again it is a most uncommon mark.
40b		1822–33	A smaller version of 40 and 40a which has a variation in the letter face of Stoke upon Trent. Another rare mark.

Reference Number	Mark	Probable years of use	Description and usage
41		1822–33	The most usual form of the felspar porcelain mark. At least two sizes were engraved.
42		After 1822	Mark no. 42 is a variation of no.1 with the names of Spode and Copeland replacing Spode at the head and LONDON added at the foot. No piece of any sort has yet been recorded with this variation, although the Bat copperplate remains at the Works.
47		1813 and perhaps to 1833	The pseudo-Chinese seal mark used on stone china. It is problematical whether the mark or the body continued long after the introduction of SPODE'S NEWSTONE body in 1822.
48		1815–22 and perhaps to 1833	A trimmed down version of mark 47 and introduced at a slightly later date. Probably made to fit items too small for mark 47. Has been found with Grasshopper P621 pattern on eggcups and teacups.
49		About 1824–33	An improved body of ivory appearance often used in conjunction with Gadroon shaped wares. Blue Rose P822, introduced in 1825, was often transferred to this body.
50		1826, or a little later, to 1833	Another new body similar to Spode's Imperial. The mark with several variations in size and minor detail is usually found on printed wares with added painted decoration.
63		1830–1833	This special cartouche for Floral P901 pattern shows the increased awareness of the advertising value of pattern names and makers' marks.

Reference Number	Mark	Probable years of use	Description and usage
64		1831–1833	Each scene was named in a similar cartouche in this multi-pattern scene P907. After 1833, the name of SPODE was erased and the cartouche was used with a separate COPELAND & GARRETT mark. The design and marks are commonly found in green but they were also issued in blue and in black.
65			A short-lived promotional mark, a forerunner of 'Buy British'. Two versions are known with the second omitting the word WHEAL which is Cornish for mine. Found on Spode's most up to date patterns of that time, India P623 and occasionally Tower P714, both first produced in 1815 and Italian P710 introduced in 1816.
66			This is an example of the titles used with a quite separate maker's mark on the various scenes of Indian Sporting pattern P904. The use of these titles, an added expense, seems to have gradually lapsed. Their use is less likely on the later productions of Indian Sporting prints particularly in those made in the Copeland & Garrett and Copeland periods.

Workman's marks appear on underglaze printed wares in the same three forms as do the maker's marks, impressed, painted and printed. Of the first group singularly little is certainly known. The most common impressed workman's marks on earthenware are numerals usually placed close to the impressed maker mark. Their significance is unclear but it is most likely that they were used in the clay department as a mark for the piecework count after first firing. Bone china and felspar porcelain are rarely found with impressed marks except marks 16, 17 and 18 which are already tabled as body marks. In addition, Old Oval shape teapots and sugar boxes are sometimes found with one-, two- or three-figure numbers following a dot impressed deeply and centrally. The covers also have an impressed number but usually not the same as that on the main piece. Neither are ever the pattern number of the decoration, and their purpose is unknown, except perhaps possible use for the workman's piecework count.

The second group, consisting of small underglaze painted marks, is probably the most helpful in attribution of underglaze blue printed pieces found without a Spode maker's mark. It seems likely that each printer, with his transferring team, had his own individual mark, again used for identification at the piecework count after firing of the ware. Some workman's marks first occur on early ware and continue on to later pieces; others occur briefly and are rarely seen. No doubt some printers stayed long in the employ of the Company and others quickly moved on, thus explaining the very noticeable difference in frequency with which various workman's marks are found. By no means all the early underglaze printed wares received Spode's maker's marks, but many that did also have a simple painted workman's mark and similar marks are found on pieces without maker's marks.

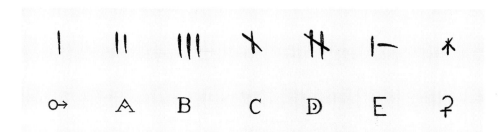

Underglaze blue workman's marks. The first seven on the top line are painted, with the first five being the earliest. The remainder are printed marks.

The third group of workman's marks are those printed in underglaze blue. Their purpose seems to have been the same as the painted marks: to identify the printer and his transferring team for payment of piece-rates. They are found on later printed wares and were simply a quicker way of marking more complicated shapes than could be done by hand painting. Capital letters are frequently seen that are obviously printed, but it is not always easy to be sure whether some marks were painted or printed, nor is it of great moment as they served the same purpose.

Similar workman's marks are found on other manufacturers' wares since payment by the piece 'good from the oven' was universal throughout the trade. Over fifty painted and printed workman's marks have been recorded on Spode's wares which gives some indication of the printing operation in Spode's time. A selection of the more often seen are illustrated but similar workman's marks found on pieces without a maker's mark can only clinch the attribution as manufactured by Spode if the pattern, body, shape and glaze also fit Spode wares.

No painted or printed workman's marks have been noted on on-glaze Bat prints nor with Pluck and Dust printing. Perhaps Bat printers' work was counted differently or a printer specialised in a single subject to the exclusion of all else, thus making counting a simple business.

Having now examined all aspects of the three printing methods employed in Spode Works during the ownership of the Spode family, it may be a matter of some regret to find that only underglaze blue printed ware has survived to continue the long tradition of excellence founded by Josiah Spode the first in 1784.

General Index

(Page numbers in **bold** refer to illustrations)

ackey, 193, 194
Argyll, Duke of, 265
Arms and Badge Books, 60, 64, 80
art forms (see Chapter 3), 43–59
Astbury-Jackfield ware, 81, 88, 146
Astbury-type, 163

Badge and Proof Book, 151
Balsam of Capivi, 65
Banks, William, 19, 22
Barker, Elizabeth, 23
Barker, J., 18
Bartolozzi, Francesco, 32, 121
Bat printed coppers, 48, 54,
Bat printed decoration, 54, 75, 165
Bat printed ware, 88, 155
Bat printing, 33, **33**, 34, **34**, 35, 38, 41, 54, 165
Bat prints, catalogue of, 94–155
Battam, Thomas, 32, 35, 36, 37, 38, 75, 171
Battersea Enamel Works, 31
Bell, George, 80, 84
Bell, Richard, 80, 84, 174
Bird prints, 92
'black printing', 32, 84, 171
Bloomfield, Robert, 124, 125
blue printed dinner plates, comparison of, 194–196
Bolton, James, 179
bone china shapes, 69
bone china, 60, 76, 89, 92, 94, 146, 147, **147**, 150, 157, 161, 162, 163, 164, 165, 166, 167, 168, 169, 185, 189, 199, 201, 279, 281, 284, **284**, 297, **297**
breakfast cup, 159, **159**
Brooks, John, 31, 43
Bruce, George, 80, 84
Bruce, Kate, 80
Buffon's Natural History, 146, 147, 148
burin or graver, **45**, **46**, 47, 48, 94
Burns, Robert, 117
Bute shape, 68, **68**, 69, 76, 88, 89, 159, 163, **163**, 199, **199**
Bute shape tea wares, 125, 157, 159, **159**, 160, **160**, 175, **175**, 178, **178**, 203, 219, **219**, 281, 284, **284**, 287, **287**, 289, **289**, 290, **290**
Byerly, Thomas, 72

Cabinet of Quadrupeds, 147
Catalogue of underglaze blue prints, 197–257
Caughley, 32, 50
Caxton, William, 31
chalcedony body, 161, **161**
Chamberlain's Worcester, 54, 108
charcoal grey, 43, 56, 76, 84, 86, 92, 157, 159, 160, 161, 162, 163, 164, 165, 166, 169
Chinese art, 55, 175, **175**
Chinese imports, 88
Chinese porcelain, 43
Church, John, 146, 147
Cinque Port Volunteers, 135
Coalport, 208
cobalt blue, 43, 44, 45, 55, 56, **61**, 76, 77, 172, 186–189, 193, 194
Colour Match Book, 166
Colour Mixing Book, 81, **81**, 84
Colour Recipe Books, 159, 174
Common shape, 159, **159**
Copeland and Garrett, 64, 178, 197, 198, 230, 324
Copeland, William Taylor, 26, 28, 29, 32, 64, 80, 255
Copperplate Magazine, 108, 116, 117
copperplate makers, 56–58
copperplate makers' marks, 58–59
copperplate room, **55**
Cowper, William, 124

creamware, 19, 30, 31, 63, 67, 110, 155, 165, 166, 177, 185, **185**, 256, **256**
Cruikshank, Isaac, 141, **141**

dates and dating, 313–325
Davenport, 208, 287
drabware, 91, **91**, 146, 163, **163**, 169, 170, **170**, 185
Dudley, Charles, 84, 85
Dudley, Hester (née Savory), 86
Dutch jug, 130, 131, 137, **137**, 139, **139**, 170, **170**, 179, **179**, 220, 293, **293**, 306, **306**, 307, **307**, 315, **315**

engraver's tools, 45, **45**
Engravers Badge Crest and Letter Book (1868), 60, 70, **71**, 71
Engraving Shop Badge and Proof Book, 64, **65**
engraving techniques (see Chapter 3) 43–59
Etruria, 72
Etruscan shape, 164, **164**, 284, **284**
Exhibition Catalogue, 1851, 171

felspar porcelain, 163, **163**, 164, **164**, 178, **178**, 185, 189, 211, 285, **285**, 286, **286**
Fenton, Thomas, 29
Finedon, William, 124
Flight, Barr and Barr, 125

Garner, Robert, 18
Garrett, Thomas, 29
Gentleman's Magazine, 141
George Barnett's Pocketbook, 74
George III, 132, **132**, 133, **133**
gilded decoration, 79, **79**, 157, 160, 161, 162, 166, 168, 172, 179, **179**, 180, **180**, 184, 278, **278**, 289, **289**, 310, **310**
glost firing, 171
glost oven, 174, 187
glue (recipe for), 73
glue bats, 42, 73, 74
Godden, Geoffrey, 206
gold Bat printing, 77, 90, **90**, 91, **91**
graver or burin, **45**, **46**, 47, 48, 76, 94
Great Invasion Scare (1803), 92, 130, 143, 144
Greatbatch, William, 18
Green, Guy, 31
Grocott, Thomas, 52, 67, 189, 224

Harlow, John, 58
Harris & Co., 57
Harris & Eastwood, 57
Harris, G., 54
Harrison Spode & Co., 24
History of the Staffordshire Potteries (1829), 18, 32, 50, 186
Holden's Annual London and County Directory, 58
Holden's Triennial Directory, 58
Holdway, Paul, 35, 46, **46**, 47, **47**, 191, 218, 244
hot printing process, 50
Howitt, Samuel, 43, 146, 147, **147**, 148, **148**

Industrial Revolution, 15, 20, 25, 38

Jewitt, Llewellyn, 50, 52
Josiah Wedgwood's Common Place Book, 74

Keele University Library, 69
Kent's Directory, 56, 58

Lamb, Charles, 84
lampblack, 47, 65, 173, **173**
Lane Delph, 17
Large, Thomas, 56
lead poisoning ('potter's rot'), 171, 187

Leeds Catalogue of Creamware, 269
Light Horse Volunteers, 137
London Gazette, 24
London shape, 99, 100, 162, **162**, 173, 284, 311, **311**
Low Oval shape, 287, **287**

marks and marking, 313–325
marks, impressed, 319–320
marks, painted, 321
marks, transfer printed, 321–324
marks, workman's, 324–325
Masons, Miles, 54, 108, 208
Middle Brook, 44, 71
Ming porcelain, 186
Minton, Thomas, 50, 52, 307
Morland, George, 146, 150, **150**
Mountford & Spode, 22, 32
Mountford, Elizabeth, 22
Mountford, Thomas, 15, 22, 23, 24

Napoleonic Bat prints, 12
Napoleonic cartoons, 130–144, **130–144**
Napoleonic mugs and jugs, 84
Napoleonic prints, 56, 79, 92, 93, 94, 121
Nelson, Admiral Lord, 93, 129, **129**
Nelson, Lady, 129
New Hall, 54, 77, 91, 108, 113, 126
New Oval shape, 85, 90, **90**, 99, 124, 125, 150, 156, 157, 158, 159, **159**, 160, **160**, 161, **161**, 184, **184**, 203, **203**, 281, **281**
Newcastle and General Pottery and Commercial Directory, The, (1822–23), 58, 80
Norfolk cup, 159, **159**
Northcote, James, 128, **128**

Oil of Swallows, 65
Old Oval shape, 76, 85, 89, 92,150, 157, 158, 159, **159**, 205, **205**, 279, **279**, 280, **280**, 288, **288**
on-glaze Bat printing, 11, 32, 40, 41, 76, 88
on-glaze black printing, 88
on-glaze glue Bat printing (see Chapter 5), 73–93
on-glaze Pluck and Dust printing, 54, (see Chapter 6), 171–185
on-glaze printed patterns, 62
Oriental art tradition, 43, 88, 101
Outrim, William, 52

Pattern Books, 12, 60, 61, **61**, 62, 63, **63**, 64, 76, 77, 80, 81, 82, **82**, 88, 89, 92, 100, 101, 121, 123, 125, 146, 153, 157, 164, 166, 172, 173, 174, 175, 176, 178, 185, 194, 211, 220, 226, 229, 286
patterns and proofs (see Chapter 4), 60–72
Payne's grey, 193
Peace of Amiens, 131
Pembroke Flower Sprays, 92
Pembroke shape, 89, 92, 94, 99, 100, 118, 151, 153, 164, **164**, 286, **286**
Penkhull, 11
Penny Magazine, 36, **36**, 258
Pillement, Jean, 93, 94
Pluck and Dust coppers, 50
Pluck and Dust printing, 11, 32, 42,76, 78, 87
Pluck and Dust printed ware, 83, **83**, 175–183
Pollard, Robert, 146, 149, **149**
Poole, Charles, 31
Post Office London Directory, The, 58
Pottery Troop of Volunteers, 92, 130
Pratt, Felix, 193
Prince of Wales feather mark, 83, 165, 184
printing, history of at Spode Works 1784–1833, 13–15

Prints for Pembroke Shape Wares P278 to P282, **118–119**
Proof Books, 60
Pull and Dust, 42
punch, 76, 94

Queensware, 31

Ranelagh Gardens, 191, **191**, 192, **192**
Recipe Books, 60, 64, 66, **66**, 73, 80, 81, **81**, 88, 189
Red Shop, 171
redware, 88
Revived Jackfield ware, 169, 170, **170**
Roden, Peter F.C., 17

Sadler, John, 31, 76
Savory, Hester (service) P276 and P277, 84, 85, 108, 118, **118**, 158, 164, 167
Savory, Joseph, 84
Sayer, Robert, 93
Scott, Sir Walter, 168
Sentinel Directory, 80
Shafe, John, 58, 126,
Shape Book (1820), 60, 68, **68**, 68, 69, 162, 168, 169, 276, 292, 297, 299, 300, **300**, 304, 305, 310
Shape Book, shapes and sizes (see Chapter 4), 60–72
shapes of wares decorated with Pluck and Dust prints, 184–185,
shapes of wares decorated with underglaze blue prints, 258–312
shapes: Bute, London and Pembroke, 156
Sharpe's *Poets*, 124, 125

Shaw, Simeon, 18, 23, 28, 32, 36, 50, 52, 186
Sherborne Castle P269, 117, **117**, **213**
single punching, 48
sizes: Teacup, Norfolk and breakfast cup, 156
Smith, Jeremiah, 22
Spode & Copeland, 26, 28
Spode & Tomlinson, 22, 32
Spode I, Josiah, **10**, 11, 17, 18, 22, 23, 24, 26, 28, 32, 50, 52, 56, 67
Spode II, Josiah, 11, **11**, 19, 22, 23, 24, 25, 26, 28, 29, 60, 64, 68, 89, 92, 130, 160, 190
Spode III, Josiah, 24, 25, 28, 29, 64, 80
Spode IV, Josiah, 29
Spode Museum, 52, 279, 303
Spode Museum Trust, 214
Spode Society Recorder, 242
Spode Society Review, 11
Spode, Copeland & Son, 26
Sporting Magazine, The, 147
Sprig Proof Book, 175
Staffordshire General Commercial Directory, The, 53, 58
Staffordshire Pottery Volunteers, 24
Staffordshire Sentinel, 52
stipple dots, 76
stipple engraving, 49, 54, 114, 122, 150
stipple punched, 49, 76, 93, 94, 146

Tam o' Shanter, 44, 71
The Ceramic Art of Great Britain, 50
Times, The, 24
Tomlinson, 15, 22, 32
Trafalgar, Battle of, 93, 129, **129**
transfer printing processes (see Chapter 2), 31–42

Turner, Thomas, 32, 50, 186

UK International Genealogical Index, 56
underglaze blue printed pearlware, 69
underglaze blue printing, 11, 50, 35, **35**, 40, 43, 54, 62, 63
underglaze printing, 186–196
Universal Directory, 56, 57

Views of Rome and its Vicinity, 215

Wales, Prince of, 28
Walmer Castle, 135
Warburton, Peter, 77, 78, 91
Water of Ayr, 44, 71
Wedgwood, Josiah, 108, 175, 180
Wedgwood I, Josiah, 31, 52, 71
Wedgwood II, Josiah, 71, 72
Wedgwood, Ralph, 108
West Clandon Park, 116
West Wycombe Park, 116, 118, **118**
Westall, Richard, 124, 125
Whieldon, Thomas, 17, 18, 19, 52
Whiter, Leonard, 61, 85, 89, 153, 164, 197, 207, 211, 229, 286, 311
Whittow & Harris, 57
Whittow & Son, 57
Whittow, Benjamin, 54, 56
Williamson, Hugh, 29, 195, 197, 201, **201**, 206, 261, **261**, 267, **267**, 274, **274**, 275, **275**, 278, **278**
Winterthur Museum, USA, 68

Yuan dynasty, 186

Pattern Index

(Page numbers in **bold** refer to illustrations)

Aesop's Fables (P907), 46, 195, 230, 250–252, **250–252**
Animals (P400), 168
Animals, Birds, Sporting subjects and Armorial bat prints P400 series, 146–155
Armorial Bat Prints (P490), P152, P159, 155
Autumn (P336), 125, **125**

Bamboo (P501), 83, **83**, 172, 173, 175, **175**, 181, 184, **184**
Bat printed landscapes P220 series, 120
Beggar at the Gate (P341), 74, **74**
Birds in Branches (P400), 164
Birds on Branches (P460–P476), 153–154
Birds in Garden Landscapes (P440 to P451), 92, 151–153
Birds in Garden Landscapes (2nd series) (P460–P476), 92
Bisham Abbey (P268), 116, **117**
Blue Rose (P822), 71, 181, 196, 225, **225**
Bolton's Birds (P529), 173, 177, 179, **179**, 183
Bone of Contention or the English Bulldog and the Corsican Monkey, The (P381), 131, **131**
Botanical (P903), 181, 195, 230, 232, 233, **233**
Botanical Flowers, (P531), 180, **180**, 183
Bothwell Castle (P275), 117, **118**
Bowpot (P813), 222, **222**
Britannia Blowing up the Corsican Bottle Conjurer (P391), 141, **141**
British Flowers (P902), 232, **232**
Broseley (P614), **45**, 190, 204, **204**, 283, **283**, 284, **284**, 288, **288**, 290, **290**

Bud and Flower (P636), 211, **211**
Buffalo (P616), **71**, 205, **205**
Bullfinch (P529-1), 179, **179**
Bungalow (P617), 200, 205, **205**, 289, **289**
Butterflies and Moths with Sea Shells (P506), 176, **176**, 182

Canary Bird, The, (P529-5), 179, **179**
Caramanian (P905), 56, 87, **87**, 189, 195, 216, 217, 230, 242–247, **242–247**, 260, **260**, 271, **271**, 273, **273**, 274, **274**, 295, **295**, 298, **298**, 303, **303**, 305, **305**, 306, **306**
Castle (P711), 53, 189, 215, **215**, 261, **261**, 267, **267**, 269, **269**, 271, **271**, 276, **276**, 292, **292**, 298, **298**, 306, **306**
Centinel at his Post, or Boney's peep into Walmer Castle, The (P385), 135, **135**,
Chantilly Sprig (P810), 221, **221**
Chinese Flowers (P816), 223, **223**
Chinese Garden (P631), 210, **210**, 288, **288**
Chinese of Rank (P632), 210, **210**
Chinoiserie (P637), 211, 312, **312**
Chrysanthemum and Bamboo (P833), 228, **228**
Classical and Contemporary Humanity P300 Series, 89, 121–145
Cock and Bull Story, A (P383), 133, **133**
Contemporary Humanity (P300), 162, **162**
Convolvulus (P819), 195
Convolvulus border (P525), **81**, 178, **178**
Conway Castle (P272), 117, **117**
Cottages (P250 to P263), 114–116, **113–116**
Country Scene (P704), 213, **213**

Country Scenes (P216 to P234), **110–113**
Curtis flowers (P530), 176, **180**

Dagger landscape first (P603), 198, **198**
Dagger landscape second (P604), 198, **198**
Dagger landscape third (Mandarin) (P605), 199, **199**
Daisy (P805), 190, 219, **215**
Daisy and Bead (P827), 226, **226**
Dragons first (P626), 208, **208**
Dragons second (P627), 208, **208**
Dragons third (P528), 172, 173, 178, **178**, 183, 185
Dresden Border (P719), 217, **217**
Dunrobin Castle (P265), 167, **167**

End of Bonaparte, The (P384), 134, **134**,
English Sprays (P815), 181, 223, **213**, 286, **286**
European and Mediterranean subjects P700 series, 211–218

Fence (P809), 221, **221**, 290, **290**
Fibre (P532), 180, **180**, 183
Filigree (P818), 65, 223, **223**, 260, **260**, 262, **262**, 266, **266**, 300, **300**, 311, **311**
Flying Pennant (P610-1), 202, **202**
Floral (P901), 189
Floral Patterns P800 series, 218–229
Flower Cross (P804), 219, **219**, 273, **273**, 302, **302**, 308, **308**
Flower Sprays (P835), 229, **229**
Flowers and Fruit P100 series, 94–107

Pattern Index

Forest Landscape (P607), 187, **187**, 188, **188**, 195, 197, 200, **200**, 201, **201**, 301, **301**, 302, **302**
French Birds (P718), 217, **217**
Fruit and Flowers (P817), 22, 223, **223**, 286, **286**, 288, **288**
Fruits (P100), 160, **160**

Geometric border first (P526), 178, **178**, 183
Geometric border second (P527), 178, **178**, 183
Geranium (P821), 163, **163**, 181, 193, 224, **224**, 253, **253**, 255, **255**, 257, **257**, 266, **266**, 284, **284**, 288, **288**, 311, **311**
Girl at Well (P701), 181, 190, 211, **211**, 225, 285, **285**, 300, **300**
Gloucester (P811), 221, **221**, 280, **280**
Goldfinch (P529-2), 179, **179**
Goldfinch in its Nest (P529-3), 179, **179**
Gothic Castle (P708), 214, **214**, 303, **303**
Grand Triumphal Entry of the Chief Consul into London, The (P387), 137, **137**,
Grapes (Uva) (P834), 228, **228**
Grasshopper (P621-1), 167, 206, **206**, 262, **262**, 264, **264**
Greek (P906), 43, **51**, 181, 195, 230, 248–250, **248–250**, 253, **253**, 264, **264**, 265, **265**, 272, **272**, 273, **273**
Group (P814), 222, **222**

Honeysuckle and Parsley (P829), 226, **226**
Humanity, (P300), 81, 160, 161

India (P623), 71, 207, **207**, 263, **263**, 268, **268**, 290, **290**
Indian Sporting (P904), **48**, 53, 189, 197, 230, 235–241, **235–241**, 261, **261**, 262, **262**, 265, **265**, 277, **277**, 300, **300**, 307, **307**
Island Near Henley (P281), 118, **118**
Italian (P710), 49, 53, 65, 190, 214, **214**, 266, **266**, 270, **270**, 272, **272**, 287, **287**, 292, **292**, 294, **294**, 297, **297**, 303, **303**, 304, **304**, 305, **305**, 306, **306**, 307, **307**, 309, **309**
Italian Church, (P709), 190

Japan (P625), 207, **207**, 262, **262**, 290, **290**
Jasmine (P820), 71, 196, 224, **224**, 255, **255**, 276, **276**, 300, **300**
John Bull extinguishing a Firebrand (P394), 144, **144**
John Bull giving Boney a Pull (P380), 130, **130**
John Bull guarding the Toy-Shop or Boney crying for some more Playthings (P389), 139, **139**

King of Brobdingnag and Gulliver, The (P382), 132, **132**,

Landscapes P200 series, 108, 163, **163**, 165, **165**, 167, 168, **168**
Landscape (P201 to P285), 54
Lange Lijsen (Long Elisa) (Jumping Boy) (P622), 207, **207**, 264, **264**, 265, **265**, 267, **267**, 305, **305**
Last Litter, The (P417), 150, **150**, 159, **159**,
Lattice Scroll (P803), 219, **219**, 257, **257**, 263, **263**, 273, **273**
Leaf (P806), 190, 220, **220**
Lily (P801), 190, 218, **218**
Lindertis (P284), 119, **119**
Long Bridge (P619), 197, 206, **206**
Love Chase (P717), 43, 211, 217, **217**, 287, **287**

Love Chase border (P524), 178, **178**, 182
Lucano (P712), 53, 215, **215**, 304, **304**
Lyre, (P802), 190, 219, **219**

Mandarin (P605-1), 278, **278**, 287, **287**
Marble (Mosaic) (Cracked Ice and Prunus) (P807), 220, **220**, 293, **293**
Milkmaid, (P702), 190, 212, **212**, 216, 299, **299**, 306, **306**, 312, **312**
Monkey (P381), 131, **131**
Morning or the Benevolent Sportsman (P422), 150, **151**
Multi-scene patterns P900 Series, 230–257
Musicians (P706), 213, **213**, 305, **305**

National Contrasts or Bulky & Boney (P392), 142, **142**
Net (P620), 71, 206, **206**
Nettle (P826), 226, **226**
Notable Buildings (P264 to P277 and P284), **116–118**

Oak Border (P523), 83, **83**, 173
Old Peacock (P624), 207, **207**
Old Performer playing on a New Instrument or one of the 42nd Touching the Invincible (P386), 136, **136**

Oriental Birds (P633), 210, **210**, 260, **260**

Pagoda (P635), 211, **211**
Parasol figure (P606), 199, **199**, 275, **275**
Pattern Books, 12, 60, 61, 61, 62, 63, 63, 64, 76, 77, 80, 81, 82, 82, 88, 89, 92, 100, 101, 121, 123, 125, 146, 153, 157, 164, 166, 172, 173, 174, 175, 176, 178, 185, 194, 211, 220, 226, 229, 286
Patterns with Animals, Birds, Sporting subjects and Armorial prints P400 series,155
Peony (P808), 220, **220**, 308, **308**
Peony and Willow (P634), 210, **210**
Peplow (P812), 222, **222**
Pidcock's Grand Menagerie, Exeter Change with an exact representation of Bonaparte...on or before Christmas (P388), 138, **138**
Portland Vase (P720), 189, 195, 218, **218**

Queen Charlotte (P612-1), 203, **203**, 258, 266, **266**, 272, **272**, 283, **283**, 307, **307**, 310, **310**

Radiating Leaves (Patience) (P831), 228, **228**
Red Birds first (P504), 176, **176**, 182
Red Birds second (P505), 176, **176**, 182
Red Flowers (P503), 176, **176**, 182
Red Plant centre with Insect and Shell border (P530), 180, **180**, 183
Red Plants and Insects (P502), 175, **175**, 182
Redpole (Redpoll) (P529-4), 179, **179**
Retirement (P332), 124, **124**
Rivalx [sic] *Abbey* (P273), 117, **117**
Rock (P608-1), 210, **201**
Rome (P713), 195, 216, **216**, 261, **261**, 263, **263**, 268, **268**, 271, **271**, 274, **274**, 292, **292**, 301, **301**, 302, **302**
Rose border (P521), 172, 173, 177, **177**, 179, **179**, 182, 185
Rose and Flowers (P836), 229, **229**
Rotunda, (P707), 54, 148, 191, **191**, 192, **192**, 195, 211, 213, **213**
Ruins (P201 to P215), **108–210**

Rural Felicity (P308), 121, 122, **122**

Sailor's Farewell, The (P350), 80, 82, **82**
Senatus Consultum on Bonaparte...Conquest of the World, A (P393), 143, **143**
Sherborne Castle (P269), 117, **117**
Shepherdess (P705), 189, 213, **213**
Sleeping Dog (P410), 54
Sleeping Maiden (P365), 129, **129**
Special and Armorial productions P950 series, 253–255, **253–255**
Spotted Flycatcher (P529-7), 179, **179**
Spring (P331), 124, **124**
Star Flower (P830), 227, **227**, 300, **300**
Stoppage to a Stride over the Globe, A (P390), 140, **140**
Starship (P838), 229, **229**
Summer (P357), 127, **128**
Sunflower (Convolvulus) (P819), 224, **224**

Tall Door (P615), 205, **205**, 287, **287**, 288, **288**, 289, **289**
Tea Party, The (P355), 127, **127**
Temple (P613), 190, 203, **203**, 281, **281**, 292, **292**, 297, **297**
Temple Landscape first (Buddleia) (P601), 198, **198**
Temple Landscape second (P611-1), 199, 202, **202**, 310, **310**
Tower (P714), 55, 190, 212, 216, **216**, 263, **263**, 264, **264**, 265, **265**, 269, **269**, 272, **272**, 291, **291**, 293, **293**, 294, **294**, 295, **295**, 296, **296**, 298, **298**, 299, **299**, 305, **305**, 306, **306**, 307, **307**, 308, **308**, 311, **311**, 312, **312**
Trench Mortar (P618, 205), **205**, 279, **279**, 280, **280**
Trophies Dagger (Fitzhugh) (P630-1), 209, **209**
Trophies Dagger (P630-3), 262, **262**
Trophies Etruscan (P629), 208, **208**, 266, **266**, 273, **273**
Trophies Nankin (P628), 208, **208**
Turk, The (P715), 189, 216, **216**, 217
Turkish Castle (P716), 189, 217, **217**
Two figures (P602), 198, **198**

Union Sprays (P143), 166
Union Wreath first (P823), 190, 225, **225**, 229, 254, **254**, 256, 285, **285**, 826, **826**
Union Wreath second (P824), 196, 225, **225**, 254, **254**, 256
Union Wreath third (P825), 211, 225, **225**, 229, 268, **268**, 269, **269**, 273, **273**, 296, **296**, 306, **306**
Union Wreath fourth (P837), 229, **229**

Vandyke, (P828), 181, 226, **226**
Vine and Oak borders (P522 and P523), 62, 83, **83**, 173, 174, 177, **177**, 182, 185, **185**

Waterloo (P709), **46**, **47**, 289, **289**
West Clandon Park (P266), 116
West Wycombe Park (P277), 116, 118, **118**, 164, **164**
Willow (P609), 195, 197, 201, **201**, 206, 261, **261**, 267, **267**, 274, **274**, 275, **275**, 278, **278**
Woodman (P703), 212, **212**
Wood Warbler, (P529-6), 179, **179**
Worcester Wheel (P832), 228, **228**